Perfect Days in...

ANDALUCÍA

C000001033

Travel with Insider Tips

MARCO◉POLO

Contents

 TOP 10   4

That Andalucían Feeling   6

For chapters: see inside front cover

TOP 10:

Not to be missed!
Our top hits – from the absolute No. 1 to No. 10 –
help you plan your tour of the most important sights.

⭐1 GRANADA ➤ 82

Tales of 1001 Nights spring to mind inside the Alhambra (photo left), the Moors' last royal residence on Spanish soil. The Albaicín district opposite is also part of their legacy.

⭐2 CÓRDOBA ➤ 114

The Mezquita, once the main mosque in Western Islam seats 25,000 worshippers, and is Spain's most eminent example of Moorish religious architecture.

⭐3 SEVILLA ➤ 144

Next to Giralda, Seville's famous landmark tower, stands the largest Gothic church in the world. A king had Spain's most beautiful monument to Mudéjar architecture built on the foundations of the former Moorish fortress.

⭐4 RONDA ➤ 50

One of the most imposing edifices in the town regarded as the cradle of bullfighting, Puente Nuevo offers an awesome view of the surrounding cliffs.

⭐5 ÚBEDA ➤ 122

Affluent citizens once had magnificent palaces built here. The result is a unique and well-rounded city tribute to the Renaissance.

⭐6 CARMONA ➤ 158

A highlight of Carmona, apart from the beautiful city centre, is the Necrópolis Romana, Spain's most important Roman burial site. Some of the tombs resemble subterranean palaces.

⭐7 JEREZ DE LA FRONTERA ➤ 53

In the "world capital of sherry", the numerous wine cellars are very inviting. The town is equally famous for its royal Andalucían School of Riding, where you can watch horses "dance".

⭐8 LAS ALPUJARRAS ➤ 94

The magnificent mountain world of the Alpujarras with its steep valley and many white villages offers a tremendous range of possibilities for mountain sports.

⭐9 PARQUE NACIONAL COTO DE DOÑANA ➤ 160

The Park ranks among the most beautiful nature reserves in Europe and offers migrant birds a superb winter hideaway.

⭐10 COSTA DEL SOL ➤ 56

The "sun coast" between Málaga de Estepona is a paradise for those who enjoy partying all night and lazing on the beach all day.

THAT
ANDALUCÍAN

Find out what makes Andalucía tick, experience its unique flair – just like the Andalucíans themselves.

IR DE COPAS

Many Spaniards love strolling from bar to bar, in order to drink a *caña*, a small beer, a glass of red wine or a *fino* as they tuck into a tasty *tapa*. You should try it too; it is a fun, albeit small, evening-meal option. Look for the bar with the largest crowd! That is where you will find the best *tapas*, and you will soon get into conversation with the other guests. Top *tapa* towns are Almería, Córdoba, Granada, Málaga and Seville.

FIESTAS

Seville's Semana Santa and Feria de Abril, Spain's two largest fiestas, offer an ideal way to get a feel for the Andalucían soul, with all its religious fervour and festive exuberance. Yet every village festival offers visitors a similar experience, because every Andalucían community organises an annual celebration for its patron saint. The programme generally starts with a church mass or procession followed by a nice meal, dancing and fireworks.

EL ROCÍO

For 362 days in the year, El Rocío (► 166) is a dusty little town with about 800 inhabitants. But over the Whitsun weekend, Andalucia's most famous pilgrimage takes place here, the Romería del Rocío. Thousands of pilgrims from all over Spain flock to the town, many in horse-drawn wagons. In festive garb (the women in colourful flamenco dresses), they accompany the procession behind the garland-festooned Virgen del Rocio (Virgin of the Dew) through the Parque Nacional Coto de Doñana. At night, there is a lot of dancing and alcohol flows freely. The final procession in El Rocío takes place to the ear-piercing accompaniment of musical instruments and fire crackers.

FLAMENCO

Flamenco is typically Andalucían. Málaga, Ronda, Jerez de la Frontera, Cádiz (► 63), Córdoba (► 114) and Seville (► 144) are regarded as main centres of this

FEELING

Elegance, grace and passion: a dancer at the World Flamenco Fair in Seville

That Andalucían Feeling

art. To avoid ending up in some "dive" with an inferior, run-of-the-mill show and extortionate prices, ask in the tourist office for reputable flamenco venues. The more authentic the presentation with the musicians, singers, dances and dancing, the more the Andalucían audience let's themselves be caught up in the spirit of the occasion! It is fun watching that, too.

ARABIAN

The Moorish legacy is not only tangible in architectural highlights, such as the Alhambra or the Mezquita, you can also experience it in the Hammam Baños Árabes of Córdoba (► 138) or in the restaurants of Granada, which serve traditional Arab meals.

SHOPPING

Zara, Mango, Desigual? Everyone had heard of these innovative Spanish fashion labels, which also have international chains. There are also numerous shops that sell traditional products such as leather, ceramics, basketwork, flamenco guitars and the like, some of which you can actually watch being made.

MERCADOS

Throughout Andalucía, the *mercado* (weekly market) offers the best shopping experience, regardless whether in the large cities, the small villages by the Mediterranean or up in the mountains. On Saturdays – mainly in the morning – the stands around the churches and main squares bow under the weight of the fresh apples, ham, clothing and household goods. The roofed market halls also provide a nice alternative. Here, too, the sales people are happy to chat to visitors, even with the help of pantomime gestures where necessary. Trying things is generally quite acceptable. Crabs, olives, best ham …

Bullfighting arena in Málaga

CORRIDA

These days, bullfighting also has a lot of opponents in Spain itself. Yet in Andalucía, especially in Ronda, Málaga, Jerez (► 53), Córdoba (► 114) und Seville (► 144), you will still find keen supporters who regard the Corrida as part of their special cultural heritage and cherish it as an art form. Should you find the spectacle too gory, then concentrate your attention on the Andalucían spectators – also a show well worth watching.

The Magazine

10

Restaurants in the Albaicín quarter in Granada (above) also exude Arab flair.
Left: The intricate detail of the Myrtle Courtyard in the Alhambra in Granada makes it
one of the most exquisite examples of the Moorish style

Moorish
Andalucía

**Many different cultures have left their mark on Andalucía: the
Phoenicians, Greeks Carthaginians, Celts, Romans and
Visigoths. Yet the Moors undoubtedly had the most lasting
influence. Under their reign, Andalucía experienced a golden
age of the arts.**

The name Moor derives from the word *amaurós* ("dark"), used by the Greeks
and Romans to describe those Berber tribes living in North Africa who were
converted to the Muslim faith by the Arabs in the 7th century and provided
armed support during the conquest of the Iberian peninsula. In AD 711,
the Arab commander Tariq Ibn Ziyad crossed the Strait of Gibraltar with
an army of 7,000 men and landed near the town now known as Tarifa,
the most southern settlement of the European mainland.

  The invaders stayed for nearly 800 years. The legacy of their subtle and
beautiful craftsmanship and their social and political skills is seen everywhere in Andalucía today, but especially in the starry fretwork and swirling
arabesques of great buildings such as the Alhambra in Granada, the
Mezquita in Córdoba and Seville's Giralda tower.

ARTESONADO OR AZULEJOS?

You'll frequently see the following terms used to describe Andalucía's architecture in literature about the region.

- **Artesonado** Intricate, coffered wooden ceiling.
- **Azulejos** Glazed ceramic tiles in vivid colours and designs.
- **Mudéjar** During the Christian Reconquest of Al-Andalus, many Muslims were expelled, but those with building and craft skills were allowed to stay. They were known by the name *mudéjar* (meaning "those permitted to remain"). The word was later applied to the architectural style that these craftspeople developed by merging Islamic and Christian forms..
- **Muqarnas** Masonry and plasterwork with stalactite effect.

Water is Life

The Moors who came to Andalucía found the kind of earthly paradise that they had only dreamt of in the desert wastes of their Moroccan home, the Maghrib. The key ingredient was plentiful water; it transformed arid lands into green oases and furnished Moorish palaces and modest homes alike with lush gardens enriched by music of fountains and the glitter of pools.

The Moors had long called the land across the Straits of Gibraltar, Al-Andalus. One suggested origin of the name relates to the Vandals who occupied Spain and parts of North Africa during the 5th century. Other sources believe that it may have derived from a phrase used by the Muslims of the east to describe "Western Islam", and was first applied to all of Spain as the Moors advanced northwards until checked on the banks of the River Loire near Poitiers by Charles Martel. As soon as the Moors retreated south across the Pyrenees, the Christian Reconquest of Al-Andalus began. It took seven centuries to achieve, chiefly because the forces of Christian Spain were sparse, fragmented and often at odds with each other.

A Golden Age

After their initial sweep through Spain and into France in the 8th century, the Moors dug in their heels in the region now known as Andalucía. In this contracted Al-Andalus they tolerated other religions, and made wise agreements and concessions with Christian neighbours. The Moors created a Golden Age within their Spanish lands. Córdoba became the Moorish capital of Al-Andalus, and its rulers, or caliphs, rivalled those of Baghdad and Damascus for their wealth and accomplishments. In 756 the building of Córdoba's Great Mosque, the Mezquita, began, and over the next 200 years the city became enriched by trade in gold and silver, leather, silk, perfumes and spices, becoming a beacon of scientific and artistic achievement.

The Charm of the Moors' Al-Andalus

By the beginning of the 11th century, factionalism and internal rivalries brought an end to the Golden Age of the Córdoban caliphate, and Al-Andalus fragmented into a number of small independent Muslim kingdoms called *taifas*. The last such kingdom, the Kingdom of Granada, founded in 1238 by Mohammed Ibn al-Ahmar, a descendant of Beni Nasr, was able to hold out for some time. The kingdom stretched from Gibraltar to Almería, and its capital was the richest town on the peninsula and at the same time its cultural centre. With the Alhambra, built in the 14th century, the Nasrid dynasty left behind an outstanding monument to their reign. With the marriage of Isabel de Castilla and Fernando de Aragón (the "Catholic Monarchs") in 1469, the foundation stone was laid for the unification of the two large Spanish kingdoms. The couple was determined to banish all the Muslims. On 2 January 1492, the Catholic monarchs moved into Granada. The last Moorish ruler Boabdil fled to Africa. His departure marked the end of almost eight centuries of Islamic culture in southern Spain. The following expulsion of many hundreds of thousands of Moors and Jews meant a heavy setback for the further economic development and cultural life of Spain. Yet, as you travel through Andalucía, it is the persuasive magic of Moorish Al-Andalus that still grips and captivates.

The reign of the Catholic monarchs to whom these elaborate tombs are dedicated, ended Moorish dominion in Andalucía

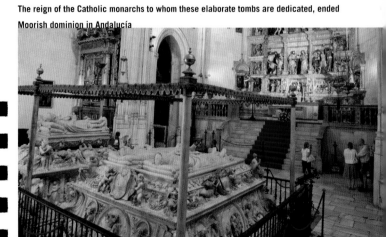

Romantic
Andalucía

Nineteenth-century visitors to Andalucía
conjured up an image of the region as a seductive
other world, a world of heat and passion,
of scented orange groves, of raffish characters
and mountain brigands, of licentious
Don Juans and alluring Carmens.

It was an image that was self-perpetuating because many of these visitors exaggerated their experiences to make them sound more romantic in what was easily portrayed as an exotic and even dangerous land. This had been the Al-Andalus of the Moors after all, a land where Europe gave way to Africa, an exciting alternative to what seemed the staid predictability of northern Europe.

The English writer Richard Ford described Spain as an escape to "racy freshness" from the "dull uniformity" of Europe. Ford wrote superbly of the Andalucía of his day. He first came to Spain in 1830 and over the next few years produced his epic *Handbook for Travellers in Spain and Readers at Home*, published in 1845 and still revered as one of the finest evocations of Spain ever written – exhaustive, witty and opinionated. Washington Irving came to Spain to work for the American Legation in Madrid in 1826, and in 1828 set off on a tour of Andalucía. He lived for some time in the semi-derelict Alhambra and there wrote *The Conquest of Granada* before beginning his famous work *The Alhambra: A Series of Tales*. The book mixes romantic stories of the Alhambra's Moorish past with vivid portrayals of the palace's decaying grandeur. It triggered movements in Spain and in northern Europe that led to the Alhambra's preservation, and fuelled interest in the palace.

George Bizet's opera Carmen is also inextricably linked to the region's romantic image. First performed in 1875, the popular opera still features on the annual venue of the world's leading theatres. The music composed by Bizet (who actually never set a foot inside Spain) represented a revolutionary break with opera tradition of that time while the short story by Prosper Merimee on which it was based fulfilled all the clichés: Carmen, a gypsy heroine of sultry good looks who worked in Seville's

THE REAL CARMEN

The image of scantily dressed female workers in the stifling heat of Seville's 19th-century tobacco factory excited the prurient rather than the romantic interest of more than one male traveller. "Most of them were young, and some were very pretty." said Théophile Gautier for example in his *Un Voyage en Espagne* (1843), adding: "The extreme carelessness of their dress enables us to appreciate their charms at ease."

George Dennis was far less charming (*A Summer in Andalusia*, 1839) "I have never beheld such an assemblage of ugliness." In truth the women worked in dreadful conditions, which no visitor paying any attention could fail to observe.

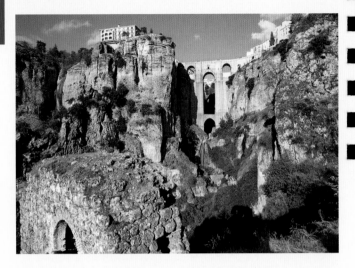

Andalucía's 19th-century bandoleros lived in remote areas, including the Serranía de Ronda

tobacco factory, a notorious bandit from the Ronda mountains, and a dashing bullfighter, all three locked into a passionate story of love, betrayal and death.

Carmen's male counterpart was the fictional Don Juan – a legendary figure who became the definition of the ladykiller per se. In turn, the Don Juan legend was immortalised by subsequent adaptations, not least by Mozart's opera *Don Giovanni*. The visitor's image of the passionate lover and seducer shines as brightly as the Andalucían sun – a romantic fantasy that has little to do with reality.

BEGGING FOR BANDITS

Andalucían bandits were all the rage among 19th-century travellers, who arrived in the region with their heads filled with the imaginative tales of previous visitors. There were certainly lawless *bandoleros* in the Sierras of Andalucía, but records show that foreigners were generally left in peace, even if some of them obviously cherished the idea of a romantic adventure. The French novelist Alexandre Dumas is said to have sent money to an Andalucían bandit chief in return for a promise that he and his party would be held up as they crossed wild country – with the proviso that no harm would be done to them. And the Danish writer Hans Christian Andersen expressed great disappointment that he passed unchallenged through the hills of the Sierra Morena.

The Bullfight
Art, Sport or Outrage?

To the *aficionado*, bullfighting is an art rather than a sport. Bullfight reviews come under the arts pages in Spanish newspapers, with the *corrida* receiving the same superlatives as stage and ballet productions.

The classic setting of the bullfight is Andalucia, although of course matadors also stride out to face the beast in all of Spain's major towns, in some countries in Latin America and in the south of France. While Madrid can boast the largest arena, Plaza de Toros, it is Andalucía's Ronda that is the oldest. It is thus not very surprising that the most famous toreros were and are Andalucíans: Manolete, Lagartijo, Joselito, Paquirri und El Cordobés – some of whom lost their lives in the arena. The *toros bravos*, those half-wild creatures bursting with energy, are for the main part the product of Anadalucian breeders. The provinces of Seville,

Matadors such as Salvador Vega, shown here during a bullfight in Malaga, see their profession as an artistic – but at the same time bloody – ritual

The Magazine

LADY IN LIGHTS

There were several accomplished female bullfighters prior to 1908, when a ban was placed on them becoming *toreras*. One such was Martina García, who took part in her last bullfight in 1880 at the age of 76. When the ban was lifted after the death of General Franco (on 20 November 1975 in Madrid), one woman who donned the *traje de luces*, the bullfighter's glittering costume, was Cristina Sánchez. She outshone many of her male peers and at one memorable *corrida* killed all six bulls. Sánchez retired early in 1997, on the grounds that she was finding difficulty in securing top-level fights because so many big-name male bullfighters refused to share the bill with her.

Huelva and Cádiz are home to these enormous estates, which are and remain the definition of the good old days of the Señorito.

Battle of Life or Death

For many Spaniards, giving up bullfighting would be like giving up a piece of their deeply entrenched culture, almost tantamount to losing a piece of their own identity. There are still plenty of opportunities to see bullfighting in Andalucía. The season runs from Easter to October, although *novilladas*, novice fights, take place in Costa del Sol bullrings as late as November. The major bullrings, such as Seville's Maestranza (► 172), are the places to experience the atmosphere of the bullfight at its most intense; and it is in the main rings that you are likely to see the best *matadores* confronting the biggest and fiercest Andalucían fighting bulls. Even the smallest villages try to stage a *corrida* at least once a year. Death, for *matador* as well as bull, is still the price to pay in any bullring, great or small.

DIRTY TRICKS

Opponents of bullfighting condemn the spectacle outright, but even enthusiasts argue that the modern *corrida* has become debased, not least by such practices as shaving the tips of a bull's horns to reduce its accuracy and sensitivity to movement. There are hints of worse practices being inflicted on "dangerous" bulls, before they are released into the ring, in order to reduce their potential lethality. *Aficionados* complain that this no longer has anything to do with the so-called *arte de lidiar*, the true art of good bullfighting.

FLAMENCO
Fire in the Blood

Flamenco is the soul music of Andalucía, a fusion of voice, guitar and dance that rarely fails to set the blood tingling. There is nothing quite like the raw, deep singing *(cante jondo)*, the hand-clapping *(palmas)* and the rippling guitar that accompany the staccato footwork and sinuous movements of the flamenco dancer.

The origin of flamenco is as varied as the history of Andalucía itself. Moorish influences and allusions to Byzantine liturgical music have been discovered in it as have elements of medieval romances. The only thing really known is that the *gitanos* (Romani) of Andalucia had the greatest influence on this art form; even today, the best flamenco artists come from this ethnic group, which call themselves *Kale and are a subgroup of the long-established Romani on the Iberian peninsula.* About 200 years ago, they began the original form of today's flamenco. Like the song and the guitar playing, the

Not "only" music, dance and song: flamenco is also an expression of one's attitude to life

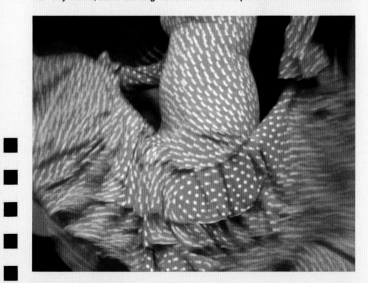

dance has since developed into an extremely demanding art form. There are flamenco schools in practically every town of Andalucía. In Seville alone there are more than 30. Some offer day and weekly courses and are thus suitable for tourists who just want to get a taste of what it involves (www.tallerflamenco.com, www.flamenco-carmendetorres.com).

Flamenco Secret

The finest flamenco singers are said to possess *duende* – the soul, the "ghost", the inspirational gift that transforms an ordinary performance into something sublime. Before achieving *duende,* singers may wait for hours, during which they massage their vocal chords with endless smoking and glassfuls of the fiery liqueur *aguardiente*, a combination that would render most people speechless, if not songless.

In its purest form flamenco is *cante jondo* (deep song), especially when performed by the best *cantadores* (singers), whose scorched voices express real grief, yet with a triumphant reaffirmation of the human spirit. For most visitors to Andalucía, however, it is the magical combination of *el cante* with *el toque*, the guitar, and *el baile*, the dance, that gives flamenco its appeal.

Emotional Depth in Music, Dance and Song

A distinction is made in flamenco between about 30 different kinds of song, not all of which are suited to dance. They have their origin in the Andalucían provinces. The *Buleria* comes from Jerez, for example, the *Alegría* from Cádix and the *Malagueña* is mainly sung In Málaga. What all these forms have in common, however, is the emotional depth of the music and the song. The songs are about the fears and anxieties of every-day life, about happiness and grief and, of course, predominantly love. Full of metaphorical allusions, the words are as clear as they are haunting.

FINDING FLAMENCO

Ask for details of flamenco *tablaos* and *peñas* at tourist offices. Hotels often have information about flamenco shows, but these may be "variety" performances or stylised cabaret, with a meal as part of the bill. There is accessible flamenco at the following venues: **Tablao Cardenal** and **La Bulería** (Córdoba, ➤ 138), **Tarantos** (Granada, ➤ 108), **Teatro Miguel de Cervantes** (Málaga, ➤ 76), **Casa Lara** (Ronda, ➤ 76), **La Taberna Flamenca** (Jerez de la Frontera, ➤ 76), **La Cava** (Cádiz, ➤ 76), **Los Gallos** and **El Tamboril** (Seville, ➤ 172)

FAMOUS FLAMENCO NAMES

Carmen Amaya (1913–63), was born in the poor district of Somorrostro in Barcelona (today Vila Olímpica) and started dancing at the age of seven. In 1929 she made her debut in Paris, which launched her career as one of the best flamenco dancers of all times.

Manolo Caracol (Manolo the Snail, 1909–73), a gypsy from the Seville province. He began his career aged just 11, at a flamenco event in the Alhambra of Granada staged by the Spanish composer Manuel de Falla, the poet Federico García Lorca and the guitarist Andrés Segovia.

Camarón de la Isla (the Shrimp of the Island, 1950–92), was the son of a blacksmith from the Isla del León/San Fernando in the province of Cádiz. He made his first appearance as a singer at the age of eight, but even then the experts realised that the youngster was on the path to a top career as a *cantador*.

Paco de Lucía, born in Algeciras in 1947 and originally christened Francisco Sánchez Gómez, is the most important flamenco guitarist of the present day. Blessed with a grandiose technique, he is both a fascinating solo guitarist and superb accompanist for flamenco singers. As a cross-border musician, he has also worked with jazz greats such as Al DiMeola, Larry Corryell and John McLaughlin. He also wrote the music for Carlos Saura's film Carmen.

Joaquín Cortés, born in 1969 in Córdoba became a soloist for the Spanish National Ballet at the age of 15 and founded his own ballet company in 1992 with which he has successfully performed all around the world. He is also known for his work with pop stars such as Jennifer Lopez und Alicia Keys.

Emotions are also expressed in the dance. The staccato of the boots symbolises anger and pride, the graceful movements of hands and fingers indicate seduction and tenderness. Just as the aim is for the audience to become one with the feelings of the singer and for a frisson to take hold of some that is released in the choral "Olé" at the end of the song, the audience is also expected to really "feel" the movements of the dancers. That is when the lines between song and dance are crossed and the flamenco has found its "demons", according to the writer Federico Garcia Lorca.

Experts will tell you that the real thing emerges spontaneously, and usually in the early hours of the morning, in hidden-away bars and in semi-private all-night parties called *juergas*. The next best thing to an impromptu flamenco event are *tablaos*, performances of "classical" flamenco by trained artistes. Flamenco clubs and associations called *peñas* are also open to visits. Perhaps the best experience for a visitor to Andalucía is to come across spontaneous flamenco at a village *fiesta*. You'll hear it before you see it, and you'll never forget it.

Festival Diary

The *fiesta* originated as a rural holiday and the *feria* as a country fair, and even in big cities their outdoor nature survives, with horses and bulls still figuring largely in the proceedings. And then there are religious festivals.

FEBRUARY

Carnaval Spectacular carnivals in Cádiz and Málaga and, to a lesser extent, Córdoba, Carmona, Nerja and many other towns and villages, are held in the days preceding the beginning of Lent.

MARCH/APRIL

Semana Santa Religious processions are staged in all the main cities and in many country towns and villages throughout Holy Week, which precedes Easter.

APRIL

Feria de Abril Seville's April festival, held about two weeks after Easter, is a week-long celebration. It is the biggest and most colourful festival in Spain.

MAY

Feria del Caballo Colourful horse fair, with marvellous displays of equestrianism (Jerez de la Frontera, early May).

"Moors and Christians" Carnival Mock battles (Pampaneira, Las Alpujarras, 3 May).

Fiesta de los Patios Many of Córdoba's beautiful private patios open to the public (early May).

Romería del Rocío The biggest religious pilgrimage and festival in Spain (El Rocío, seventh week after Easter, ➤ 166).

Feria de Primavera Puerta de Santa María wine festival (last week in May).

Feria de la Manzanilla Sanlúcar de Barrameda wine festival (last week in May).

Corpus Christi Processions and celebrations in many places (late May/early June).

FUN AND SUN

Andalucíans have long been noted for their love of festival and fun. "Every day seems to be a holiday," commented the 19th-century writer Richard Ford, in a rather sniffily English way, on his first visit.

The English politician and writer Benjamin Disraeli was more enthusiastic. "It is all the Sun," he exclaimed when he visited Andalucía in 1830 after an illness and felt rejuvenated.

JUNE

Feria de San Bernabé Marbella's very lavish festival (second week in June).

Fiestas Patronales de San Antonio Festival with mock battles between "Moors" and "Christians" (Trevélez, Las Alpujarras, 13–14 June).

"Moors and Christians" Fiesta Mojácar (10 June).

International Guitar Festival Córdoba (two weeks June/July).

JULY

International Festival of Music and Dance at the Alhambra (Granada, late June/early July).

Virgen de la Mar Almería's lively summer festival (last week in July).

AUGUST

Feria de Málaga Málaga's summer festival (mid-Aug).

The most important event in the church calendar is Semana Santa, the week before Easter (below: the procession in Úbeda)

Sanlúcar de Barrameda Horse Races Horse races along the beach at Sanlúcar (last two weeks in Aug).

Feria de Grazalema Cillage festival includes bull-running through the streets (last week in Aug).

Fiestas Patronales San Augustín Mojácar festival (last week in Aug).

SEPTEMBER

Fiesta de la Vendimia Major wine festival at Jerez de la Frontera (first/second week in Sep).

Romería del Cristo de la Yedra Baeza's main festival (7 Sep).

Feria y Fiesta de Pedro Romero Ronda festival featuring bullfighters in traditional 18th-century costume, plus flamenco (first two weeks in Sep).

OCTOBER

Fiesta de San Miguel Festival at Úbeda and in many other towns and villages (1 Oct).

Feria de San Lucas Jaén's main festival (mid-Oct).

HEROES & VILLAINS

The surrender of Granada to Los Reyes Católicos on 22 January 1492

The First and Last of the Moors

Tariq Ibn Ziyad, the Governor of Tangier in Morocco, was the man who first gained a military foothold in southern Spain by landing at Gibraltar in 711. The famous Rock was named after him: Jabal Tariq, the "mountain of Tariq". Abur Abd Allah, known as **Boabdil**, was the last of the Nasrid dynasty of sultans of Granada, and the last Moorish ruler of any substance in Spain. The story goes that, as he made his sad withdrawal from Granada, he kept looking back, much to his proud and severe mother's despair. The place where he caught his final regretful glimpse of the city is still known as Puerta del Suspiro – the Pass of the Sigh.

Los Reyes Católicos

It was the marriage of **Isabel I de Castilla** and **Fernando V de Aragón** in 1469 that heralded the end of Islamic authority in Spain. Prior to the uniting of these most powerful of the Catholic kingdoms, the Christian Spanish had been far too divided to mount a complete Reconquest of Islamic Al-Andalus. Isabel and Fernando, still revered in Spain as

HARD HEADED

The Catholic Monarchs, **Isabel and Fernando**, are buried in the crypt of the Capilla Real, adjoining Granada cathedral (▶ 90). The royal pair are represented by recumbent effigies in marble, the centrepiece of the chapel. Isabel's head is more deeply sunk into her marble cushion than is Fernando's, a subtle conceit that is said to represent the well-attested fact that Isabel had a much "heavier" brain, and a much harder head, than did her husband.

Los Reyes Católicos, the Catholic Monarchs, brought renewed vigour to the ideal of a wholly Christian Spain. To their non-Christian subjects, who were initially allowed religious freedom and later hounded out of the country when they did not convert, they represented one of the most terrifying double acts in history. Following the Reconquest, the notorious Spanish Inquisition was established. Using threats of torture and the confiscation of property, the Inquisition was able to ensure the loyalty of those who had converted to Christianity.

Artistic Andalucía

Francisco de Zurbarán (1598–1664) was born in Andalucía's neighbouring province of Extremadura but based for most of his life in Seville. Zurbarán's haunting paintings of robed monks and saints reflect an austere nature rarely associated with Andalucía, yet even 17th-century Seville was a harsh enough place: Zurbarán lost the children of his second marriage to the Seville plague of 1649.

Most famous of all the region's artistic sons is **Pablo Ruiz y Picasso** (1881–1973), who was born in Málaga (he moved with his family at the age of nine to Galicia and then to Barcelona, and lived for most of his life in France). You can see examples of his work in Málaga's **Museo Picasso** (▶61).

Literary Andalucía

Miguel de Cervantes Saavedra (1547–1616) was born near Madrid, but worked as a tax collector in Andalucía during the 1590s. He was jailed for a time because of alleged financial "inaccuracies" and, ever resourceful, is said to have written much of his great novel *Don Quixote* while in prison.

Federico García Lorca (1898–1936), a poet and playwright of immense lyrical gifts, was one of Andalucía's greatest writers. Lorca was born in Granada, but his relationship with his native city was uneasy; he was a homosexual and liked to mix with the *gitanos,* who, for him, represented the true spirit of Andalucía.. Lorca's most famous works include the plays *Bodas de Sangre* (Blood Wedding) and *La Casa de Bernarda Alba* (The House of Bernarda Alba).

TRAGIC FALL

In his early years **Esteban Murillo** (1617–82) produced richly colourful and often sentimental Madonnas as well as numerous picturesque urchins, although his later work reflected a darker side. The lives of 17th-century painters could be hazardous. Murillo fell from scaffolding while painting an altarpiece in a church in Cádiz and later died from the injuries he sustained. He was 64 years old when the accident happened (in an era when lifespans were far shorter).

Liquid Gold
The Sherry Experience

In Andalucía, you don't simply drink sherry, you experience the entire sherry culture that goes with it – as befits one of the world's most exquisite wines.

By international law the wine can only be labelled as "sherry" if it is produced within the "Sherry Triangle", the corner of land that lies in the northwestern part of Cádiz province between the towns of Jerez de la Frontera, Sanlúcar de Barrameda and El Puerto de Santa María.

The Jerez area was producing wine from the time of the Phoenicians, but the specialised production of sherry began in the 16th century when British adventurers, exiled from Protestant England because of their Catholicism, became involved in wine production in the south of Spain, intermarried with local families and founded sherry dynasties. Sherry had been known as "sack" to the medieval English, and it became a favourite tipple after Sir Francis Drake and the Earl of Essex attacked Cádiz in the 1580s and 1590s and carried off thousands of barrels of sherry. The British are still the biggest consumers of the sweetened "cream" sherry.

Sherry is produced from three types of white grape: palomino, the basis of all sherry production, and muscat and Pedro Ximénez, both used in the blending of different types of sherry. The secret of sherry-making lies in

A wine expert judges the taste and clarity of the sherry. It is believed that even back in 1000 BC the Phoenicians planted vines in the region around Jerez. However, it was not until the Vino de Jerez – the wine from Sherish, as the Moors referred to the town – was discovered by the English and renamed Sherry that the area attained real acclaim

SHERRY BULLISHNESS

On hilltops overlooking main roads all over Spain, you'll see huge metal silhouettes of fighting bulls (below). They were erected by the Osborne sherry company of El Puerto de Santa María from the 1950s onwards. When roadside advertising was banned in the late 1980s, Osborne removed its name from the bulls, but left the silhouettes in place. There was a national outcry when the authorities threatened to dismantle them, and about 100 of the original 500 "sherry" bulls remain defiantly in place.

the time-honoured system of fortifying the palomino grape with alcohol, then storing it in huge casks of American oak. The yeast retained in the wine creates a surface film called *velo de flor* (veil of flowers) which prevents oxidation. It is this "locking in" of the wine that preserves the pale colour of *fino*, the most popular sherry in Spain, and creates its dryness and distinctive bouquet. In the absence of *flor*, oxidation takes place, producing darker and fuller *amontillado* and *oloroso* sherries, which are often blended with the sweet wines made from muscat and Pedro Ximénez grapes to create pale, medium and cream sherries.

If you take a tour of one of the warehouses *(bodegas)* of famous-name sherry empires such as Domecq, González Byass, Sandeman and Osborne (➤ 53), you'll see thousands of casks, in rows called *criaderas* up to five casks high, where the sherry remains for between three and seven years. Sherry for bottling is drawn off at intervals from the ground-level row of casks, the *solera*. The amount taken is made up from the casks above, and the eventual shortfall in the top casks is then replenished with new wine. The results of this blending are the delicious sherries of the officially denominated *Jerez-Xéres-Sherry y Manzanilla-Sanlúcar de Barrameda*. And if you can get your tongue around that, you fully deserve another glass of liquid gold.

Land of
OLIVES

Say Andalucía and most people will immediately think of Costa del Sol, Alhambra, Mezquita, flamenco and Carmen. Yet, anyone driving north of Granada soon lands in the middle of España Incognita: in the Jaen province. And there the visitor's attention is focused on the many uses of Andalucían oil.

The olive tree is veiled in a sort of mystique; it gives life, can live several hundred years and still bear fruit like it did in its younger years. Some people dream of planting an olive tree and the Phoenicians had exactly the same idea over 2,500 years ago when they planted the first trees. In the following years, the Romans cultivated the oil and improved the production methods. Dealers ensured that it was shipped to harbours throughout the Roman Empire and sent the best oils to Rome. At the time, the oil tree enjoyed a special reputation and its wood was used for carving images of the gods. Olive groves were sacred and carrying and an olive branch was believed to protect the carrier from danger. In ancient times, olive oil served as an important foodstuff, but also as medicine, body lotion and for lighting, since oil lamps were popular for a long time before candles appeared.

In Rank and File
The olive trees stand atop the flat, rolling hills of Jaén province in neat rows, just as if they are about to take part in a parade. They need a lot of care, and at harvest time, there is little scope for daydreaming – even when, for example, the age-old trees near Martos are called "Romeo and Juliet", owing to the tender entwinement of the shimmering silver branches over the ochre-coloured grounds. Almost half of the annual harvest is exported. Abroad though few people know that most of the olives come from the Jaén province. When travelling between Jaén and Úbeda the only interruption to the row after row of olives tree is a pylon or two, so visitors soon work out that Jaén is the largest olive oil producer

in Spain and the world – pure monoculture, yet nonetheless extremely efficient. In order to establish the exact number of trees for the subsidies from the EU, aerial shots were taken of the province. The figure is amazing: over 60 million!

Star Chefs Swear by the Andalucían Olive Oil

The oval fruits of the tree are processed in modern factories into *Virgen Extra* and ordinary *Aceite de Oliva* while the crushed stones are used in the heating systems of quite a few health resorts. The "Region's Gold" is also used for cosmetics, in arts and crafts and, of course, in the kitchen. Even ice cream is made from it, although people tend to either like or hate the result. The Piscual olive from Jaén province is particularly well known, and this popular, savoury oil is a must in many local dishes, such as marinated partridge, pork tenderloin, roast lamb, dried cod or the garlicky *ajoatao* stew. Even Spain's star chefs, such as Ferran Adrià and Juan Mari Arzak from the distant Catalonia or the Basque region swear by the oil.

A Very Special Experience...

Oil-tasting is an experience in itself. In the special *Catas de Aceite*, visitors can smell and taste the valuable oil and then evaluate it. If the colour, taste and smell are first-class, the oil receives the top mark: *Aceite Virgin Extra!* To neutralise the palate between oils, you eat apple and not bread.

Around 6.1. million oval fruits are harvested in Spain – the world's largest olive oil producer – each year. And 80 percent of the olive trees are in Andalucía.

Left page and above: In Gallo Azul in Jerez de la Frontera the tapas may be master-pieces with shrimps or simpler works of art, but both are absolutely delicious. And at the bar, the next difficult choice awaits you...

TIME for **TAPAS**

Eat Andalucían and you eat tapas. These little dishes of food are a delicious accompaniment to a *copa de fino*, a glass of dry sherry.

In Andalucían bars, people come and go, order at their leisure, have a chat and generally don't tend to stay too long. When you order beer, sherry or wine, they come with two or three little dishes of tasty appetizers that are set out in a row in front of you. They can and should not be regarded as a full meal; *tapa* does not describe the type, but rather the amount of food. However, if you stroll from bar to bar and try out a different *tapa* delicacy each time, you will not only realise how much choice there is, but also have absolutely no problem skipping a main meal.

The literal meaning of *tapa* is "lid" or "cover", and its evolution as a culinary term is said to come from the old Andalucían habit of placing a small dish on a glass of sherry to protect it from flies and dust. Bar staff got into the habit of dropping morsels of bread and cheese and a couple of olives onto the dish and the custom grew. Today a good *tapas* bar will often have honey-coloured cured hams hanging from the ceiling, a row of stainless steel dishes filled with a selection of cold and hot *tapas*, a great choice of sherries and other drinks, and an atmosphere of enjoyment and good cheer.

You can order them as a *ración* (whole dish) for several people or as a *media ración* (half a dish) for just one person. Very traditional establishments

SOME TASTY TAPAS

Here are some tasty and popular *tapas* to start you off (although different bars may serve them under slightly different names).

FISH AND MEAT

Gambas a la plancha grilled prawns

Puntillitas fritas deep-fried baby squid

Boquerones fritos deep-fried anchovies

Cazón en adobo fish marinated in vinegar, lemon, spices, and then deep fried

Croquetas croquettes filled with anything from ham to spinach

Jamón Serrano fabled cured ham of the mountains. Usually expensive

Habas con jamón broad beans and ham

Lomo al Jerez fresh loin of pork cooked with sherry

Flamenquin casero sliced pork, boiled egg and vegetables, rolled tightly in breadcrumb batter

Pollo al ajillo chicken in garlic

Pincho muruño small meat kebabs

Pimientos rellenos stuffed peppers with tuna

VEGETARIAN

Aceitunas olives

Ensalada mixta mixed salad

Revueltos scrambled eggs with delicious additions, such as asparagus

Champiñones a la plancha grilled mushrooms with garlic

Patatas ali-oli diced potatoes in a garlic mayonnaise dressing

Tortilla de patatas potato omelette

Arroz rice

still work out what is owed by adding together the various drinks scrawled in chalk on the bar. Some *tapas* bars have menus in several languages, but where the menu is in Spanish only, be careful; if you don't speak the language, you may end up playing *tapas* roulette. Choosing "blind" can bring enjoyable surprises, but it can also lead to the cruel reality of finding that the *criadillas* or *sesos* that you ordered, and that sounded so delicious, are actually fried testicles of pig and scrambled brains. When in doubt, ask.

FIVE BEST TAPAS BARS

- **Bar Logüeno**, Málaga (➤ 71): best in town (possibly even in Andalucía) for sheer variety, with more than 75 *tapas* to choose from.
- **Matahambre**, Torremolinos (➤ 72) best for classy *tapas* accompanied by a superb choice of wines.
- **El Faro** (➤ 73): best seafood *tapas* in Cádiz with an upmarket atmosphere.
- **La Gran Taberna**, Granada (➤ 105): best for its traditional atmosphere, with hams curing above the bar and seating around giant barrels.
- **El Patio**, Seville (➤ 169): famous *tapas* bar, serving a wide range of *tapas*.

Finding Your Feet

First Two Hours

Arriving in Málaga

Málaga International Airport

The airport (tel: 902 40 47 04), 8km (5 mi) west of Málaga city and 4km
(2.5 mi) east of Torremolinos, is the main point of entry for most visitors.

- An **electric train service** (Línea C-1) between Málaga city and Fuengirola
  connects with the airport, Torremolinos and Benalmádena. This is the
  best option for getting to and from the airport by public transport. For
  the airport station (Aeropuerto), turn right outside the airport building
  upper-level exit and follow signs over a footbridge to the station. Tickets
  are obtained from a machine by the end of the footbridge. You will pay
  more if you buy your ticket on the train. Trains to Málaga city run from
  7am, then on the half hour until midnight; journey time: 12 minutes.
  First train for Torremolinos and Fuengirola: at 5:45am, then at 45 and
  50 minutes past the hour until 11:45pm; journey time: Torremolinos
  10 minutes, Fuengirola 29 minutes.

- **Bus service** Línea A Exprés runs between the airport and Málaga city every
  30 minutes, 7am–midnight. Journey time is about 15 minutes (around
  €3). The end destination in the town centre is Plaza del General Torrijos).

- A **taxi** to Málaga city costs about €18.50 (weekdays) and €23 (at night,
  weekends); to Marbella €65 to €77. Licensed taxis (usually white) line
  up outside the airport exit.

- Leaving the airport **by car**, follow the exit road. Approaching the N340,
  the left-hand lane will take you across a flyover and on to Málaga and
  the Málaga Ring Road (Ronda de Málaga) for Granada, Almería and
  destinations north and east of Málaga city; the right-hand lane will take
  you on to the N340 (and subsequently the A7/AP7) heading west for the
  Costa del Sol and onwards to Cádiz and Seville.

Málaga Railway Station (Málaga RENFE)

The main railway station (tel: 902 32 03 20) lies 750m from Málaga city
centre. **Electric train** (Línea C-1) connects to Alameda Centro; Buses 1, 2,
6, 7, 8, 9, 10, 17, 21, 23, 26, 30, 31, 38 go to Alameda Principal.

Málaga Bus Station

The bus station (tel: 952 35 00 61) is adjacent to the railway station. For
connections to the city centre see Railway Station above.

Arriving in Almería

Almería Airport

Almería Airport (tel: 902 40 47 04) lies about 9km (5.5 mi) east of Almería
city. **Bus** No 22 runs between the airport and the city centre approximately
every 70 min., from 7:25am to 10:25pm. A **taxi** to the Puerta de Purchena
costs €15–€22.

Almería Railway Station and Bus Station

The railway station (Estación de Ferrocarril, tel: 902 42 22 42) and bus station
(Estación de Autobuses, tel: 950 26 20 98) share the arrival/departure
concourse on Plaza de la Estación. It is a short walk of about 700m to the
seaward end of Avenida Federico García Lorca (Rambla de Belén).

Arriving in Granada

Granada Airport
The airport (tel: 902 40 47 04), about 15km (9.25mi) west of Granada city, is for internal flights only. After flight arrivals **city buses** No 3, 10 and 33 go from the airport to Plaza Isabel la Católica at the end of Gran Vía de Colón in the city centre. A taxi to the city centre costs about €28.

Granada Railway Station
The station (tel: 902 24 02 02), on Avenida de Andaluces, is about 1.5km (1 mi) from the city centre. Nine bus lines run between the station and Gran Vía de Colón and Los Reyes Católicos at the city centre. **Taxis** cost about €6 to Los Reyes Católicos.

Granada Bus Station
Carretera de Jaén (tel: 902 42 22 42), about 3km (2 miles) from the city centre. City buses No 3, 10 and 33 run to city centre.

Arriving in Córdoba

Córdoba Railway Station
The station (tel: 902 24 05 05) is about 1.25km (0.75 miles) from central Córdoba. **Bus No 3** connects to Plaza de las Tendillas and continues to the riverside in front of the Mezquita. **Taxis** cost about €6 to the Mezquita area.

Córdoba Bus Station
Bus No 3 (see above) takes arrivals from the bus station (tel: 957 40 43 83) to the city centre.

Arriving in Seville

Seville Airport
The airport (tel: 902 40 47 04) handles internal flights and international flights. It lies about 8km (5 mi) northeast of Seville city centre. **Bus** to city centre runs from about 5:20am to 1:15am at least every hour. **Taxi** to the city centre costs about €22.

Seville Railway Station
Bus No C1 takes you from the station (tel: 954 90 80 40) to Avenida Carlos V, just a short walk from the cathedral area. **Taxis** to the cathedral area cost about €8, plus €2 for luggage. The **tourism information desk** can book hotels.

Seville Bus Station
Seville has two bus stations. International arrivals and arrivals from other Spanish cities outside Andalucía come in at Plaza de Armas (tel: 954 90 77 37/90 80 40). Buses from Andalucía's other main cities arrive at Prado de San Sebastián (tel: 954 41 71 11).

Tourist Information Offices
There are two types of tourist office: the regional **Oficinas de Turismo de la Junta de Andalucía (J de A)**, which deals mainly with city tourism, and the city or municipal tourist office – **Oficina Municipal de Turismo (OMT)** which deals with city and regional tourism.

Getting Around

Public Transport

Train

There are train connections to all major towns in Andalucía. High-speed train services run to Córdoba, Seville and Málaga. **RENFE** (Red Nacional de Ferrocaril de España) is the national rail network. Services between main cities are generally fast, comfortable and efficient. Services to smaller towns and throughout rural areas are much slower, but are often scenic. Stations and halts in rural areas can be several kilometres from the main settlement that they serve; public transport is usually not available and you may need to phone for a taxi.

- For general enquiries about RENFE services throughout Andalucía, tel: 902 32 03 20. The RENFE website is in Spanish and English, www.renfe.es
- It is advisable to **reserve a seat** on mainline trains. You can buy **tickets** and reserve seats at city-centre travel agents that display the RENFE sign. Most city railway stations have a queuing system at ticket desks: you must first take a numbered slip from a machine signed *"Venta anticipada su turno"*, then watch for your number to appear on indicators above the desks.
- For details of **railway stations** in Málaga, Almería, Granada and Seville, ► 34–35.

Types of Train

- **Cercanías** are city and suburban link trains, though services may extend to nearby provincial towns. They are fast and fairly cheap.
- **Media Distancia** are intercity links. They are being upgraded to what are known as TRDs (Trenes Regionales Diésel) and are fast and comfortable.
- **Larga Distancia**, known as AVE (Tren Alta Velocidad) is the national high-speed service into Andalucía from Madrid to Córdoba and Seville.

Bus

Andalucía has an excellent regional bus service run by a number of companies. Buses, in general, are reliable and comfortable (with air conditioning on intercity buses) and fares are usually about 25 per cent less than for similar journeys by train. In rural areas bus travel is often faster than train or is the only option.

- For details of **bus stations** in main cities, including telephone information numbers, ► 34–35.
- Buy **tickets** as early as possible (preferably the day before) for bus journeys between main cities and towns. If you arrive within minutes of departure without a ticket, you will probably be given a ticket for a later bus. There can be long queues, especially in the mornings.
- Some bus stations sell all tickets from one desk, but at **Málaga bus station** the Alsina Graells company ticket office handles main services inland and the Automóviles Portillo company handles Costa del Sol, Cádiz and coastal routes to the east.
- Services are greatly reduced on Sundays and public holidays.
- Luggage goes in the hold, but there is room under the seat in front of you for a normal-size case or pack, if you want to keep an eye on your luggage.

Taxi

Taxis in Andalucían have metres. Fares are generally cheaper than in northern Europe. Make sure the metre is operating, but expect a change to an increased rate as soon as you leave city limits, or late at night, at weekends and during holidays. A surcharge is also likely for luggage carried.

Driving

Avoid, where possible, driving right into the cities, especially into the historic centres, which are often a labyrinth of narrow, one-way streets that make progress very slow. In most towns, you will have to pay a parking fee for the blue designated spaces; you are not allowed to park on yellow lines. Pay the parking attendant or feed the machine, as applicable. Driving in Andalucía is fairly stress-free away from cities and towns, although the high speeds and congestion of the **N340** main road along the Costa del Sol can be daunting.

- Drive on the **right-hand side** of the road. When **turning left** outside localities, you will find that the more major roads have their own lanes, which first go off to the right and then cross the main street *(raqueta)*.

- **Seat belts** must be worn in front seats and in rear seats where fitted.

- **Fuel** (*gasolina*) is available in four grades: *normal*, *super*, *sin plomo* (unleaded) and *gasoleo/gasoil* (diesel). Most garages take credit cards, but rural garages often prefer cash.

- The **speed limit** on the *autopistas* (toll motorways) and *autovías* (free motorways) is 120kph (75mph). On dual carriageways and roads with periodic overtaking lanes it is 100kph (62mph) and on rural roads 90kph (56mph). The maximum speed on urban roads is 50kph (31mph) and 25kph (16mph) in residential areas.

- Breath testing is random. The blood alcohol limit is 0.5 percent. If you drink, don't drive.

- In cities and larger towns particularly (but also in smaller places), check whether you have parked in a **pay-for area**. Penalties range from a fine to towing away.

- You must carry a **warning triangle**, a **set of replacement bulbs** and a **reflective jacket**.

Hiring a Car

- **Book ahead** at peak times. From the UK, try **Budget** (tel: 08701 56 56 56, www.budget.co.uk) or **Europcar** (tel: 08706 07 50 00, www.europcar.com).

- **On-the-spot hiring** can be done at airports and at most city railway stations. If you can speak some Spanish you can get good deals and often friendlier service from local companies. A good hire company is **ATA S L Rent a Car** (www.atarentacar.com) with offices in Seville (tel: 954 22 09 57) and Cardelmar (www.cardelmar.es, tel: 807 17 07 27, €0.42/min.). These offices can also put you in contact with their regional outlets (in Cádiz and Marbella, for example).

- Always **check** bodywork, tyres, undercarriage and inside trimmings of your hire car and indicate any damage to the hirer before driving off.

- In the event of a **breakdown**, follow the instructions on your car-rental agreement. Make certain that there are portable warning symbols with your hire car and use these to warn other traffic no matter where you break down. If using your own car use the procedures outlined in your insurance or motoring association membership.

- You will be expected to return the car with the **petrol** tank at the same level as when you left.

Accommodation

This guide recommends a cross-section of places to stay, ranging from *paradores* (the state-owned chain of top-quality hotels) to small family-run *hostales* (modest hotels). In the more popular tourist destinations, it is advisable to book ahead.

Finding a Room

- If you have not reserved a room, the local tourist office will have a list of accommodation; most are prepared to call ahead to check if there is a room available. Note, most hotels are only required to retain a reserved room until 6pm unless you have given your credit-card details in advance.
- If there is no tourist office, or it is closed, then look for the main plaza or the centre of town as the most likely area for hotels and *hostales*.
- If you have a pet or small child with you, inform the hotel when booking.

Checking In and Out

- You will be asked to produce your passport when you check in; this will be used to complete a registration form.
- Check-out time is normally noon in hotels, although at some *hostales* and *pensiones* it is 11am; always find out in advance, to avoid paying an extra day. If you are staying in cheaper accommodation and plan to leave early, advise the front desk.
- Hotels will normally store your luggage until the end of the day.

Types of Accommodation

Paradores

Paradores are an expensive but special option. They tend to be converted castles, palaces and monasteries and most successfully retain the historical character of the building, while incorporating modern bathrooms, air conditioning and all the luxurious trimmings that you'd expect from a five-star hotel. They are often furnished with magnificent antiques and original works of art. There are some 16 *paradores* in Andalucía. Advance booking is recommended; to reserve a room at any *parador*, contact: **Central de Reservas**, Calle José Abascal 2–4, 28003, Madrid, tel: 902 54 79 79, www.parador.es

Hotels

Spanish hotels are officially classified with one to five stars (*estrellas*) by the Ministry of Tourism, depending on the amenities.

- A **five-star** hotel is truly luxurious with a price to match. You can expect facilities such as a WiFi, tennis court, swimming pool and gym, as well as nightly entertainment.
- A **four-star** hotel is slightly less deluxe, but still first-class.
- A **three-star** hotel is considerably lower in price but the rooms are perfectly adequate and will include TV and air conditioning.
- A **one- or two-star** hotel is more basic and relatively inexpensive. When booking such accommodation, enquire about the exact location and facilities provided, as standards can vary.
- Many hotels have family rooms with extra beds for children costing roughly 30 per cent more than the double room rate.

Hostales

Hostales often provide better accommodation and value for money than cheap hotels. Not to be confused with a youth hostel, a Spanish *hostal* is essentially a small hotel, often family run and officially categorised from none to three stars. An *hostal* with **three stars** is roughly the equivalent of a two-star hotel. With few exceptions they provide straightforward accommodation at a reasonable price, with the option of en-suite bathroom. There are some charming small *hostales* in Andalucía, particularly in the major cities where they are invariably situated in the historic quarter of town.

Pensiones

There is not a great deal of difference between an *hostal* and a *pensión*, except that the latter is more like a boarding house and will often have a shared bathroom. A *pensión* will usually require you to take either full board or half board. You can expect your room to be clean but spartan and you will have to supply your own soap and shampoo, although towels and blankets should be provided.

Budget Accommodation

Camas or **habitaciones** are the closest Spanish equivalent to a B&B, usually advertised in the windows of private houses and the upper floors of bars and *ventas* (➤ 41), perhaps with the phrase *"camas y comidas"* (bed and meals). Don't expect an en-suite bathroom. A **fonda** is a small inn offering basic no-frills accommodation. Most **Youth hostels** *(albergues juveniles)* are housed in old buildings that lack modern plumbing or air conditioning and possibly are unheated in winter. They are also usually situated out of town and can be packed with schoolchildren during holiday periods.

Camping

Andalucía has some excellent campsites. These are routinely inspected and approved by the Spanish tourist authority, and classified under four categories: L (luxury), then first, second and third class, according to their amenities. However, even the most basic campsite must have 24-hour surveillance, be within a fenced area, provide unlimited drinking water, have first-aid and fire-prevention facilities, and toilets and showers. There is usually an extra charge for hot water. Camping is forbidden on beaches and may result in a fine.

Seasonal Rates

Minimum and maximum rates are established according to the season, as well as the facilities provided. In popular summer resorts, such as those of the Costa del Sol, July and August are the high season *(temporada alta)* when room rates can increase by 25 per cent. In winter resorts, as in the Sierra Nevada, high season is, logically, winter. During national holidays and local *fiestas* such as Seville's Feria de Abril, accommodation costs more and is harder to find, (➤ 22 for more information on festivals). Outside the main season, many hotels offer discounts, and some will have reduced prices at weekends. *Paradores* can be particularly good value then.

Accommodation Prices

Prices are for a double room per night.

€ up to €60   €€ €60–€90   €€€ €90–€140   €€€€ over €140

Food and Drink

Andalucía has the climate, coast and terrain to produce a wonderful range of raw ingredients: swordfish *(pez espada)*, mussels *(mejillones)*, cockles *(coquinas and almejas)* and fresh anchovies *(boquerones)* for seafood lovers; baby goat *(choto)* and rabbit *(conejo)*, both popular in this part of Spain, for meat eaters; and beautiful fruit and vegetables according to season – purple figs, glossy red peppers, curly green chard or brilliant orange pumpkin.

Meal Timetable

■ **Breakfast** *(desayuno)* usually consists of coffee with toast *(tostada)* which locals prefer topped with olive oil instead of butter. Other toppings include pork lard *(manteca)*, coloured a lurid orange by the addition of paprika, and crushed tomato with olive oil *(tomate y aceite)*. Spiral-shaped *churros* and hot chocolate are another popular choice. However, most Spaniards drink coffee in the morning, either strong and black *(café solo)*, with hot milk *(café con leche)*, or black with a dash of milk *(café cortado)*. If you find the coffee too strong, you may prefer the more diluted *americano*.

■ **Lunch** *(almuerzo)* is the most important meal of the day, eaten by the Spanish at 2pm, although most restaurants will serve until 4pm. There are usually three or four courses, starting with soup and/or salad, followed by a seafood or meat dish with vegetables. Vegetarians tend to be restricted to *gazpacho*, followed by a Spanish *tortilla* (see Andalucían Cuisine, below) or omelette with salad. Often the choice of desserts is limited to caramel custard *(flan)*, ice cream or fresh fruit. Most average restaurants offer an economical menu of the day *(menú del día)*.

■ **Tapas** are an integral part of the local culinary tradition (▶30).

■ **Dinner** *(cena)* is generally a lighter meal than lunch. Few restaurants offer their cut-price menu in the evening. The normal dinner hour is late compared to northern Europe, starting anywhere between 9 and 10:30pm, although in the popular resorts you can usually dine at 8pm.

Andalucían Cuisine

■ **Soups** *(sopas)*: The best-known soup is *gazpacho*, served cold in summer and made from blended tomatoes, cucumbers, peppers, garlic, bread, vinegar and olive oil. A thicker version, known as *salmorejo* in Córdoba and *porra antequerana* around Málaga, is also popular, while *ajo blanco*, a chilled soup made with almonds, garlic and grapes, is often found at better restaurants.

■ **Eggs** *(huevos)*: Potatoes, onions and eggs are the simple ingredients for a Spanish omelette *(tortilla)*. A plain omelette is a *tortilla francesa*.

■ **Seafood** *(mariscos)*: **Chiringuitos** (▶41), located on beaches, are the best places to find economically priced fish such as fresh charcoal-grilled anchovies *(boquerones)*. Paella is another all-time favourite, made with shellfish and garnished with red peppers and lemon wedges.

■ **Meat** *(carne)*: Popular meat dishes include loin of pork *(lomo de cerdo)*, chops *(chuletas)*, spicy sausage *(chorizo)* and roast suckling pig *(cochinillo)*. Some of the best Spanish mountain ham *(jamón serrano)* originates from the Alpujarras region of Granada province. Spit-roasted chicken is very popular and sold on the spot at small open-fronted shops *(asador)*.

■ **Vegetables** *(verdura)*: Salads tend to be a combination of lettuce, tomatoes and onion. Many vegetable dishes are seasonal, such as oyster mushrooms *(setas)* fried with garlic and parsley, and fresh asparagus prepared with scrambled eggs *(revuelto)*.

■ **Desserts** *(postres)*: As well as caramel custard with cream *(crema catalan)* and ice cream *(helado)*, you may find rice pudding *(arroz con leche)*, vanilla whip *(natillas)* and fresh fruit on the menu.

Where to Eat

■ **Ventas**, rural restaurants that traditionally catered to farm workers and travellers, still serve hearty home-style cooking, though nowadays the clientele is a mix of construction workers, business people and, on weekends, families. Chiringuitos are beachside restaurants serving fresh seafood.

■ There's plenty of choice when it comes to **cafés** and **bars**, including *tascas* that specialise in *tapas*, and *bodegas* where you can sample wine or sherry straight from the barrel.

■ **Restaurants**, ranging from sophisticated places serving international cuisine to ethnic and fast-food joints, are found in the Costa resorts and main cities. Restaurants tend to specialise in seafood, game and meat dishes.

■ **Teterías** are Moroccan-style tea shops serving a wide choice of herb teas *(infusiones)*, accompanied by traditional Arab pastries.

Tipping

The Spanish tip is an average of five per cent but there is rarely any arithmetic involved. It's more a matter of just leaving spare change. Most foreigners tip as they would in their own countries.

What to Drink

■ **Beer** *(cerveza)* is extremely popular – many Spaniards prefer it to wine. A *cervecería* is a bar that specialises in beer and usually has several brands on tap, plus a wide range of bottled and imported beers. Spanish beer is fairly strong, usually around five per cent alcohol by volume. For something lighter, try a shandy *(clara)*.

■ Rioja is perhaps the most famous of Spanish **wines**, but there are 40 other wine denominations in Spain. You may want to try a house wine *(vino de la casa)* or, for a refreshing alternative, a *tinto de verano*: red wine with lemonade *(gaseosa)*. Red wine is *tinto*, white wine *blanco*. The sweet Málaga wine is made from muscat grapes grown in the Axarquia region.

■ **Sherry** *(fino, manzanilla, amontillado, oloroso)* is produced in Andalucía and is a popular aperitif (►26).

■ **Sangría** is a delicious red wine punch that combines wine, cognac, other liqueurs and *gaseosa* with slices of citrus fruit.

■ **Cocktails and spirits** are much cheaper in Spain than in most other countries and the measures are generous. Many Andalucíans will have a brandy *(coñac)* or *anís* with their morning coffee.

■ The usual choice of fizzy soft drinks is available. Other **non-alcoholic drinks** include fruit juice *(zumo)* and *Bitter Kas*, the latter similar in flavour to Campari. For something different, try ice-cold *horchata*, a nutty milk-like beverage made from tiger nuts *(chufas)*.

Restaurant Prices

Price per person for a three-course meal, including wine and service.

€ up to €15   €€ €15–€40   €€€ over €40

Shopping

In Andalucía's glitzy coastal resorts and major cities, top-name fashion salons exist side by side with shops selling traditional flamenco wear. In every region, you'll find *alfarerías* (pottery workshops) and *talleres* (craft studios) producing colourful ceramics and fabrics, leatherwork and silverware (craft traditions that have their origins in the region's Moorish past). You'll also find tempting delicatessens, wine shops and pâtisseries in every city, and colourful local markets, where you can buy a range of regional specialities.

Where to Shop

Fashion

All of Andalucía's main cities – Málaga, Granada, Seville, Córdoba and Cádiz – and the chic Costa del Sol resorts of Marbella and Puerto Banús, have a huge number of clothes and shoe shops. You can buy anything from top-of-the-range Armani or Gucci to affordable and bargain clothes and accessories.

There are many jewellery shops in the Costa del Sol resorts, although with some outlets you would be wise to know something about what you are buying. Long-established jewellers are also found in the main shopping areas of cities and larger towns.

Souvenirs

You can buy souvenirs that range from tacky T-shirts to traditional pottery in just about every city and large town in Andalucía. Most shops that are wholly dedicated to mass-produced souvenirs are concentrated around major attractions, such as Córdoba's Mezquita and Seville's Barrio Santa Cruz area. The more authentic outlets that sell fine pottery and other traditional Andalucían craftwork can still be found (the Where to… Shop sections throughout the guide give some suggestions). The main streets and seafront *paseos* of the major Costa del Sol resorts are lined with gift shops, and at peak season an additional layer of pavement stalls hawk cheap souvenirs. There's quality around as well, however, and you can often find entertaining items amid the relentless trash. (See also the sections below on antiques and art, crafts and village shops.)

Antiques and Art

For interesting pieces with a genuine Spanish pedigree – a cut above the usual "souvenir" – search the antiques and fine-arts shops scattered throughout the centres of main cities like Granada and Seville. Most of the pieces on display may be too hefty to cart back home, but there are often worthwhile smaller items.

Crafts

Andalucían **ceramics** reach international standards, not least in such regional centres as Úbeda (▶122) and Níjar (▶101). Andalucía is particularly noted for vivid and colourful tile work in a tradition that goes back to the Moorish era. In Córdoba you will find outstanding **leatherwork** and **filigree silverware**, while Granada is a centre for **marquetry**. The mountain areas of Andalucía, especially the Alpujarras (▶94) and the Sierra de Grazalema (▶66), are good places to find traditional fabrics and clothing such as ponchos, as well as small rugs and bedcovers, known as *jarapas*.

Food and Drink

The hill regions of the Alpujarras in Granada province and the Sierra Morena in Seville province are famous for their *jamón serrano* and *jamón ibérico* (cured ham) respectively; villages such as Trevélez (►96) in the Alpujarras, and Aracena (►162) and Jabugo (►188) in the Sierra Morena, have shops devoted to *jamón* and other meats. You can find own-label brands of **sherry** in the big-name *bodegas* of Jerez de la Frontera (►53), El Puerto de Santa María (►67) and Sanlúcar de Barrameda (►67), while in specialist shops in main towns and wine-producing areas, you will find every kind of sherry, wine and liqueur on sale.

Department Stores

Spain's shopping success story is the **El Corte Inglés** chain of mega-stores, which has branches in Seville, Granada, Córdoba, Málaga and the Costa del Sol. Some, like Malaga's, are crammed with departments that specialise in just about anything you could want.

Markets

Town and village markets are excellent sources of fresh food. Colourful, noisy, good-natured and, above all, bursting with life, they can be an entertainment in themselves.

Best Markets

For fish: Sanlúcar de Barrameda (►67), Almería (►98)

For mixed fish, meat, fruit and vegetables: Cádiz (►63), Málaga (►60)

For clothing and general goods: Fuengirola (►57), Córdoba (►114)

Village Shops

Village hardware and general goods shops can sell anything from local pottery to straw hats, spices and condiments, colourful shawls and neckties. You'll pay a fraction of the price for such items that you would pay in town, while they have a far more authentic pedigree than a typical resort souvenir.

Insider Tip

Opening Hours

Most shops in Andalucía open 9–2 and 4:30–8:30 Monday to Saturday, although there is individual flexibility at either end. Large department stores open all day from about 9:30am to as late as 10pm. Saturday afternoon and all-day Sunday closing is general outside coastal resorts.

Payment

In main cities and larger towns, credit cards are accepted in most shops and stores. In village shops and other rural outlets, cash payment is still expected.

Etiquette

Andalucíans enjoy browsing in shops and you will have no problems about doing so as a visitor. To avoid any misunderstandings, shoppers should ask the assistant's permission before handling goods. However, in chic fashion salons you will be assumed to be serious about buying and here you may receive one-to-one attention as soon as you enter. In the wall-to-wall shopping of the resorts, shopkeepers and stallholders are sometimes overly attentive.

Entertainment

There is no lack of organised evening entertainment in Andalucía's towns and villages, from nightclubbing to flamenco watching. Most cities have cinemas and the Costa del Sol has a number of casinos. For the outdoor enthusiast there are plenty of activities, and children are more than catered for on the Costa del Sol where there is a whole range of fun parks (➤ 65).

Nightlife

- The main **clubbing circuit** is on the Costa del Sol. Most clubs **open** their doors at 10 or 11pm, but you'll have the place to yourself until at least 1am, and things often don't really get going until 3 or 4am.
- There are **cinemas** in all the major cities and in most large towns. Most foreign-language films are dubbed into Spanish rather than subtitled. Cinemas in Málaga, Fuengirola and Marbella show original version films.
- There are plenty of opportunities to see **flamenco** (➤ 19).

Special Events

- **Festivals** are an essential and exuberant part of Andalucían life. The calendar of events is fullest from Easter through to June (➤ 22).
- The main **bullfight** season runs from Easter to October, but there are novice fights into November on the Costa del Sol. Bullfights are advertised by garish posters about three weeks before the event, and resort hotels often organise bus pickups. For major rings, tickets are often booked well ahead by locals. Prices can be as high as €140 but start at about €15. Even Costa del Sol *novilladas* may cost you from €30 to €60, although they should be much less. For more information ➤ 17.

Outdoor Activities

- The windier Atlantic coast, especially at Tarifa (➤ 68), between Gibraltar and Cádiz, is one of the world's best **windsurfing** and **kitesurfing** venues, while the opportunities for **scuba diving**, **waterskiing** and **paragliding** are increasing. Boat trips are an enjoyable option and in the Gibraltar and Tarifa area, there are special **dolphin-watching** boat trips available.
- Specialist "golf villages" proliferate on the Costa del Sol. On the Costa courses in general you may find that you need to book well in advance for a round, and provide a handicap certificate. Fees vary, but can be hefty on some of the more upmarket courses where you may even have difficulty in making a casual booking (➤ 76 for details). A good source of information about golf in Andalucía is the **Real Federacíon Andaluza de Golf** (Sierra de Grazalema 33-5-1B, Málaga, tel: 952 22 55 90, http://rfga.org).
- Andalucía's magnificent mountains offer endless opportunities for adventure holidaying, whether it's basic **walking** along the numerous tracks and paths in Las Alpujarras (➤ 94), the Sierra de Grazalema (➤ 66) and the Sierras de Cazorla y Segura (➤ 128) or **horse riding** and **cycling** on organised trips with expert guides. Ask at tourist offices. For information on angling, contact **Spanish Fishing Federation** (tel: 915 32 83 53, www.fepyc.es). You can also go for the wilder edges of **adventure sport** and try rock climbing, abseiling, canoeing, paragliding and hang-gliding.

Useful Publications

At most city tourist offices, you can pick up a copy of *Qué Hacer? – Guía de Ocio de Andalucía*, a monthly entertainments guide, in Spanish and English.

Málaga and Cádiz

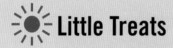 **Little Treats**

The Wild Blue Yonder
Anyone who visits **Júzcar** (➤ 52) experiences the wild blue yonder in its literal sense: Here, the typical white houses of Andalucía, *pueblos blancos*, were all painted blue as an advertising gag for the world premiere of *The Smurfs*.

Whale Watching
The narrow Strait of Gibraltar offers a perfect place to go out on a boat **whale-watching**, e.g. with FIRMM (www.firmm.org) in **Tarifa** (➤ 68).

Cry with the Wolves
See wolves from a different side! Daniel Weigend and Alexandra Stieber make this possible with tours through their **Lobo Park** (➤ 66) in the mountains of Antequera.

Getting Your Bearings

Málaga and Cádiz are Andalucía's most visited provinces, not only because of the popular appeal of Málaga's Costa del Sol, but for their spectacular landscapes, old Moorish villages and historic cities and towns.

Málaga province provides an ideal introduction to the extraordinary diversity of Andalucía. The vibrant, everyday life of its capital, Málaga, is a refreshing contrast to the conspicuous tourism of the neighbouring Costa del Sol's crowded resorts. North of Málaga and the Costa lie the forested valleys and rugged mountains of a different Andalucía, seen at its most dramatic in the bone-white limestone pinnacles and wooded ravines of the Parque Natural del Torcal near the historic town of Antequera. There is also dramatic scenery further west, in the Serranía de Ronda, especially at the clifftop town of Ronda. To the south and west of Ronda, where Málaga and Cádiz provinces meet, villages of whitewashed houses known as the *pueblos blancos* (white towns) dot the mountains of the Sierra de Grazalema and the wooded hills of the area known as El Alcornocales.

On the western border of Cádiz province, between Jerez de la Frontera, Sanlúcar de Barrameda and El Puerto de Santa María, lies a grape-growing area known as the "Sherry Triangle". The ancient, labyrinthine city of Cádiz lies on a promontory to the south. To its southeast are the undeveloped beaches of the Costa de la Luz and old Moorish towns such as hilltop Vejer de la Frontera and Spain's most southerly town, Tarifa. Further east again is the dramatic punctuation mark of the Rock of Gibraltar.

Sanlúcar de Barrameda **17**

Jerez de la Frontera

16

El Puerto de Santa María **18**

Arcos la Fror

Cádiz **12**

San Fernando

Los Caños de Meca

Costa de la Luz **19**

Ta

TOP 10

Don't Miss

At Your Leisure

**At Jerez de la Frontera's
famous riding school**

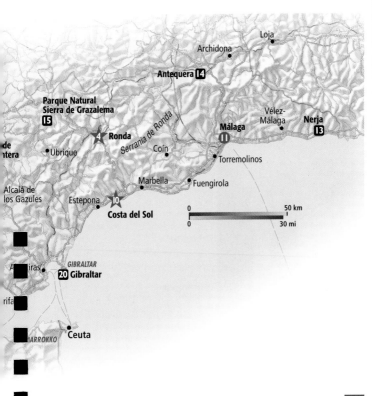

Four Perfect Days

From Málaga follow dramatic mountain roads to Ronda and the "white towns", then head for the sherry capital, Jerez, and historic Cádiz, before following the coast road back to Málaga. For more information see the main entries (➤ 50–69).

Day One

Morning
Visit ❶ **Málaga's** (➤ 60) colourful morning market, the **Mercado Atarazanas** (➤ 62), then down the Marqués de Larios (right), the marble-surfaced main shopping street, and surrounding narrow streets to the Moorish citadel, the **Alcazaba** (➤ 60). Drop into the **cathedral** (➤ 61) to see its Renaissance interior before lunchtime *tapas* at Bar Logüeno (➤ 71).

Afternoon
Visit the **Museo Picasso** (➤ 61) for a feast of works by Málaga's most famous son. In the late afternoon head through wooded, rocky mountains to ★**Ronda** (below, ➤ 50), perched to either side of its stupendous gorge (left).

Enjoy Ronda in the evening when the gorge is bathed in golden sunlight. Stay overnight.

Day Two

Morning
Visit **Iglesia de Santa María Mayor** (➤ 50) with its exquisite traces of the Moorish mosque it supplanted. Go on to the clifftop **Palacio de Mondragón** for its museum (➤ 51), decorative patios and spectacular views.

Afternoon
Drive through the 🔟 **Sierra de Grazalema** (➤ 66), stopping at beautiful Grazalema itself or at Zahara de la Sierra. Continue through the mountains to reach ★**Jerez de la Frontera** (➤ 53) for an overnight stay.

Day Three

Morning

Visit the **Royal Andalucían School of Equestrian Art** (➤ 53), then take a tour of one of the town's sherry *bodegas* before a late lunch at a *tapas* bar.

Afternoon

Set off south for an overnight stay in ❶❷ **Cádiz** (➤ 63). See the city's great **cathedral**, then stroll through narrow streets full of early evening shoppers to the **Museo de Cádiz** (➤ 63) for absorbing displays (right) of Phoenician and Roman history, and paintings by Spanish masters. Wander along the seafront in the glorious evening light.

Day Four

Morning

Breakfast in the colourful **Plaza de las Flores** (left, ➤ 63), then drop into the adjoining market on your way to the **Torre Tavira** (➤ 63) for great views over the city. In the late morning, take the road east along the ❶❾ **Costa de la Luz** (➤ 68). If you have time, visit the old Moorish town of **Vejer de la Frontera** (➤ 68), then continue to **Tarifa** (➤ 68) over the coastal hills of the Sierra del Cabrito with dramatic views of ❷⓿ **Gibraltar's** (➤ 69) mighty rock. Aim for a late lunch at **Estepona** (➤ 56).

Afternoon

Relax on Estepona's splendid beach before heading for **Marbella** (➤ 56) and an evening at one of the Costa del Sol's many all-in-one food and entertainment venues. Or continue to ❶❶ **Málaga** (➤ 60) to catch the evening *paseo* along Paseo del Parque, followed, perhaps, by a *tapas* and sherry crawl.

⭐4 Ronda

Ronda is irresistible if only because of its spectacular position above the Río Guadalevín's rocky gorge, El Tajo, whose towering walls seem to be prised apart by the spectacular 18th-century Puente Nuevo. The town has been popular with tourists since the 19th century, when it became an essential destination on the itinerary of travellers from northern Europe.

The town can become very crowded during the middle part of the day as streams of coaches, packed with day visitors, arrive from the Costa del Sol, but by visiting the most popular sights during the early part of the morning, or in the evening, you can escape the worst of the overcrowding.

El Tajo is over 100m (109yd) deep and splits the town into two parts. Where the Guadalevín enters and emerges from the depths of the gorge, the vast walls extend as escarpments to either side. Brown and white buildings cluster along the edges of the great cliffs like carved and painted extensions of the natural rock. The spectacular bridge, the **Puente Nuevo**, spans the gorge at its narrowest point and offers great views of the awesome walls, although you may have to jostle for position with crowds of camera-wielding fellow visitors. You can enjoy even better views of El Tajo and the escarpment by heading for the cliff-edge gardens of the Paseo Blas Infante, reached from Ronda's main square, Plaza de España, on the north side of the Puente Nuevo.

The Old Town

Ronda's most interesting sights lie on the south side of the gorge in the **Ciudad**, or Old Town, where you can discover mosques, churches and Renaissance palaces as you thread your way through the side streets. The focus of the Old Town is the Plaza Duquesa de Parcent, a leafy square surrounded by handsome buildings and dominated by **Iglesia de Santa María Mayor**. The church stands on the site of a mosque,

Ronda, perched on two sides of a rocky gorge, commands spectacular views of the surrounding countryside

Ronda's 18th-century bullring, an architectural treasure

and Moorish features survive within the exquisite Gothic and baroque fabric of the building. The belfry crowns a fragment of an old minaret.

Just round the corner from the church, along Calle Manuel Montero, is the 14th-century **Palacio de Mondragón**. Originally a Moorish palace, it was altered after the Reconquest, but some *mudéjar* (late Moorish) architecture survives: there are three small patios that in their decoration and style are superb examples of Islamic artistry. Take in the stupendous views from the garden terraces; and as you climb the main staircase, pause and look up at the brilliantly colourful cupola. Palacio de Mondragón doubles as the Municipal Museum and there are imaginative displays outlining Ronda's pre-Moorish history.

Nearby is the **Casa Juan Bosco**. The glory of this 19th-century mansion is its ornamental garden, with mosaics, fountains and clifftop views. In Calle Armiñán, the main street of the Ciudad, is the **Museo del Bandolero** (Bandit Museum), which tells the story of the 19th-century youthful *bandoleros* (bandits) who lived by their wits in the mountains (➤ 16).

Insider Tip

The Mercadillo

On the north side of the gorge is the **Mercadillo**, the Ronda of smart hotels, restaurants, bars and souvenir shops. The **Plaza de Toros** here is the second oldest bullring in Spain, and is where the legendary matador Pedro Romero established the rules and ornate moves of bullfighting in the mid-18th century. A museum within the handsome walls of the bullring is crammed with memorabilia of famous bull-fighters and bulls and notable *aficionados*, such as American actor Orson Welles and writer Ernest Hemingway.

Opposite the bullring is the start of Ronda's main shopping street, the pedestrianised Carrera Espinel, flanked on either side by souvenir shops of varying quality, seductive delicatessens, and boutiques. Part-way up Espinel, on the left, is Plaza del Socorro with numerous restaurants, bars and cafés.

TAKING A BREAK

For a spectacular view of Ronda's dramatic gorge and the Puente Nuevo, stop for a drink or snack at **Don Miguel** (Calle Villanueva 4, tel: 952 87 10 90), a classic Spanish restaurant.

✚ 199 E2

Tourist Information
✉ Municipal Office, Paseo de Blas Infante (OMT)
☎ 952 18 71 19 ✉ Plaza de España 1 (J de A) ☎ 952 87 12 72

Parking
Central car park at Paseo de Blas Infante, just off Virgen de la Paz and behind the bullring. Multi-storey car park just off Plaza de la Merced at the west end of Virgen de la Paz.

Iglesia de Santa María Mayor
✉ Plaza Duquesa de Parcent ⏰ Mon–Sat 10–7, Sun 10–12:30, 2–7 💶 €4

Palacio de Mondragón
✉ Plaza de Mondragón, Calle Manuel Montero
☎ 952 87 84 50 ⏰ Mon–Fri 10–6, Sat, Sun and public hols 10–3 💶 €3

Casa Juan Bosco
✉ Calle Tenorio 20 ☎ 952 87 86 69 ⏰ Daily 9–6

Museo del Bandolero
✉ Calle Armiñán 65 ☎ 952 87 77 85 ⏰ Summer 10:30–8:30, winter 10:45–7
💶 €3.50

Plaza de Toros and Museo Taurino
✉ Calle Virgen de la Paz ☎ 952 87 41 32 ⏰ Daily 10–6 💶 €6.50

INSIDER INFO

- Stay **overnight in Ronda** and enjoy the town outside the very busy period.
- Stroll through the **Jardines Ciudad de Cuenca**. This cliffside terraced garden is on the north side of the gorge and can be reached from Plaza de España along Calle Nueva, turning right down Los Remedios and then right again down Calle Mina.
- At the eastern entrance to the gorge of El Tajo are two other bridges, the medieval **Puente Viejo** and the Moorish **Puente de San Miguel**, with dramatic views along the bed of the gorge. Close to the Puente de San Miguel are the **Baños Arabes** (Arab Baths) dating from the 13th and 14th centuries (Calle San Miguel, open ⏰ Mon–Sat 11–6/7, Sun 10–1/3. 💶 €3).
- **Júzcar**, *el pueblo pitufo*, the smurf village, 21km (13mi) south of Ronda, is quite a sensation. The houses in an idyllic tree-covered mountain setting were painted blue as part of an advertising campaign for the Hollywood film "The Smurfs" and have since become a tourist attraction in their own right.

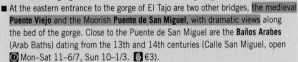

★7 Jerez de la Frontera

Jerez is renowned as the sherry capital of the world and a centre for stylish equestrianism and flamenco. However, it also has enough fine plazas, fashionable shops, and lively bars and restaurants to make it one of Andalucía's most enjoyable provincial towns.

The solera process is used in sherry production; it entails aging the sherry by blending together a mixture of different vintages

The Sherry Experience

Wine production in Jerez goes back to Phoenician and Roman times, when the rich chalky soil of the surrounding area was found to be ideal for vine growing. Today, in the city's palatial sherry *bodegas*, fermented wine is transformed into sherry and fine Spanish brandy. A tour of one or other of the *bodegas* is *de rigueur* and you'll find it an enjoyable experience, even if you do feel a little like a captive as liveried guides march you through vast wine stores or decant you briskly from "road trains" at each stage of the tour. A tasting session at the end is a satisfying lesson in the differences between the types of sherry. The city's

FROM XERES TO SHERRY

Jerez's very name reflects its most important industry. An original settlement was known to the Romans as Xeres. The Moors adapted the name to Sheriss, which, in turn, became Jerez ("de la Frontera" was added when Jerez became a border settlement of the Moorish kingdom of Granada in the late 14th century). Wine was produced in the area as early as Roman times, but it was not until the 18th and 19th centuries, that the name sherry was used to describe them.

bodegas include such famous names as González Byass (Tío Pepe), Domecq-Harveys, Sandeman and Williams & Humbert, but the tours of the González Byass and Domecq-Harveys bodegas are the most lavish. Both are like self-contained villages with lush gardens, covered patios and cobbled streets. At the Williams & Humbert bodega you get flamenco and falconry too.

Horses and More

Jerez's association with horses dates from the 18th century, when the monks of the nearby La Cartuja monastery began the selective breeding of Cartujano horses, which were noted for their elegant lines and obedience. The Jerez area is still the premier horse-breeding district of Spain. At

the **Real Escuela Andaluza del Arte Ecuestre** (Royal Andalucían School of Equestrian Art) you can watch the Sinfonía a Caballo displays of choreographed equestrianism or visit the school's training area and stables. If you have a little more time at your disposal, pay a visit to the 12th-century Moorish **Alcázar**, a walled complex of beautiful gardens that includes a restored mosque and bathhouse. You enter the Alcázar through the Puerta de la Ciudad. Inside you will discover a well-preserved domed mosque with a restored mihrâb as well as Arab baths dating back to the 14th century. The Palacio de Villavicencio, renovated in the style of the Renaissance, has a camera obscura in its tower that offers a 360-degree view of the town through lenses and mirrors. Alcázar offers a good view of the rear of the Colegiata de San Salvador Cathedral, built in 1695, in the baroque style. Admire the free-standing belfry, the protruding buttresses built as protection against earthquakes, the dome decorated with sculptures as well as the beautiful baroque steps leading up to the main façade.

The acclaimed **Centro Andaluz de Flamenco** (Andalucían Centre for Flamenco) is also worth a visit if you are interested

Displays at the Real Escuela Andaluza del Arte Ecuestre show equestrian skills of the highest calibre

Flamenco demands stylish dress

in flamenco. The centre lies at the heart of the Barrio de Santiago, Jerez's old gypsy quarter and one of the acknowledged cradles of flamenco in its purest form. You can request showings of videos and there is an audiovisual theatre, which screens excellent films of flamenco greats such as the late Manolo Caracol (➤ 21). If you visit the barrio in the morning you may hear the evocative clatter of heels and the ripple of guitar music echoing from local flamenco schools.

For the best of modern Jerez, explore the busy streets to the west of the main street, pedestrianised Calle Larga, stopping at serene Plaza de la Asunción, known locally as Plaza San Dionisio after its handsome 15th-century church. The entire area is well supplied with excellent *tapas* bars.

TAKING A BREAK

At **La Maceta Bar** (27 Calle Lancería), a typical local bar but with more character than most, you can enjoy an ice-cold *fino* (sherry) accompanied by pickled mussels or a more substantial sandwich. Sit *al fresco* or in the bar.

✚ 198 C2
ℹ️ Tourist Information
✉️ Plaza del Arenal ☎ 956 33 88 74; www.turismojerez.com

Alcázar
✉️ Alameda Vieja ☎ 956 14 99 55 🕐 March–June and mid-Sep, Oct Mon–Fri 9:30–18; July–mid-Sep 9:30–8; rest of the year and Sat, Sun until 3 ✋ €5

Real Escuela Andaluza del Arte Ecuestre
✉️ Avenida Duque de Abrantes ☎ 956 31 96 35 (reservations); www.realescuela.org 🕐 Sinfonía a Caballo (riding displays): March–mid-Dec Tue noon. Training sessions and stable visits: non-show days 10–1 ✋ €21–€27 (main show); €11 (training sessions)

Centro Andaluz de Flamenco
✉️ Palacio Pemartín, Plaza de San Juan, Barrio de Santiago ☎ 956 90 21 34; www.centroandaluzdeflamenco.es 🕐 Mon–Fri 9–2 ✋ Free

INSIDER INFO

- Book well ahead for the show at the Real Escuela Andaluza del Arte Ecuestre (www.realescuela.org).
- The collections in the **Museo Arqueológico** (Plaza del Mercado, tel: 956 33 33 16 open Tue–Fri 10–2, 4–7, Sat, Sun 10–2. Admission €5), covering prehistoric Andalucía to the Moorish period, are excellent.
- If you intend visiting a **sherry** bodega, check at the tourist information office for the times of the tours conducted in your national language.

⭐ Costa del Sol

The tourist mecca on the coast stretching from Málaga to Estepona is regarded as Europe's largest holiday "playground". Until the 1950s hardly anyone strayed here, but then the tourist industry discovered the coast on which the sun shines for 320 days a year, and visitors have been swarming here ever since.

Estepona, Marbella and Puerto Banús

The most westerly of the Costa del Sol's main resorts, the former fishing village **Estepona**, grew phenomenally with the arrival of mass tourism in the 1960s, although the pretty centre has been retained. The long seafront is entirely urban, but sensible planning has created a pleasant *cordón sanitaire* of aromatic flower beds, palm trees and shrubs between the main street, Avenida de España, and the broad promenade that runs alongside Estepona's fine beach. The old heart of the town is the Plaza de las Flores, a small jasmine-scented square that evokes 19th-century Andalucía. There are numerous bars, cafés and restaurants in the town centre, but few other diversions; Estepona's beach is the main attraction. At the west end of the resort are an old lighthouse, the fishing harbour, a yacht marina and – a few kilometres further west – **Costa Natura**, Spain's longest-established nudist beach.

East from Estepona the ubiquitous *urbanizaciones*, the "fill-in" residential estates of the Costa del Sol, cling to either side of the highway as far as **Marbella**, the next main resort. The Phoenicians first founded a settlement here called Salduba (Salt town). In 1485, the Catholic monarch Queen Isabel is said to have cried: "Qué mar bella!" when she saw the sea – which is how the town got its name. Marbella's promotion to in-place followed in 1953 when Prinz Alfonso

On the Playa del Salon (Nerja)

von Hohenlohe founded the Marbella Club, which became the hub of the high society for many years. The town's generally subdued air by day is surprising, but you can expect lively nightlife, especially around the yacht harbour of Puerto Deportivo and in Plaza Puente Ronda in the carefully manicured Old Town, the Casco Antiguo. The Casco Antiguo has not been robbed entirely of its traditional character. At its heart is the Plaza de los Naranjos, created in the 14th century by demolishing the old Moorish quarter. Today it is an intimate tree-lined square with several pricey restaurants. The alleyways that radiate from the plaza are full of upmarket clothes shops and craft galleries. Just east of the square is Plaza de la Iglesia, where the handsome church of Nuestra Señora de la Encarnación rubs shoulders with part of Marbella's Moorish walls. South of Plaza de los Naranjos the Old Town gives way to the busy through-road of Avenida Ramón y Cajal, on the other side of which lies the Plaza de **In the heart of** la Alameda with its big central fountain. From the far side of **Estepona** the plaza a walkway, the Avenida del Mar, descends to the

seafront past a succession of eccentric Salvador Dalí sculptures. Marbella's beach offers the inevitable mix of churned-up sand and seafront *chiringuitos* (fish restaurants), souvenir shops, bars and cafés. Keep heading west along the seafront for a few kilometres to reach the marina resort of **Puerto Banús**, with pseudo-Moorish apartment blocks, floating gin palaces, expensive shops and restaurants, and an often elusive celebrity circus.

Fuengirola and Torremolinos

About 25km (40mi) east of Marbella is **Fuengirola**, perhaps the least favoured of the Costa resorts because of the high-rise hotels that crowd the seafront. This said, Fuengirola is a wholeheartedly fun resort as well as a genuine Spanish working town. The long, narrow beach is packed with sunbeds hired out, for a king's ransom, by adjoining bars and restaurants.

🎡 COSTA FUN PARKS

Selwo Aventura (tel: 902 19 04 82, www.selwo.es, June–Aug 10–8; rest of the year 10–6; €24.50), located 6km (3.75mi) east of Estepona, is a safari park with 200 animals. There's a walk-through canyon filled with exotic birds. **Sea Life**, Puerto Marina, Benalmádena Costa (tel: 952 56 01 50, open daily 10–midnight; www.visitsealife. com; €16.25). Submarine view of Mediterranean sea life from tiny shrimps and shellfish to sharks. **Tivoli World**, Arroyo de la Miel, Benalmádena Costa (www.tivoli.es; from noon until 6pm (summer) until 7pm–2am (summer). Rides and amusements, Wild West shows and flamenco spectaculars. **Aqualand Torremolinos** (tel: 952 38 88 88; www.aqualand.es/torremolinos; May, June, Sep 11–6, July, Aug 10–7; €26). A huge complex with lots of water slides and numerous other attractions.

INSIDER INFO

- **Torremolinos** and **Fuengirola** are on the **electric rail line** to Málaga Airport and Málaga city. The train takes you right into the heart of both resorts, making car-free day visits an easy option. If you **walk** some distance to either side of the main beaches of the Costa resorts, you'll find less crowded sections of beach.
- Marbella's **Museo del Grabado Contemporáneo** (Museum of Lithographic Art), housed in a pleasant Renaissance building, contains work by Joan Miró and Picasso as well as contemporary Spanish graphics.
- **Costa Excursions:** In the mountains behind the Costa del Sol there are many attractive hill villages. Casares lies in the Sierra Bermeja about 18km (11mi) in and from Estepona, its whitewashed houses overlooked by a Moorish castle. *Insider Tip* The pretty village of Mijas lies 8km (5mi) north of Fuengirola. Although touristy and crowded during the day, it still retains much of its charm, and this is especially apparent when you walk through the town in the evening. There are regular bus services to both villages from the main resorts.

Torremolinos, probably the most visited (and developed) of the Costa resorts, is 20km (12.5mi) northeast of Fuengirola. The place is a mass of souvenir shops, bars, cafés and restaurants, although fragments of an older Torremolinos survive. At peak season the main streets of the resort are dense with people and the beaches are carpeted with sunbeds. You can keep moving along the resort's delightful promenade, the Paseo Marítimo. It runs for about 5km (3mi), passing the pleasant beaches of La Carihuela and de Montemar, before reaching **Benalmádena Costa**'s kitsch Arab harbour complex with layered terraces and whipped-cream domes. All the way along the Paseo Marítimo are tempting beachside *chiringuitos* sizzling with barbecued sardines and glittering with cool, beaded glasses.

Yacht harbours on the coast of Marbella

Playground of
the rich and
beautiful: on
the Costa del
Sol

TAKING A BREAK

Splash out on an extortionately expensive drink at the famous
Sinatra Bar in Puerto Banús for a little celebrity spotting.
This front-line bar is a traditional hang-out for the Marbella
jet-set, and if you get tired of the poseurs you can admire
the luxury yachts, or do a little window shopping instead.

Estepona Tourist Information
✚ 199 E2 ✉ Avenida San Lorenzo 1 ☎ 952 80 20 02; www.infoestepona.com

Marbella Tourist Information
✚ 199 E2 ✉ Salinas 4 ☎ 952 76 11 97; www.marbellaexclusive.com
✉ Glorieta de la Fontanilla

Fuengirola Tourist Information
✚ 199 F2 ✉ Avenida Jesús Santos Rein 6
☎ 952 46 74 57; www.visitafuengirola.com

Torremolinos Tourist Information
✚ 199 F2 ✉ Plaza de las Comunidades Autónomas
☎ 952 37 19 09; www.portaltorremolinos.com

⓴ Málaga

Andalucía's second-largest town at the foot of the Montes de Málaga is the economic and cultural centre of the Costa del Sol and enjoys 300 days of sunshine a year.

Málaga was founded by the Phoenicians who used it as a trading centre for salted fish, and this probably inspired the name of the town: the Phoenician *malak* derives from the word *malac,* the verb "to salt". Málaga is the second most important city of Andalucía, after Seville. It has a busy port and a thriving financial sector, which underpins the mass tourism of its coastal hinterland as well as the city's textile and food-processing industries. The Guadalmedina river divides the town into two districts: in the west, there is the new part of town with the main station and battalion of tower blocks, and in the east, the Old Town. Yet at its heart lie 19th-century streets and squares, crammed with bars and cafés as well as many shops and art and craft galleries. Scattered throughout are historic monuments that reflect Málaga's long history as a port and trading centre. A fine example is the Moorish Alcazaba on the lower slopes of Monte del Faro (Lighthouse Hill).

The Sights

The building of **Alcazaba** fortress began on the Roman remains in the 11th century and saw substantial improvements under the Nasrid dynasty in the 14th century which put it almost on a par with the Alhambra of Granada. After the demise of the Moors,

Peerless evening scene: the beautifully illuminated Alcazaba in Málaga

the fortress fell into disrepair, and it was not until 1931 that serious reconstruction work began. Now, the palace rises above the cramped streets in a series of buildings linked by cobbled ramps and archways and with terraces where elegant cypress trees stand beside fountains and pools. Alongside the entrance gateway are the impressive remains of a Roman theatre uncovered in the 1950s; numerous marble columns and capitals from the Roman period are embedded in the red brickwork of the palace's Moorish walls. As you climb higher into the Alcazaba, the views become spectacular.

The renovated 14th-century **Castillo de Gibralfaro** (Gibralfaro Castle) stands on the summit of Monte del Faro above the Alcazaba. There are magnificent views from the ramparts and there is a small military museum. It is a stiff uphill walk to Castillo de Gibralfaro (head along the road to the right of the Alcazaba entrance), albeit by a surfaced path through pleasant gardens; but you can catch Bus No 35 from Avenida de Cervantes, or take a taxi, and then stroll back down with terrific views for company.

Near the Alcazaba is Málaga's **cathedral**, begun in 1582 and completed in 1783. It is known as La Manquita, "the one-armed old woman", because its west front has only one tower. The cathedral's exterior is mainly baroque, a style enhanced by the dark stone of its crumbling façades, which have been magnificently renovated.

Housed in the elegant 16th-century Palacio de Buenavista, the **Museo Picasso** is a superb celebration of Pablo Picasso (► 25). The design of the museum is a fine merging of the old and new. A permanent collection of Picasso's works is on display, plus temporary exhibitions by international artists. Over 200 paintings from Baroness Carmen Thyssen

Málaga and Cádiz

Bornemisza's collection are housed in Palacio Villalón in the **Museo Carmen Thyssen** (Calle Compañía 10). The collection focuses on 19th-century Spanish art. The CAC, a museum for modern art, offers a permanent exhibition of paintings, photography and sculptures.

Soaking up the Atmosphere

Málaga is a wonderful city in which to wander. The pedestrian Calle Marqués de Larios, lined with smart shops and cafés, leads to lively Plaza de la Constitución at the heart of the Old Town. West of here, a tangle of narrow streets and squares is overlooked by tall, balconied buildings and historic churches.

TAKING A BREAK

There is only one place that you will find the true Malageño enjoying his afternoon coffee, a glass of wine or a tapa and that is **El Pimpi**, a bar encompassing two floors in the Calle Granada. The bodega does not open until 5pm though.

✚ 199 F2
🛈 Tourist Information; www.malagaturismo.com ✉ Pasaje de Chinitas 4
☎ C951 30 89 11 ✉ Avenida de Cervantes 1 (OMT) ☎ 952 13 47 31

Alcazaba
✉ Calle Alcazabilla ☎ 952 22 72 30
🕒 Tue–Sun 9:30–7 or 8pm 💶 €2.20

Catedral
✉ Calle Molina Larios 9 ☎ 952 22 03 45 🕒 Cathedral: Mon–Fri 10–6, Sat
10–5: Iglesia del Sagrario: Tue–Sat 9:30–12:30, 6:30–7:30 💶 €5

Museo Picasso
✉ Calle San Agustín ☎ 902 44 33 77; www.museopicassomalaga.org
🕒 Tue–Thu, Sun and public hols 10–8, Fri, Sat 10–9 💶 €6

Parking: Underground car parks are reached from the Alameda Principal and the Plaza de la Marina.

INSIDER INFO

- Join the locals at the morning market, **Mercado Atarazanas**, to the west of Calle Marqués de Larios – a cornucopia of fresh fish, meat, vegetables and fruit.

- See the **Iglesia del Sagrario** adjoining Málaga's cathedral. It has a splendid Gothic portal and a beautiful altarpiece.

- Before the opening of the Museo Picasso, the main shrine to Picasso was his birthplace. The **Casa Natal de Picasso** in Plaza de la Merced (daily 9:30–8; €2) is still worth a visit for an uncanny sense of the Picasso spirit.

- The **Museo de Artes y Costumbres Populares**, in a restored 17th-century inn, displays traditional artefacts from the rural and seagoing life of old Málaga province (Pasillo de Santa Isabel 10, tel: 952 21 71 37, open Mon–Fri 10–5, Sat 10–2; €4).

⑫ Cádiz

The harbour town sits atop limestone rock at the end of a 9km (5.5mi) long isthmus that stretches like a tongue into the bay on the Atlantic coast. The city's one-time wealth is reflected in the great cathedral and other baroque buildings and churches, but much of the pleasure of a visit comes from wandering through its narrow, cobbled streets and out to the brilliant light of seafront promenades.

A constant, cool breeze flows along the streets, making a visit agreeable even in the height of summer and creating a shimmering clear light that has earned the town the nickname "una tazita de plata" ("little silver cup"). Although Cádiz was an important port for Phoenicians, Romans and Visigoths, it declined under Moorish control and what you see today dates essentially from the 18th century, when the Spanish-American gold and silver trade revived the city's fortunes. The **Museo de Cádiz** is a good place to start your exploration of the city. The museum, which is housed in a restored 18th-century mansion, is one of the best in Spain; the archaeological section includes superb Phoenician jewellery and glassware and a reconstruction of the wreck of a Roman trading vessel. The first floor contains the city's art treasures, including work by Murillo and Rubens and a series of 17th-century religious panels by Zurbarán (▶ 25). The city's canyon-like streets are linked by pleasing squares such as the Plaza Topete, known also as **Plaza de las Flores**, site of a flower market and encircled by cafés and restaurants. Adjoining the plaza is Cádiz's food market. Narrow streets draw you on irresistibly, the shady labyrinth punctuated at intervals by surprises like the **Torre Tavira**, one of Cádiz's ancient watchtowers and now a maritime museum and camera obscura. The **Oratorio de San Felipe Neri** is also worth a visit. Its oval interior soars triumphantly to a sky-blue dome encircled by tiers of railed galleries. Exuberant side chapels punctuate the walls and Murillo's luminous painting, *The Inmaculate Conception,* graces the high altar.

The beautiful interior of the Oratorio de San Felipe Neri

From the cathedral's octagonal twin towers, the sound of the bells echoes across the roofs of the town

Málaga and Cádiz

The monumental **Catedral Nueva** is Spain's only completely baroque cathedral. Its main front dominates the broad **Plaza de la Catedral** and its interior is a vast arena of baroque architecture, all in plain stone and marble. The cathedral's central, so-called "gilded" dome is in fact faced with yellow tiles rather than precious metal, but the effect is still glorious, especially when you see it from the seafront promenades.

The golden dome of Cádiz Cathedral

TAKING A BREAK

"La Gorda te da de comer" (Insider Tip) ("The fat lady feeds you") is the name of a *tapas* bar in the Old Town slightly away from the main tourist routes in the direction of the harbour (Calle del General Luque 1). There is always a lively atmosphere in the bar, and the tapas are tasty and good value.

✚ 198 C2 ℹ️ Tourist Information; www.turismo.cadiz.es ✉️ Avenida José León de Carranza s/n ☎ 956 28 56 01 ✉️ Paseo de Canalejas ☎ 956 24 10 01

Parking: Visitors are advised not to drive through the heart of Cádiz. There are car parks on Plaza San Juan de Dias, adjacent to the railway station and on the nearby Cuesta de las Calesas. Parking is also possible along parts of the seafront.

Museo de Cádiz
✉️ Plaza de Mina 5 ☎ 856 10 50 23 🕐 Tue–Sat 9–3 (winter 10–8:30), Sun 10–5 🎫 free for EU passport holders

Oratorio de San Felipe Neri
✉️ Calle San José ☎ 956 22 91 20 🕐 Tue–Fri 10–1:45, 5–7:45, Sat 10–1:45, Sun 11–1:45 🎫 free

Catedral Nueva
✉️ Plaza de la Catedral ☎ 956 28 61 54

INSIDER INFO

- Catch the lively evening *paseo* (promenade) on pretty Plaza San Francisco, near the *ayuntamiento*, with its orange trees and traditional yellow-and-white houses.
- Visit the **top floor of the Museo de Cádiz** where there are exhibitions of craftwork and an interesting display of antique marionettes representing the city's traditional puppet theatre.
- The **Capilla** (chapel) in the former **Hospital de Mujeres** (Calle Hospital de Mujeres, Mon–Fri 8–2:30, 5:30–8:30, Sat 10–1:30) is a treasure, though you may have to persevere before the porter finally relents and unlocks its door. Within its glorious baroque interior, you'll find El Greco's painting *The Ecstasy of St Francis*.
- The **cathedral museum** (in Plaza de Fray Félix not far from the cathedral) is included in the ticket price for the cathedral, but unless you are interested in vestments and church plate, paintings and relics, give it a miss.

🕐 Mon–Sat 10–6:30, Sun 1:30–6:30 🎫 €5

At Your Leisure

Nerja's beaches are smaller and quieter than those on the neighbouring Costa del Sol

13 Nerja

Seaside Nerja, 56km (35mi) east of Málaga, makes a refreshing change from the Costa del Sol's main resorts. Nerja's best-known feature is the **Balcón de Europa**, a palm-fringed promenade overlooking the sea. The smallish beaches either side become crowded; the best and biggest beach is **Burriana**, east of the Balcón along the Paseo de los Carabineros.

TIPS FOR KIDS
- Cueva de Nerja (► 65)
- Parque Natural del Torcal (► 66)
- Tarifa: dolphin/whale cruise (► 68)
- Gibraltar: cable car, Barbary apes, dolphin cruise (► 69)

About 3km (2mi) to the east of Nerja are the popular **Cueva de Nerja**, a complex of limestone caverns. Tours are stagey affairs involving special lighting and piped music, but they provide an entertaining escape from the heat.

🗺 200 B1 🛈 Tourist Information:
✉ Carmen 1 (in the town hall)
☎ 952 52 15 31; www.nerja.es/turismo

Cueva de Nerja
🗺 200 B2 🛈 www.cuevadenerja.es 🕐 July–Aug 10–7:30; Sep–June 10–2, 4–6:30 💶 €8.50

14 Antequera
Historic sights in Antequera range from prehistoric burial chambers to Moorish ruins and fine churches. Oldest of all are a remarkable group

The Bronze Age Menga dolmens in Antequera

of Neolithic to Bronze Age burial chambers: the **Menga** and **Viera** dolmens, off Camino del Cementerio on the northeastern outskirts. In the highest part of the town, above central Plaza San Sebastián, stands the **Arco de**

Málaga and Cádiz

Los Gigantes, a 16th-century gateway incorporating Roman sculpture in its stonework. The dignified Renaissance façade of the church of Santa María dominates the adjoining plaza, and above it are the vestigial ruins of the town's Moorish Alcazaba, now a pine-scented, terraced garden.

Just north of the Arco de Los Gigantes is the 17th-century church of Nuestra Señora del Carmen, its baroque altarpiece a feast of carved and painted figures. About 14km (9mi) south of Antequera is 🔟 Parque Natural del Torcal, a striking natural landscape of tall limestone pinnacles and wooded ravines. In Lobo Park (LCtra. Antequera–Álora – A343 –, km 16, www.lobo park.com, daily 10–6, €11), you can visit the wolves and watch them in natural surroundings.

✚ 200 A2
🛈 Tourist Information:
✉ Plaza de San Sebastián 7
☎ 952 70 25 05; http://turismo.antequera.es

Menga and Viera Dolmens
✚ 200 A2
🕐 Tue–Sat 9–3:30, Sun 10–5
✋ Free

🔟 Parque Natural del Torcal
✚ 200 A2

OFF THE BEATEN TRACK

If you have time to spare and crave peace, head for the Parque Natural de los Alcornocales, a region of hills and mountains clothed in cork oak forests north of Tarifa. The walking is good, and the area has some charming villages – Medina-Sidonia, Alcalá de los Gazules and Jimena de la Frontera.

🔟 Parque Natural Sierra de Grazalema

The Sierra de Grazalema is a range of craggy limestone peaks swathed in forests of oak and the rare Spanish fir, the pinsapo. Tortuous roads wind through the mountains and link villages such as Grazalema, Zahara de la Sierra and Benaocaz, classic examples of the *pueblos blancos*. Zahara de la Sierra (► 182), with its clifftop castle and sweeping views, is one of the most dramatic. The entire Sierra is a wildlife reserve, and you can sample horse riding, cycling, rock climbing, canoeing, and even paragliding, with experienced guides and instructors (► 76). There are numerous walking routes that you can tackle on your own or on a guided trip. The park information offices at El Bosque and Grazalema have route maps to the area. You need to obtain a permit from the El Bosque or Grazalema office if you wish to enter certain areas such as the Garganta Verde, a mighty river gorge near Zahara (► 181), and one of the main roosting sites of the magnificent griffin vulture.

✚ 199 D2
🛈 Tourist Information:
✉ Federico García Lorca 1, El Bosque
☎ 956 70 97 33
✉ Plaza Asomaderos 3, Grazalema
☎ 956 13 20 52

🔟 Arcos de la Frontera

Arcos de la Frontera tumbles downhill in a careless sprawl from the spectacular clifftop site of its old Moorish quarter. The Old Town's alleys surround the two main churches, San Pedro and Santa María de la Asunción. San Pedro is a quiet haven; the highlight of the late Gothic interior is a fine 16th-century altarpiece showing Saint Peter and Saint Jerome. Santa María dominates the central square, Plaza del Cabildo, and has a splendid Renaissance façade and a richly decorative interior full of pleasant gloom and Gothic extravagance. As you take in the vista across the plain from the plaza's viewpoint, look for the kestrels that drift along the cliff face. Then descend to mix with the boisterous life of the bars and restaurants of the lower town.

➕ 198 C2 ℹ️ Tourist Information:
✉️ Plaza del Cabildo ☎ 956 70 22 64

🔟7 Sanlúcar de Barrameda

Great seafood restaurants and dry *manzanilla* wine, which has a different flavour from Jerez *fino* and is claimed to be of superior quality, are Sanlúcar de Barrameda's specialities. The town stands at the mouth of the Río Guadalquivir opposite the southern edge of the Doñana National Park (➤ 160), which is accessible from here by boat. The morning market in Calle Bretones, close to the main square, Plaza del Cabildo, is a colourful, raucous affair. Stroll uphill from the market for a look at Sanlúcar's town hall, located in the 19th-century Palacio de Orleáns y Bourbon, a showpiece of extravagant decoration in neo-Moorish style (Mon–Fri 10:45–1:30, Sat 10:30, 11:30). For background information on the town's historic churches ask at the tourist office for their useful Spanish/English leaflet guide. For the *manzanilla* experience, visit the **Bodegas Barbadillo** in Calle Sevilla or, better still, the long-established **Bodegas La Cigarrera** in Plaza Madre de Dios near the market. In the old fishing district of Bajo de Guía, at the western end of the riverfront, you'll find numerous fish restaurants.

Insider Tip

➕ 198 C2 ℹ️ Tourist Information:
✉️ Calzada Duquesa Isabel ☎ 956 36 61 10; www.sanlucardebarrameda.es

🔟8 El Puerto de Santa María

The river port of El Puerto de Santa María is at the southernmost angle of the "Sherry Triangle", and has a reputation for excellent sherry and seafood. It is a useful base for exploring the region: Sanlúcar de

San Pedro church in Arcos de la Frontera stands on the site of a Moorish fortress

Málaga and Cádiz

Barrameda (➤ 67) is a short bus ride away, and Jerez de la Frontera (➤ 53) a mere 15 minutes by train, while Cádiz (➤ 63) is 10km (6.25mi) across the estuary by the venerable ferry, *Motonave Adriano III*, known affectionately to locals as *El Vapor* (The Steamer).

The finest of El Puerto's many churches is the **Iglesia Mayor Prioral** in Plaza de España, and there are several ornate 18th-century palaces scattered around the town. **Castillo de San Marcos** is a 13th-century fortress built on the site of a mosque. The pedestrianised main street, Calle Luna, has a number of cheerful bars, and the waterfront area is

View of Tarifa

A Fountain in Vejer de la Frontera

full of life in the evenings. **Sherry bodegas** with famous names such as Osborne, Luis Caballero and Duff Gordon, are open to visitors.

✚ 198 C2
🛈 Tourist Information:
✉ Plaza del Castillo
☎ 956 48 37 15; www.turismoelpuerto.com

🔟 Costa de la Luz (Cádiz)

Cádiz's Costa de la Luz, which means the "Coast of Light", is far less developed than the Costa del Sol. There are excellent beaches at **Los Caños de Meca** and **Zahara de los Atunes**, where broad stretches of golden sand still offer you room to breathe. This is an Atlantic coast, however, and the sea can be chillier and choppier than on the Mediterranean Costas. Inland from the coast the hilltop settlement of **Vejer de la Frontera** preserves its secretive Moorish character.

The beaches at breezy **Tarifa**, the most southerly town in Spain, are a windsurfer's paradise. From Tarifa, the Rif Mountains of Morocco seem only a stone's throw away across the Strait of Gibraltar. You can take a one-day or two-day trip to Tangier from Tarifa; or try windsurfing, kite-surfing, join a 🐬**dolphin- and whale-watching cruise**, or take a diving trip with experts (➤ 76).

✚ 198 B2

Vejer de la Frontera Tourist Information
✚ 198 C1 ✉ Avenida Los Remedios
☎ 956 45 17 36; www.turismovejer.com

Tarifa Tourist Information
✚ 199 D1 ✉ Paseo de la Alameda s/n
☎ 956 68 09 93; www.tarifaweb.com

🔢 🚠 Gibraltar

A visit to Gibraltar, one of the UK's last remaining colonies, is like finding yourself in Britain at the heart of Mediterranean Spain. The vast Rock is invariably packed with expat Brits from the Costa del Sol in search of tax-free British goods. The **Old Town** (North Town) begins on the other side of the airport with Casemates Square. Towering above it in the east, you can see the ruins of Moorish Castle, which dates back to the 8th century and was rebuilt by the Almohads in the 14th century. The market and the harbour, constructed in 1309 and substantially extended in past years, are just to the northwest of the castle. Main Street, on which you will find most of the hotels, shops, pubs and public buildings, leads from Casemates Square to the post office and stock exchange with the adjoining town hall at the rear, and on to the Roman Catholic Cathedral, once a mosque that underwent a Gothic facelift in 1502.

Following Bomb House Lane that leads off to the right, you come to the **Gibraltar Museum**, which apart from providing all sorts of facts about the town history also includes a 30m² (39yd²) model of "the Rock" from 1865 as well as the very well preserved Moorish Baths. On Cathedral Square, you will find the Anglican Church of England built in 1821 in Moorish style. At the south end of Main Street, on the right-hand side, is the Governor's Palace (The Convent) built on the foundations of a 1531 Franciscan monastery.

An exciting 🚠 **cable-car ride** (daily 9:30–7:15, in winter until 5:15) whisks you away from the far end of Main Street to the Upper Rock, where you can visit the famous Barbary apes. See, too, the vast **St Michael's Cave**, venue for occasional musicals and dance shows, and the **Upper Galleries** or "Great Siege Tunnels", a vast labyrinth excavated for military defence in the 18th century.

The Gibraltar tourist information offices are the best sources for information about tours, dolphin-watching trips and sightseeing cruises. It is inadvisable to take a car on to Gibraltar's extremely crowded streets.
✚ 199 D1
🛈 Tourist Information:
✉ Duke of Kent House, Cathedral Square
☎ 350 20 07 49 50; www.visitgibraltar.gi

The Rock of Gibraltar, a dramatic and contentious symbol of British presence in Spain

THE BARBARY APES

Gibraltar's "apes" are a breed of tailless monkey. They may have been brought over by Moorish settlers or introduced as pets by British colonists. There is a myth that Gibraltar will cease to be British if the apes ever leave the Rock. Fears of this happening during World War II prompted British officials to import more of the animals.

Where to...
Stay

Prices
Expect to pay per double room per night
€ up to €60   €€ €60–€90   €€€ €90–€140   €€€€ over €140

MÁLAGA

Castilla €
This inexpensive little *hostal* is in a superb location, between the city's main artery, the Alameda, and the port. The rooms have no frills but are spick and span; some of them have some balconies overlooking the relatively quiet side street. There is an underground garage, a real boon in this town, and plenty of bars and restaurants are to be found nearby.

✚ 199 F2 ✉ Calle Córdoba 7
☎ 952 21 86 35; www.hotelcastillaguerrero.com

Insider Tip
Hotel Humaina €€
Away from the clamour of Málaga's coast, this is the perfect place to relax. The location is idyllic, in the centre of a natural park but just 16km (10mi) from the city. terracotta tiles, ochre walls and balconies in most rooms. Food is prepared with organic vegetables grown in the garden.

✚ 199 F2 ✉ Carretera del Colmenar s/n, Las Montes de Málaga
☎ 952 64 10 25; www.hotelhumaina.es

Larios €€€€
You get a top location in a swanky shopping street, yet from here it's just a short stroll to the cathedral and atmospheric old part of Málaga. Black-and-white tiles, soft beige furnishings and light wood make for an upbeat yet elegant look. There is a lovely rooftop terrace where you can enjoy a glass of wine after a busy day sightseeing.

✚ 199 F2 ✉ Marqués de Larios 2 ☎ 952 22 22 00; www.room-matehotels.com

BENALMÁDENA

La Fonda €€€
On a pretty pedestrian street in the centre of the relatively unspoilt town of Benalmádena, this hotel has a pretty rooftop terrace overlooking the Mediterranean and a wonderful outside pool. There are cool patios shaded by palms, pebbled floors and fountains, and the rooms are light and airy with terraces and views. The downstairs eating area is particularly quiet.

✚ 199 F2 ✉ Calle Santo Domingo 7
☎ 952 56 90 47; www.lafondabenalmadena.es

RONDA

Alavera de Los Baños €€€
Next to the 13th-century Baños Arabes (► 52), this German-run small hotel was featured as a backdrop for the film classic *Carmen*. It has super views of the Serranía de Ronda uplands and the city walls, plus facilities like a reading room, library and lounge. In the pleasant dining room, there is an emphasis on organically grown foods.

✚ 199 E2 ✉ Hoyo de Miguel
☎ 952 87 91 43; www.alaveradelosbanos.com

Hotel Reina Victoria €€€
Views from the Reina Victoria's cliff-top gardens, hanging over a 150m (492ft) precipice, are dramatic. The hotel (named after Queen Victoria by a patriot Brit) rose to fame in 1912 when Rainer Maria Rilke, the ailing German poet, came here to convalesce. His room is now a small museum.

The rooms are well equipped and comfortable.

➕ 199 E2 ✉ Calle Jeréz 25
☎ 952 87 12 40; www.hoteles-catalonia.com

SIERRA DE GRAZALEMA

El Molino del Santo €€

This century-old mill, on a running stream flanked by willows and olive trees, has books to read instead of TVs to watch. There is a choice of bed and breakfast or half board. Most rooms have fine views of the surrounding Grazalema park with a backdrop of mountains and pine trees. The hotel is popular as a base for walkers.

➕ 199 D2 ✉ Estación de Benaoján, Benaoján
☎ 952 16 71 51; http://molinodelsanto.com
🕒 Closed Nov–Feb

JEREZ DE LA FRONTERA

El Ancla Hotel €

El Ancla's architecture is classic Jerez, with yellow and white paint-work, wrought-iron balconies and wooden shutters. The hotel doubles as a popular local bar, which is good for atmosphere but means it can be noisy at night. Rooms are plainly furnished but comfortable, with TV and telephone. The underground car park across the street is a bonus.

➕ 198 C2 ✉ Plaza del Mamelón
☎ 956 32 12 97; www.hotelancla.es

CÁDIZ

Hostal Bahía €€

On a tree-lined pedestrian street just off the bustling Plaza de San Juan de Dios, this is a real winner with firm beds, smart bathrooms, TV, air conditioning and small balconies in most of the rooms. The lack of a dining room is compensated by the choice and proximity of bars and restaurants, including the excellent Mesón La Nueva Marina which is right next door (▶73).

➕ 198 C2 ✉ Calle Plocia 5
☎ 956 25 90 61; www.hostalbahiacadiz.com

Where to... Eat and Drink

Prices
Expect to pay for a meal, incl wine
€ up to €15
€€ €15–€40
€€€ over €40

MÁLAGA

Antonio Martin €€/€€€

Seafood and fish at its best is on offer at this long-established, family-run restaurant located right on the sea front and with the benefit of a pleasant terrace. Everything from *gambas a la plancha* (grilled prawns) and *boquerones fritos* (deep-fried anchovies), to *merluza* (hake) and *pez espada* (swordfish) is on offer. The food and atmo-sphere make this is a very popular place with locals, and it draws celebrities too, so reservations are advised.

➕ 199 F2 ✉ Playa de la Malagueta
☎ 952 22 41 53 🕒 1–4, 8–10:30

Bar Logüeno €

Shoehorned into a deceptively small space, with extra seating space across the road, this well-loved traditional *tapas* bar is tucked down a side street near Calle Larios. The L-shaped wooden bar is crammed with a tantalising 75-plus choice of *tapas*, including many Logüeno originals, like sau-téed oyster mushrooms (*setas*) with garlic, parsley and goat's cheese. There is an excellent range of Rioja wines, and service is fast and good.

Insider Tip

➕ 199 F2 ✉ Calle Marín García 12
☎ 952 22 30 48; http://www.logueno.es
🕒 Mon–Sat 1–4, 7–late

Málaga and Cádiz

Restaurante Chinitas €€

Expect traditional Andaluz décor here, with paintings of bullfighters on the walls. The cuisine is predictably macho, with oxtail a speciality, plus *serrano* hams and calf sirloin. Several dishes include Málaga sweet wine, including *solomillo al vino de Málaga* (fillet steak in a wine sauce).

➕ 199 F2 ✉ El Moreno Monroy 4

☎ 952 21 09 72; www.elchinitas.com

🕐 1–4, 8–midnight. Closed 24 and 31 Dec

ESTEPONA

Restaurante El Lido €€€

El Lido, 3km (2mi) east of Estepona, is known for its award-winning cuisine and sumptuous elegance; try to book a table overlooking the glorious gardens with ocean backdrop. The dishes are broad-spectrum Mediterranean with an emphasis on seafood and Italian specialities – such as a delicious deep-sea prawn ravioli in a spicy curry sauce. There's a ten-page wine list with some fine vintages, but prices start at an acceptable level.

➕ 199 E2 ✉ Las Dunas Beach Hotel and Spa, Boladilla Baja, Carretera de Cádiz, Km 163.5 Estepona

☎ 952 79 43 45 🕐 Wed–Sun 12:30–3, 8–11

MARBELLA

El Patio de los Perfumes €€€

This classy restaurant situated in the heart of the Old Town is a truly romantic choice. Here you can dine alfresco in the gorgeous bougainvillea-draped courtyard, complete with candles and gentle mood music, as well as twice-weekly flamenco. The food is eclectic Mediterranean with plenty of French influence with dishes like grilled *foie gras* with caramelised apple, and warm goat's cheese in a *Malagueño* wine sauce.

➕ 199 E2 ✉ Calle Aduar

☎ 952 82 86 50 🕐 Tue–Sun 8–11

FUENGIROLA

Bistro €/€€

This popular restaurant is located behind the post office in the attractive old part of Fuengirola. The décor is scrubbed pine with intimate booths and there is an outside terrace. The service is friendly and swift. Popular with local expat residents, the menu is international with plenty of soup, salad and meat choices but no seafood. Reservations are essential here.

➕ 199 F2

✉ Calle Palangreros 30

☎ 952 47 77 01 🕐 Mon–Sat 7–late

MIJAS

Restaurante La Alcababa €€

From this glass-fronted restaurant that overlooks the coastline, you can even spy Africa on a very clear day. The menu is Spanish, with a fabulous *ajo blanco* (almond and garlic soup).

➕ 199 F2

✉ Plaza de la Constitución

☎ 952 59 02 53 🕐 Tue–Sun noon–4, 7–11

TORREMOLINOS

Matahambre €

This is a stylish *tapas* bar and restaurant with a barrel vault ceiling, terracotta tiles and a warm ochre colour scheme. The menu includes lots of tasty light bites and *tablas* (larger portions to share) like *queso curado* (cured Manchego cheese) and *paté de pédiz* (pheasant paté) as well as more substantial dishes such as *morcilla de Burgos y morrones y cebollas salteada* (black pudding from Burgos with roasted peppers and onion). There is an outside terrace from where you can enjoy the panoramic sea views.

➕ 199 F2

✉ Las Mercedes 14

☎ 952 38 12 42 🕐 Daily 1–4, 7–11

RONDA

Tragabuches €€€

This fashionable restaurant in the centre of Ronda near the *parador* has an innovative menu of exquisitely prepared dishes like *tocino con jugo de almejas, morcilla y lemongrass* (pork with blood sausage in a clam-and-lemongrass sauce) and the highly adventurous white garlic ice-cream with pine nuts! The surroundings are elegant yet relaxed. Reservations are essential.

➕ 199 E2 ✉ José Aparicio 1
☎ 952 19 02 91
🕐 Tue–Sun 1:30–3:30, 8:30–10:30. No dinner Sun

THE SHERRY TRIANGLE

Las Bóvedas Restaurant €€/€€€

This is a fabulous restaurant in a gracious baroque building, now a hotel, on a narrow cobbled back street in El Puerto de Santa María. Formerly a monastery, Las Bóvedas was once the laundry room for the nuns, although it's hard to believe that such mundane pursuits took place beneath the fine vaulted ceiling. Chef Joaquín Ramírez has won several awards for his innovative cuisine, which includes an excellent variety of seafood dishes.

➕ 198 C2 ✉ Hotel Monasterio San Miguel, Virgen de los Milagros 27, El Puerto de Santa María, Cádiz
☎ 956 54 04 40 🕐 Daily 9pm–late

La Molinera €€

The restaurant belongs to Hotel Mesón de la Molinera, a former oil mill on the edge of Lake Arcos with a fantastic view of the Old Town of Arcos de la Frontera. On the menu are typical, fairly priced Andalucían specialities. Vinegar from Jerez de la Frontera is used to refine the cold dishes.

➕ 198 C2 ✉ Avenida El Sombrero de Tres Picos, Arcos de la Frontera
☎ 956 70 80 02 🕐 Daily 1–4, 8–11

La Mesa Redonda €€

This small friendly restaurant is owned by José Antonio Valdespino who produces traditional Jerez dishes with a creative twist. The seasons are marked by the specialities served: the Game Menu from October to February; the Cod Menu during Lent; the *Almadraba Tuna* from April to June and, throughout the year, a varied Seasonal Menu featuring the sherries and brandies of Jerez.

➕ 194 C2 ✉ Calle Manuel de la Quintana 3, Jerez de la Frontera ☎ 956 34 00 69 🕐 Mon–Sat 1–4, 7–11

CÁDIZ

El Faro €€/€€€

El Faro, in the city's shabby, one-time fishermen's quarter, is deservedly famous. You can opt for seafood *tapas* at the bar or really splash out in the restaurant on innovative dishes like grilled peppers stuffed with crabmeat, or the relatively pricey *menú del día*. The décor is understated Andalucían with ceramic wall tiles, marble and mahogany bar, and lots of photos of Cádiz past and present.

➕ 198 C2 ✉ Calle San Félix 15
☎ 956 21 10 68 🕐 Daily 1–4, 8–midnight

Mesón La Nueva Marina €/€€

Jamón serrano hams jostle for space with strings of garlic, dried peppers and black-and-white photos of the port in this welcoming restaurant and *tapas* bar. *Manzanilla* from nearby Sanlúcar is available on tap and the small adjoining restaurant gets packed at weekends. The menu is varied, in particular the 24-plus choice of starters which can be doubled up for a main course, and includes some mouth-watering specialities like *cazón en adobo* (marinated deep-fried white fish).

➕ 199 C2 ✉ Calle Plocia 3
☎ 956 28 93 81 🕐 Daily 1–4, 8–late. Closed 24, 25, 31 Dec, 1 Jan

Insider Tip

Where to...
Shop

MÁLAGA

Málaga's Calle Marqués de Larios is the heart of the city's fashion shopping. Try the branch of the smart Spanish fashion chain **Mango** (Larios 1, tel: 952 22 31 02), and **ZM Woman** (Nosquera 13, Tel. 952 21 04 33) for ultra-chic clothes. West of Marqués de Larios is a more traditional shopping area in the streets around Plaza Flores, Plaza de Félix Sáenz and Calle Puerta del Mar and Calle Nueva. Here you'll find shops of all kinds. Don't miss **La Mallorquina** (Plaza de Félix Sáenz), a delicatessen with a terrific selection of cured meats and other delicacies. Diagonally opposite is **La Mallorquina Regalos** run by the same company, a *licorería* (liquor shop) with a superb selection of drink including some of Málaga's distinctive sweet wines. Málaga's branch of the department store chain of **El Corte Inglés** is at Avenida de Andalucía 4–6 and is enormous. It carries a big range of foreign-language newspapers and is a good source of maps and books. Another mammoth shopping centre is the **Larios Centro** with 153 shops, distributed over two floors (Avenida de la Aurora 25).

RONDA & SIERRA DE GRAZALEMA

Ronda (►50) has many souvenir shops, a good number in the town's main shopping street, Carrera Espinal. Scattered among them, however, are some excellent shops selling *productos artesanos*, local produce of all kinds. Look for **Márquez** (Espinel 13, tel: 952 87 29 86) for everything from cured meats to wine, herbs and honey. For more upmarket craftwork and souvenirs

you'll find a sprinkling of outlets in Ronda's Old Town.

In the mountains of the Sierra de Grazalema (►66), **Artesanía Textil de Grazalema** (Carretera de Ronda; www.mantasdegrazalema.com) has a range of local clothing, carpets, pottery, and produce that includes cheeses, honey, and pears in wine. Another pleasant place to browse in Grazalema is **La Jara Cerámica Artesanal** (Calle Agua 19, tel: 956 13 20 75) for quality craftwork and gifts. On the Grazalema to Zahara de la Sierra road, stop off at **El Vínculo Molino de Aceite Alojamiento Rural** (tel: 956 12 30 02) for a chance to buy some very fine olive oil, wine and cheeses (►182).

THE SHERRY TRIANGLE

Pedestrianised Calle Larga and its surrounding streets are where you'll find the best shopping in **Jerez de la Frontera** (►53), with shops selling fashion, crafts, ceramics, leatherware and jewellery. If it's sherry you want, you'll find that, although every *bodega* sells its own product exclusively, **La Casa del Jerez** (The Sherry Shop, Divina Pastora 1, tel: 956 33 51 84) stocks all brands and you can sample happily. It is opposite the **Real Escuela Andaluza del Arte Ecuestre** (►54), where there is a souvenir shop for all things equestrian.

La Casa del Mimbre (Corredera 46), sells basketry made of esparto grass. You can browse pretty ceramic products in **Amaya Cerámica** (Avenida de Blas Infante 16).

The *manzanilla* and sherry *bodegas* in **El Puerto de Santa María** (►67) and **Sanlúcar de Barrameda** (►67) all sell their own products. For the area's food specialities, don't miss Sanlúcar's busy morning **market** off Plaza de San Roque, or the **fresh shellfish shop** attached to the Romerijo fish restaurants in Ribera del Marisco, in El Puerto de Santa María.

CÁDIZ AND BEYOND

Cádiz has a superb **morning market**, located just next to Plaza de las Flores with its colourful flower stalls. The pedestrianised Calle Francisco, Calle Rosario and Calle Ancha, together with their linking streets, form Cadiz's main shopping district, where there is a good mix of shops. Farther along the coast to the east, **Gibraltar** (►69) is famous for its VAT-free shopping, and the town's Main Street is packed with shops of every kind. Prices are cheaper than in Britain and northern Europe, but you won't necessarily find that special Andalucían gift or memento.

COSTA DEL SOL

All the main resorts confront you with ranks of souvenir outlets: you take your pick of everything from jewellery to leather accessories, but with little variation in quality or prices. For big fashion names, such as Versace, Armani, Donna Karan, Gucci, go for the smart main shopping drag **Ramón y Cajal** and **Casco Antiguo** (Old Town) in Marbella (►56), or the waterfront **Muelle Ribera** in nearby **Puerto Banús** (►57). **El Corte Inglés** department store chain has a branch on the outskirts of Puerto Banús at Carretera N340, Km 174.

Markets in this prosperous area are always worth browsing through. There are often good antiques and objets d'art lurking among the pottery, clothing and kitsch buys in **Puerto Banús's Saturday morning market** at Centro Plaza in the Nueva Andalucía district, near the bullring, or – biggest and best of all – **Fuengirola's Tuesday morning market** on Avenida Jesús Santos Rein. Fresh fish from this south Andalucían town travels as *pescado fresco de Fuengirola* to kitchens throughout Spain. If flea markets are more your thing then don't miss the Saturday morning event in the same Fuengirola location. It is huge.

Where to...
Go Out

Andalucía offers a huge variety of entertainment, from the club scene on the Costa del Sol and in the larger cities, to the more traditional cultural pursuits of flamenco, bullfighting and *fiestas*. The energetic can enjoy water sports in the coastal resorts and dry-land adventure in the mountainous interior.

PUBLICATIONS

The *Guía Marbella – Día y Noche*, a Spanish/English listings guide, and the weekly *Sur* newspaper, which has a useful entertainment section, are available from tourist offices. One or two publications, aimed at expat residents, carry useful information on current shows and events.

NIGHTLIFE

The club scene in Málaga province is at its most intense on the lively **Costa del Sol**. In Puerto Banús, the waterfront **Sinatra Bar** (Muelle Ribera 2, tel: 952 81 09 50) is a top spot for stars and celebrity wannabees. In Marbella the hottest scene is in the seafront area of Puerto Deportivo with its massed discos and bars. Fuengirola is a relentless nightlife zone; for total clubbers there's **Crazy Daisy** (Martínez Catena 37) – experience midnight-to-dawn dancing. Benalmádena Costa's big **Kiu Club** (Plaza Solymar, tel: 952 44 05 18) and the **Palladium** (Avenida Palma de Mallorca, tel: 952 38 42 89) in Torremolinos are also popular. Visit Marbella's **Casino Marbella** (Hotel H10, Plaza de Andalucía, tel: 952 81 40 00) for a stab at blackjack, roulette, poker, and slot machines in plenty. Alternatively, try your luck at **Casino**

Málaga and Cádiz

Torrequebrada (N340, Km 220, tel: 952 44 60 00, www.torrquebrada. com), where you can start your evening's entertainment at the gaming tables and then, on some days, move on to enjoy a show in the next door restaurant. Passports need to be shown at both casinos. **Málaga's** nightlife is concentrated on the area to the northeast of the cathedral around Plaza de Uncibay and the nearby streets of Granada and Beatas. In **Jerez de la Frontera**, you'll find discos and music bars in Calle Divina Pastora and around. In **Cádiz** city, head for the streets round Plaza de España.

FLAMENCO

In Málaga there are regular flamenco shows at the **Teatro Miguel de Cervantes** (Calle Ramos Marín, tel: 952 22 41 09, www.teatrocervantes. com). In Ronda there is flamenco at **Casa Lara** (Calle Armiñán 29, Tel. 952 87 1263). Jerez de la Frontera has a strong flamenco tradition (►20ff) and there are worthwhile flamenco shows at **La Taberna Flamenca** (Calle Angostillo de Santiago 3, tel: 956 32 36 93). In Cádiz try **La Cava** (Calle Antonio López, tel: 956 21 18 66, www. flamencolacava.com).

THEATRE

Theatre lovers will find excellent programmes of music, drama and dance at Málaga's **Teatro Miguel de Cervantes** (Calle Ramos Marín, tel: 952 22 41 09) and at Cádiz's **Gran Teatro Falla** (Plaza Fragela, tel: 956 22 08 28). Ask at tourist offices for current programmes.

BULLFIGHTING

All the main resorts have bullrings where *novilladas*, fights with young bulls and novice bullfighters, are staged, usually on Sunday evenings. These are advertised, and hotels

often have details. The bigger rings at Málaga, Ronda and Jerez stage major fights; booking is advised.

GOLF

Most courses are on the Costa del Sol. Many require a handicap certificate and forward booking is heavy. **Estepona Golf**, Estepona (Arroyo Vaquero, Carretera de Cádiz, Km 150, tel: 952 93 76 05), and **Golf Torrequebrada**, Benalmádena Costa (Carretera de Cádiz, N340, tel: 952 44 27 42) are moderately priced.

HORSE RIDING

On the Costa del Sol try the **Escuela del Arte Ecuestre** (Carretera Nacional 340, Km 159, Estepona, tel: 952 80 80 77). For a canter on the beach, try the **Hurricane Hotel** (Carretera Nacional 340, Km 78, Tarifa, tel: 956 68 90 92, www.hurricanehotel.com).

OUTDOOR ACTION

For hang-gliding and paragliding try **Club Escuela de Parapente Abdalajís** (Valle de Abdalajís, tel: 952 650 68 59 69). In the spectacular Sierra de Grazalema, **Horizon** (Calle Corrales Terceros 29, tel: 956 13 23 63; www. horizonaventura.co) in Grazalema (►66) offers caving, rock climbing, mountain biking and other sports.

WATER SPORTS

For scuba diving, contact **Simply Diving** (Carlota Alessandri 25, Torremolinos, tel: 600 50 65 26, www.simplydiving.com) or **Centro Buceo Tarifa** (Plaza del Mirador 1, Tarifa, tel: 956 68 06 80, www. yellowsubtarifa.com). For windsurfing try **Club Mistral** (Hotel Hurricane, Carretera Cádiz–Málaga, tel: 956 68 49 19) near Tarifa. Arrange dolphin-watching trips through **Dolphin Safari** (Marina Bay Complex, Gibraltar, tel: 956 77 19 14, www.dolphinsafari.gi).

Granada and Almería

 **Little Treats**

Sierra de Alhamilla

Hard to believe but true, this region has one of Europe's only **semi-deserts** (▶ 184). And it is in Sierra de Alhamilla that you will find Andalucía's "Western" towns.

Cabo de Gata

Black sand and only 350m (1,150ft) long, yet still a dream: the **Playa de Mónsul** (▶ 101). Volcanic stone juts up through the sand and a huge dune provides the beach backdrop.

Off the Beaten Track

In **Calle Alhamar**, Granada, you will find everything from the designer bar to the simple pub. What is also pleasant: things are less focused on mass tourism than in the Navas restaurant mile.

Getting Your Bearings

Andalucía's eastern provinces of Granada and Almería contain spectacular and diverse landscapes. In Granada, the mighty mountains of the Sierra Nevada range contrast with deeply wooded river valleys, while in Almería you'll find strange desert hills and arid coastal plains that seem more suited to North Africa than to Europe.

Such diversity extends to the towns and cities of the region. Granada city's main treasure is the Alhambra Palace, one of the world's great buildings and the most hauntingly beautiful symbol of Moorish Andalucía, but it also has a medieval quarter, the Albaicín, that seems more like a Moorish village in the heart of the Andalucían hills than a city enclave. Granada has neither the exuberant sunny nature of Seville nor the easy-going atmosphere of Málaga and Cádiz. Christian conquerors imposed a more austere Northern European style upon Granada's buildings and streets and on the habits of its citizens. Southeast of Granada, the rugged slopes of the Sierra Nevada soar to the highest peaks in Spain, and then descend in great waves to the foothills of the beautiful Alpujarras, where you can sample superb regional food and wine. In inland Almería province, parched desert buttes and gulches – Hollywood stand-ins for the Wild West – lie seared by the wind, while the arid, treeless coast offers strange lunar landscapes. The capital, Almería city, once surpassed Granada as a Moorish stronghold, and its formidable hilltop fortress, the Alcazaba, is a dramatic reminder of medieval Al-Andalus in its heyday.

Moreda

27
Guadix

★ **Granada**

Abla

Sierra Nevada

Trevélez

Pampaneira • Yegen
Lanjarón
• Órgiva **8 Las Alpujarras**

El Ejid

• Motril
Adra

| 0 | 30 km |
| 0 | 15 mi |

Left: cool, effervescent water on the patio of the Acequia in Granada's Generalife

Right: Wild, lonely wilderness in Almería

Getting Your Bearings

Serón

•Huércal-
Overa

Gérgal

Sorbas
㉕

㉔ Mojácar

Mini
Hollywood
㉖ Sierra de Alhamilla

•Carboneras

Níjar ㉓

Almería ㉑

•Roquetas
de Mar

㉒ Cabo de Gata

The Alcazaba
von Almería
provides more
elegant
evidence of
the Moors

Perfect Days in ...

Four Perfect Days

Enjoy the splendours of Granada city before heading south into the timeless wooded hills of the Alpujarras. For dramatic contrast, explore Almería city, its scorched desert hinterland, and its coast, Spain's sunniest. For more information see the main entries (➤ 82–103).

Day One

Morning
Breakfast in one of the cafés in ⭐**Granada's** bustling Plaza Nueva, then take the Alhambra bus (➤ 88) from the stop on the south side of the square to the **Alhambra** entrance. After exploring the complex (right, ➤ 83), treat yourself to lunch in the Parador de San Francisco, the plush hotel at Alhambra's very heart.

Afternoon
Linger in the gardens of the **Generalife**, then walk back down to Plaza Nueva through the cool woods of the Bosques y Paseos. Go through the Gate of the Pomegranates *(Puerta de las Granadas)* and continue down Cuesta de Gomerez, where you'll find plenty of marquetry and souvenir shops.

Day Two

Morning
Stroll through the old Moorish quarter of the **Albaicín** in the fresh morning light (➤ 87). Stop for coffee in **Plaza San Miguel el Bajo** (➤ 89). Back in central Granada visit the **Capilla Real** (➤ 90) and the adjoining **cathedral** (➤ 90).

Afternoon
Drive south from the city along the Motril road, the N323, and turn off along the A348 to Lanjarón. Continue to Órgiva, then follow the winding mountain road into ⑧**Las Alpujarras** (➤ 94), the foothills of the Sierra Nevada. Stay overnight in any one of the three lovely

villages clinging to the sides of the **Poqueira Gorge** – Pampaneira, Bubión or Capileira (➤94).

Day Three

Morning
Make an early start and set off east along the high road of the Alpujarras to **Trevélez** (above, ➤96), famous for its *jamón serrano* (cured ham). Enjoy a slice or two for lunch at one of the cafés in the village.

Afternoon
Continue east, past a string of typical Alpujarran villages – Juviles, Bérchules, Yegen… Continue to **21 Almería** city (➤98) and an overnight stay. Go on an evening *tapas* tour, starting in the Puerta de Purchena area (➤100).

Day Four

Morning
Visit Almería's Moorish fortress, the **Alcazaba** (➤98), before the sun gets too hot, then stroll back through tranquil **Plaza Vieja** (➤100) and enjoy an early lunch at the highly recommended Casa Puga (Jovellanos 7) just east of the plaza.

Afternoon
Take the Granada road north, calling in at **26 Mini Hollywood** (➤103) if you have the time; or continue to **27 Guadix** (➤103) and visit its cave district and intriguing museum before heading back to Granada.

★ Granada

Granada's Alhambra Palace is the greatest relic of Islamic Spain. As one of the most seductive monuments in the world, the Alhambra is a hard act to follow, but this compelling city has much else of beauty and interest, including the Albaicín (the old Moorish quarter), the Capilla Real (Royal Chapel) and cathedral, and some outstanding churches and museums. Beyond the modern city's traffic-bound main thoroughfares lies a leisurely world of colourful plazas and pedestrianised streets.

The former Moorish king's palace, now a UNESCO World Heritage site is idyllically situated at the foot of the Sierra Nevada between two hills that slope steeply down to the fertile valley of the Río Genil. Albaicín, Granada's old quarter, is on the northern elevation; it is separated from the rest of the town by the deep ravine of the Río Darro, which flows into the Río Genil in the south of the city. Granada was ruled from Córdoba, and then from Seville, before emerging in the 1230s as the capital of the kingdom of the gifted Nasrid dynasty founded by Muhammad I ibn Yusuf ibn Nasr. In 1246, the Nasrids became vassals of the Christian kingdom of Castile, an arrangement that helped to ensure the survival of Granada as a Moorish kingdom until the late 15th century. A succession of Nasrid sultans did much over 200 years to create the Alhambra's most beautiful buildings and their exquisitely decorated chambers, scented patios and lush gardens. In 1492, the Christian rulers Fernando and Isabel "conquered" Granada and evicted Abur Abd Allah, known to the Spanish as Boabdil, the last Nasrid sultan. The Catholic monarchs preserved much of the Alhambra's Islamic beauty, however, and they left the Moorish Albaicín intact.

Discover the Arab flair in the maze of Granada's streets

🛈 Tourist Information; www.turismodegranada.org

✚ 204 B2 ✉ Plaza del Carmen ☎ 902 40 50 45

✚ 204 B1 ✉ Plaza Mariana Pineda 10 ☎ 958 24 71 28

✚ 204 C3 ✉ Plaza de Santa Ana ☎ 958 57 52 04

Parking: There are underground car parks in La Caleta at the western end of Avenida de la Constitucíon near the railway station and in Calle San Agustín, just north of the cathedral and off Gran Vía de Colón; also one near the central post office in Puerta Real at the junction of Calle Reyes Católicos and Acero del Darro. There are car parks adjacent to the Alhambra ticket office.

The Alhambra

The Alhambra's hilltop complex is the essential and irresistible starting point of a visit to Granada. Within its large area are four main groups of buildings and gardens: the Alcazaba, the original fortress; the Palacio Nazaríes, which served as the monarchs' administrative, judicial and diplomatic headquarters as well as their private home; the Palacio de Carlos V, an early 16th-century addition; and the Palacio de Generalife, the monarchs' summer palace and gardens, where they could escape from the pressures of court life.

The distant peaks of the Sierra Nevada provide a magnificent backdrop to the Alhambra

The Generalife is immediately to the right of the main entrance to the Alhambra, while the Alcazaba and the Palacio Nazaríes lie close to each other at the far western end of the site. Given the Alhambra's size and complexity, one of the best ways of organising a visit is to head straight for the most westerly section of the site and begin by visiting the Alcazaba. From there you can work your way back via the Palacio Nazaríes and the Palacio de Carlos V to finish at the Generalife, a relaxing finale amid flowers and cooling fountains.

The Alcazaba

The Alcazaba today is essentially the shell of the 13th-century Moorish fortress, but its mighty walls and towers survive. The great tower at the western end is the **Torre de la Vela**, the Alhambra's belfry, from whose airy summit there are magnificent views over Granada, the Albaicín and the surrounding countryside known as the Vega. The poet García Lorca, a native of Granada, imagined the misty Vega as a bay of the sea, and once teased a friend by asking him if he had not seen boats bobbing below the Alhambra's towers.

On the southern edge of the Alcazaba are the lush, aromatic garden terraces of the **Jardín de los Ardaves**, with the green woods of elms and cypresses on the Alhambra hill sweeping away below, and the great massif of the Sierra Nevada rising in the distance.

The "Red Fortress"

The name Alhambra is derived from the Arabic word *Kala al-Hamra*, which means "Red Fortress", the colour that its walls and towers radiate at sunset. Alhambra encompasses not only the Nasrid palace, but the entire complex, including the palace of Carlos V, the Alcazaba and the Generalife.

❶ **Mexuar:** The Mexuar was used for meetings and the public administration of justice. Carlos V had it turned into a chapel.

❷ **Diwan or Serail:** The royal palace proper: this is where you will find the Patio de los Arrayanes (Myrtle Courtyard) with a water basin surrounded by myrtles.

❸ **Harem** In the centre is the Patio de los Leones (Lion Courtyard) with the Lion Fountain.

❹ **Patio de Mexuar:** An impressive feature of this courtyard is its warm-coloured marble and azulejo cladding, especially in the Cuarto Dorado (the Golden Room).

❺ **Torre de Comares** and **Sala de Embajadores** The 45m (147ft) high Torre de Comares is the tallest tower in the fortress. Royal audiences took place on the ground floor in the Sala de Embajadores (Ambassadors' Chamber). The ruler's throne is opposite the entrance.

❻ **Sala de la Barca:** The name for this antechamber with its seven arcades derives either from the hull-like shape of the artesonado ceiling or from the Arabic word "baraka" (blessing).

❼ **Sala de los Reyes:** A very rare glimpse of court life is revealed in these three scenes painted on leather. One picture shows a discussion between ten finely clothed men (hence the name "Chamber of the Kings").

❽ **Tocador de la Reina:** The "Queen's Dressing Room" is one of the most charming rooms: it was used by Isabel the Catholic and the wives of Carlos V and Felipe II.

❾ **Torre de las Damas:** More of an ornamental building than a fortress, it is one of the oldest structures in the Nasrid palace, erected during the reign of Mohammed III at the beginning of the 14th century.

❿ **Palace of Carlos V:** Colonnaded square with a two-floor circular structure. The Museo de la Alhambra is on the ground floor and above it is the Museo Provincial de Bellas Artes.

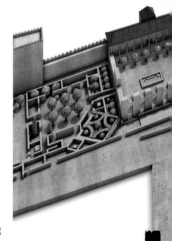

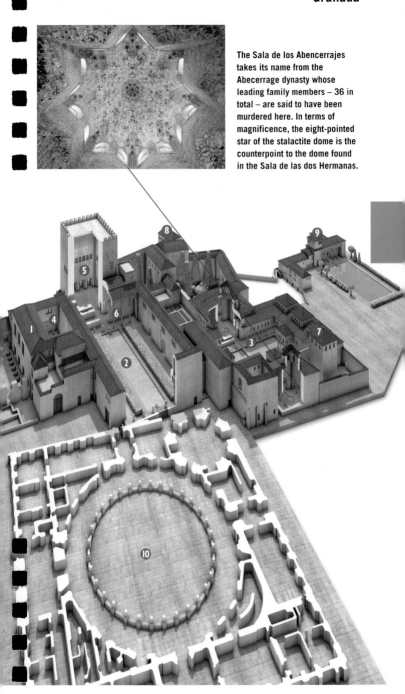

The Sala de los Abencerrajes takes its name from the Abecerrage dynasty whose leading family members – 36 in total – are said to have been murdered here. In terms of magnificence, the eight-pointed star of the stalactite dome is the counterpoint to the dome found in the Sala de las dos Hermanas.

Palacio Real

The Palacio Nazaríes, a decorative treasure house of Islamic craftsmanship in brick, wood and stucco, is the crowning glory of the Alhambra. The entire complex reflects the subtle use of space, light and cool water that was the great gift of Islamic arts and crafts. You enter through a modest doorway and first come to the **Mexuar** (Audience Hall), the public rooms of the Islamic palaces, where superb tiling and stucco work are a foretaste of what is to come.

Beyond the Mexuar lies the **Serallo**, a complex of chambers that opens off the **Patio de los Arrayanes** (Patio of the Myrtles), a rectangular courtyard with a central pool, gently splashing fountains and a border of myrtle hedges. The patio's northern arcade leads to the **Sala de la Barca** (Hall of the Boat), named for its boat-shaped ceiling, and the magnificent **Salón del Trono**, or Salón de los Embajadores (Throne Room or Hall of the Ambassadors), where the king received emissaries. The tiled and stuccoed walls soar to a ceiling dome that is a dazzling masterpiece of carved woodwork depicting the star-speckled heavens.

More austere than Islamic architecture: the Palacio de Carlos V

The next section of the palace was built as an inner sanctum for the sultans, and is where the rooms of the harem were located. The focus is the **Patio de los Leones** (Hall of the Lions), enclosed by pillared arcades of marble columns and with a fountain at its centre surrounded by 12 stone lions. On the southern side of the patio is the beautiful **Sala de los Abencerrajes**, a small room which contains some of the complex's most breathtaking crafts-manship. The ravishing dome, composed of a mass of tiny stalactites like star-bursts, and the 16-sided ceiling frieze are reflected in a fountain on the floor beneath it. The dark stains in the fountain bowl are said to represent the blood from the severed heads of 36 slaughtered princes of the Abencerraj family (after whom the room is named), whose chief had coveted Sultan Abu al-Hassan's favourite concu-bine, Zoraya. Rust is probably the more likely source of the stains, but black deeds and acts of cruelty certainly did take place amid these exquisite surroundings.

At the far end of the Patio de los Leones is a long narrow room, the **Sala de los Reyes** (Hall of the Kings), where re-cessed chambers retain paintings on their leather-covered ceilings. These are believed to depict tales of chivalry and are possibly the work of later Christian artists. The hall was used for summer entertainment, and the recesses may have served the same purpose as boxes at the theatre. Opposite the Sala de los Abencerrajes is the **Sala de las Dos Hermanas** (Hall of the Two Sisters), named for two large slabs of marble in the chamber floor. The stuccowork on the room's roof is dazzling, like an explosion of shattered crystals. Beyond lies the romantic **Sala de los Ajimeces** (Hall of the Arched Windows), the private quarters of the sultan's favourite, where a gazebo overlooks a lush patio below.

Palacio de Carlos V

From the Sala de los Ajimeces a series of rooms and passageways leads into terraced gardens interspersed with patios and Moorish towers. You leave the gardens alongside the Renaissance **Palacio de Carlos V**, a gran-diose intrusion on the Moorish complex by the Spanish monarch, who ripped out part of the Palacio Nazaríes to accommodate it. This is a building that would stand as a splendid structure in any other context. The core

NEAR RUIN

From its early days, the Alhambra was plundered of its valuables. Vandalism took many forms. Nineteenth-century collectors from Northern Europe often came armed with small hammers with which they surreptitiously removed parts of the exquisite stucco work. In the 1820s, the American writer Washington Irving set up home in the abandoned Palacio Nazaríes, where he wrote the romantic *Tales of the Alhambra*, a book that triggered huge interest in the Alhambra and prompted the Spanish authorities to protect and restore the site. A commemorative plaque in the palace indicates the rooms in which Irving resided while writing part of the book.

of the palace is a vast circular courtyard, open to the sky. It was used at one time as a bullring. The surrounding rooms contain the **Museo de la Alhambra** with outstanding artefacts from the Islamic era, finest of which is the great Jarrón de las Gacelas (Gazelle Vase), elegantly decorated in enamel. The building's upper floors house the **Museo de Bellas Artes** (➤ 92).

The cool green gardens of the Generalife are a real delight

The Generalife

On the Cerro del Sol (Hill of the Sun), at the eastern end of the Alhambra complex, is the luxurious Generalife, a world of cool fountains and pools, of garden patios and flower-filled terraces. This was the extravagant pleasure palace of the Nasrids, where banquets and theatrical performances were staged. Today you can wander through the **Patio de los Cipreses,** a walled garden containing a cypress tree that is hundreds of years old, and dip your hands in the **Camino de las Cascades**, a stone stairway where water pours down the channelled balustrades.

➕ 205 E2
✉ Alhambra Hill ☎ 958 02 79 71 ⏰ March–Oct daily 8:30–8 (also floodlit visits Tue–Sat 10– 11:30pm); Nov–Feb 8:30–6 (also floodlit visits Fri, Sat 8–9:30pm) 🍴 Restaurants (€€€); drinks and snack kiosks (€–€€)
🚌 Alhambra bus (➤ 93): Every 10 minutes from Plaza Isabel la Católica and Plaza Nueva 🎟 €13, senior citizens €8

ENTRY TO THE ALHAMBRA
Entry to the Alhambra is limited to about 6,000 visitors daily. A main ticket to the entire complex is stamped with a half-hour time slot for entrance to the Palacio Nazaríes and you must enter within that half-hour. You can remain inside for as long as you like. Tickets can be purchased at the Alhambra Entrance Pavilion (with a maximum of ten per person), but expect long queues. If you purchase a ticket at the Entrance Pavilion late in the day, all the Palacio Nazaríes time slots may be taken up. You are strongly advised to pre-book your visit. This can be done directly through the Spanish bank, the ServiCaixa at any of its many branches throughout Spain or at its offices in Paris, London, Milan and New York. Tickets can be reserved up to a maximum of one year ahead by phoning from within Spain (tel: 902 88 80 01) or from abroad (tel: 0034 92 37 50 78), or through the website www.alhambratickets.com. Payment is by Visa, MasterCard or Eurocard only. For current information check the official website, www.alhambra-patronato.es.

The Albaicín

Granada's old Moorish quarter, the Albaicín, stands on the slopes of Sacromonte hill and faces the lofty Alhambra across the valley of the Río Darro. Its roughly cobbled streets and alleyways wriggle to and fro, punctuated by tall palm trees, between whitewashed walls splashed with bougainvillaea and geraniums. Scattered throughout are leafy plazas buzzing with local life. At sudden junctions you catch glimpses of the Alhambra painted against the backdrop of the Sierra Nevada and at popular viewpoints, such as the Mirador de San Nicolás (➤ 176), you can admire the floodlit palace at dusk.

The southern edge of the Albaicín is flanked by the Carrera del Darro, the narrow street that leads alongside the Río Darro, its line of buildings pierced at intervals by the steep and narrow alleyways that lead upwards into the heart of the Albaicín. In the Carrera del Darro, you'll find the 11th-century **Baños Árabes** (Arab Baths). You enter through a minuscule patio garden, an enchanting prelude to the brick-vaulted

chambers of the baths themselves, with their starred and octagonal skylights. Nearby is Granada's excellent **Museo Arqueológico** (Archaeological Museum), with a fine collection of prehistoric, Phoenician, Roman, Visigothic and Moorish exhibits, housed in a Renaissance palace, the Casa de Castril. Its arcaded patio balcony has a view of the Alhambra above.

Other highlights of the Albaicín include **Plaza Larga**, where everyday life is focused on surrounding shops and bars, and **Plaza San Miguel el Bajo**, to the west of the Mirador de San Nicolás; here amid whispering plane trees you can linger over drinks and *tapas* at the popular Bar Lara or Bar El Yunque. Nearby is another fine viewpoint, the **Mirador de Cruz de Quirós**. The eastern heights of Sacromonte hill contain the caves where a vibrant *gitano* community once lived. Now the former dwellings only house a few establishments offering expensive flamenco shows.

Insider Tip

Wander along the side streets of Albaicín away from the clamour of the crowds

The Albaicín can be explored by a planned itinerary (➤ 174) or by wandering at random. Heading downhill will usually lead you back to central Granada. Don't wander in this area at night though, and watch for bag snatchers during the day.

Baños Árabes
✚ 205 D3 ✉ Carrera del Darro 31 ☎ 958 22 97 38
🕐 Tue–Sat 10–2 🚌 Alhambra bus (➤ 92) 💷 Free

Museo Arqueológico
✚ 205 D3 ✉ Carrera del Darro 41 ☎ 958 57 54 08
🕐 Currently closed for restoration work 🚌 Alhambrabus (➤ 93)
💷 €1.50 (free to EU passport holders)

Capilla Real & Catedral

In the centre of modern Granada, just off the busy main Gran Vía de Colón, you'll find two important post-Moorish buildings, the catedral (cathedral) and adjoining Capilla Real (Royal Chapel).

The **Capilla Real**, built in late Gothic style and located on the south side of the cathedral was built over a 15-year period, from 1505 to 1521, under the direction of Enrique de Egas and destined as the resting place of the Catholic monarchs, Isabel and Fernando. The royal couple's original wish was to be buried in Toledo, but their conquest of the Moors encouraged them to build a burial chapel for themselves beside the cathedral that would replace Granada's Great Mosque.

The chapel is richly endowed with elegant columns and arches and superb altarpieces. A splendid grille encloses the lavish mausoleum of Isabel and Fernando, whose likenesses are depicted in Carrera marble. To its right are the figures of their daughter Joana ("the Mad") and her husband Felipe. Narrow steps descend to a crypt where the lead coffins of all four lie in grim display. Whether the remains within the coffins are those of the royal family is open to question, as they were vandalised by Napoleon's troops (always irreverent) during their short stay in the city during the Napoleonic Wars.

The chapel's sacristy is an absolute joy and includes in its collection of royal artefacts Isabel's personal treasury of Italian and Flemish paintings, the latter including fine works by Hans Memling and Rogier Van der Weyden.

Towering above the maze of houses in the town centre is the **Catedral Santa María de la Encarnación**, the most important of the four large Renaissance churches in Andalucía. It started out as a Gothic structure under the direction of Enrique de Egas in 1523, acquired lavish Plateresque elements when Diego de Siloé took over in 1525 and was consecrated in 1561, although still not complete. In 1563, Juan de Orea was put in charge of continuing the work, which dragged on until 1703 when it was finally stopped without two of the towers foreseen in the plans being completed; even the tower that had been started did not reach its planned height.

The 47m-(154ft)-high central dome gives the interior of the cathedral a wonderful airiness, and there are a

The Capilla Real, Granada's finest Christian Gothic building

**Organ and
ceiling of
the nave in
the cathedral**

number of chapels that light up sporadically as visitors feed coins into switch boxes. There are fine paintings and sculptures within the cathedral, several by the 17th-century Granada-born artist Alonso Cano, who worked on the cathedral's west façade.

To the southwest of the cathedral lies an area of narrow streets and attractive plazas that is worth exploring. On its east side, across the main thoroughfare of Calle Reyes Católicos from the Corral del Carbón tourist office (itself a finely preserved 14th-century merchants' inn), is the entrance to the **Alcaicería**, a mock-Arab souk or arcade, crammed with souvenir shops. Just beyond is Calle Zacatín, a pedestrianised shopping street that leads into **Plaza Bib-Rambla**, a huge square ringed by tall buildings and well supplied with café-bars and restaurants and with a swathe of flower stalls. The streets beyond the plaza are the heart of Granada's shopping district.

TAKING A BREAK

Try the **Vía Colón** bar-restaurant at Gran Vía de Colón 13, close to the Capilla Real and cathedral. It's busy, but friendly, and great for everything including breakfasts. Don't mind the full-size baroque angel and harp that stand on the bar.

Capilla Real
✚ 204 B2 ✉ Oficios 3 ☎ 958 22 92 39 🕐 10:15 (Sun from 11) until 1:30 and 4–7:30 (winter 3:30–6:30) 🚌 Buses 1, 3, 4, 6, 7, 8, 9 💷 €4

Catedral
✚ 204 B3 ✉ Gran Vía de Colón 5 ☎ 958 22 29 59 🕐 Mon–Sat 10:45–1:30, 4–8; Sun and public hols 4–8 🚌 Buses 1, 3, 4, 6, 7, 8, 9

Granada and Almería

Monasterio de la Cartuja

Try to visit the **Monasterio de la Cartuja** (Carthusian Monastery) on the northern outskirts of the city, one of Spain's most extravagant baroque buildings. Started in 1506 on the orders of the Gran Capitán (at that time Gonzalo Fernández de Córdoba y Aguilar, General and statesman in the service of the Catholic monarchs), the monastery was not finished until 250 years later. What remain are the cloister, refectory, church and sacristy. The lavish interior is a fine example of Churrigueresque (named after the Spanish architect and sculptor José Benito de Churriguera).

Moorish plasterwork in La Madraza, the old Muslim college, located opposite the Capilla Real

⛉ Parque de las Ciencias

A visit to the city's science museum provides a modern, and futuristic, perspective of Granada. It is a treat for youngsters, who can get interactive with various hands-on installations, as well as with giant chess and water games, and there's a planetarium, a butterfly house and a plant labyrinth. The museum is 2km (1.25mi) from the centre but there are regular buses.

Monasterio de la Cartuja
✚ 204 off B5 ✉ Calle Real de Cartuja ☎ 958 16 19 32
🕑 Daily 10–1, 4–8 (winter 3–6) 🚍 Bus 8, C 💷 €4

Parque de las Ciencias
✚ 204 off A1 ✉ Avenida de la Ciencia ☎ 958 13 19 00
🕑 Tue–Sat 10–7, Sun and public hols 10–3. Planetarium: hourly shows
🚍 Buses 4, 5, 10, 11 💷 Museum: €6.50, planetarium: €2.50

INSIDER INFO

- Granada's main **tourist office** is usually very busy. The Municipal Tourist Office on **Plaza Mariana Pineda** is a useful alternative.
- Take an early evening stroll through the **university district** to the northwest of the cathedral. There is a youthful bustle in the streets and you may hear the strains of music emanating from buildings as you pass by. Look out for some splendid churches and other buildings with spectacular baroque features scattered through the area.
- Enjoy the peace of a visit to the restored 16th-century **Monasterio de San Jerónimo** in the university district (Rector López Argüeta 9, daily 10–1:30, 4–7:30). The church contains superb frescos and a classical central altarpiece rising to a barrel vault through a series of niches crammed with magnificent sculptures and reliefs. If you go in the evening you might hear the subdued chanting of the Sisters of St Jerome.
- The **Alhambra bus** (Lines 30 and 32) is a very useful circular bus service that links Plaza Nueva with the Alhambra and the Albaicín. The service runs every 10 minutes between 7am and 11pm. The Plaza Nueva terminus, where buses for both the Alhambra and the Albaicín Linea 32 depart, is near the entrance to Cuesta de Gomérez, the narrow lane that leads up to the Alhambra. The Albaicín service has an extension to Sacromonte hourly.
- Unless you are a devoted art lover, you may find the **Museo de Bellas Artes** in the upper rooms of the Alhambra's Palacio de Carlos V a museum too many; it holds some fine paintings, but nothing to take what's left of your breath away.

★⑧ Las Alpujarras

The Alpujarras, south of Granada and the Sierra Nevada, though slightly austere in places, have an attractive and very temperate mountain environment, which was rediscovered by writers and hikers at the beginning of the 20th century.

Moors settled in this region back in the 8th century and built up a lucrative silk business there in the 10th and 11th centuries. After losing Granada in 1492, the Moors retreated to the outlying villages until the majority were banished for good after several violent uprisings in 1568. Some Muslim families were allowed to stay, however, in order to help the new Christian settlers maintain the sophisticated irrigation systems and terraced gardens. The terraces are still used today for growing cereal crops, olives, citrus fruit and vegetables.

Busquístar is located at an altitude of 1160m (3806ft) on the Rio Trevélez in the Alpujarras

Go West
The approach from Granada to the Western Alpujarras is through the spa town of **Lanjarón**. At the market town of Órgiva, 18km (11mi) east of Lanjarón, turn off north to follow an exhilarating mountain road that takes you into the heart of the formidable Poqueira Gorge. This is the best of the High Alpujarras.

The Poqueira Villages
The Poqueira Gorge, a broad but steep-sided wooded valley, slices into the hills towards the second highest summit of the Sierra Nevada, Pico Veleta (3,398m/11,145ft), with the highest summit Mulhacén (3,481m/11,418ft) just out of sight to the east. The white houses of a chain of three villages climb up the terraced slopes of the valley. The first village is **Pampaneira**, a compact jumble of houses

that rises above the rugged old church of Santa Cruz in the central square, Plaza de la Libertad. On the square, you'll find Nevadensis, an excellent information centre for the Alpujarras and Sierra Nevada, along with several bars and plenty of souvenir shops selling local pottery, rugs and blankets that reflect Pampaneira's popularity with coach parties.

Above Pampaneira is the village of **Bubión**, the most tranquil and least visited of the Poqueira villages, with narrow streets spilling down the slopes below the main road to the flower-hung Plaza Iglesia. On the corner of the church square is the **Casa Tradicional Alpujarreña**, an outstanding museum of Alpujarran life. It occupies a traditional village house, left unchanged since its occupant moved away in the 1950s. On the way down to the square is the **Taller del Telar** (Weaver's Workshop, ➤ 107), where fine woollen cloth is produced on a loom that belonged to the last master weaver of Granada. The cloth, of superb quality, comes in subtle colours; it is for sale, as are other artefacts such as textile lampshades.

The highest of the Poqueira villages is **Capileira**. It is extremely popular and gets very crowded in summer. Away from the main road, however, you can wander between classic Alpujarran flat-roofed houses on narrow alleyways with covered roofs of twisted branches packed with clay.

The white-washed stone houses of the Alpujarras (below: in Pampaneira) are very typical of Moorish architecture

Then, as the lower houses of Capileira thin out, you can follow tracks that lead higher into the wooded gorge, where the Poqueira river gushes across polished boulders amid scented pinewoods.

Trevélez and Beyond

The road east from the Poqueira Gorge runs in delectable twists and turns along the great wooded shelf of hills and passes through the less visited villages of Pitres, Pórtugos and Busquístar, before turning north once more along the slopes of another deep valley to the town of **Trevélez**. This is the highest settlement in Spain and is famed for its production of cured ham, *jamón serrano*. The houses of Trevélez climb the upper slopes of the valley in a succession of *barrios*, separate quarters that have quite distinct characters. The lowest of these, the *barrio bajo*, pays the price of Trevélez's popularity. Its main square is not much more than a large car-parking area with souvenir shops, cafés, restaurants and *jamón serrano* outlets. A steep zigzagging road leads up to middle Trevélez, the *barrio medio*, then continues to the upper village, the *barrio alto*, where traffic fades away and lanes grow narrower as they climb towards the steepening mountain slopes above.

Continuing east from Trevélez takes you deeper into the Alpujarras, through a landscape of woods and streams,

INSIDER INFO

- **Driving in the Alpujarras** takes much longer than you think, so plan accordingly. It may take you the best part of a morning to drive 50km (31mi) along the area's winding roads, and with all the spectacular scenery, the temptation to stop and admire the view is irresistible. If you have time to spare, why not be adventurous? You can enjoy plant and birdwatching **walks** or longer treks, **horse riding, cycling, four-wheel drive trips**, and even **hang-gliding** throughout the area, all with experienced local guides. Most of the villages along the southern slopes of the Alpujarras are linked by the waymarked long-distance path GR-7. With careful planning you can walk sections of the route between villages and return to your starting point by bus. Ask for details at Nevadensis in Pampaneira (▶ Tourist Information, below).

- **All About the Alpujarras:** The English writer Gerald Brenan lived in Yegen during the 1920s and wrote of his experiences in *South From Granada*, an enthralling account of Alpujarran life. A plaque commemorating Brenan is fixed to the wall of the house in which he lived, now called the **Casa de Brenan**, near the village's main square. Another Alpujarran book, *Driving Over Lemons* (1999), was written by Chris Stewart, ex-drummer of the band Genesis, who set up as a small farmer near Órgiva. He also wrote *Parrot in the Pepper Tree* and the *Almond Blossom Appreciation Society*.

- Solynieve (Sun and Snow) is Granada province's winter sports resort, reached from Granada. It stands on the upper slopes of the Sierra Nevada and in summer is fairly desolate. If you ski, you could catch some late seasonal runs – with the aid of numerous snow-making machines. But unless you are really keen, you could also give it a miss!

A regional speciality from Trevélez: cured ham

dense with chestnut, poplar, evergreen oak and pine. The road takes you past old Moorish settlements, such as **Bérchules** and **Yegen**, unspoiled villages that cling to the tumbling slopes of the hills and captivate with their slow pace of life and friendly inhabitants. Beyond Yegen the road continues east until the landscape begins slowly to lose its green mantle as it gives way to the arid hills of Almería province.

TAKING A BREAK

In Pampaneira, the **Alegrías** bar-restaurant makes use of a pleasant little terrace just below the preserved public washhouse. Head uphill from the church square of Plaza de la Libertad on a cobbled lane with a central water channel. **Casa Diego** offers good food and a convivial atmosphere.

➕ 200 C2

Tourist Information
✉ Nevadensis, Plaza de la Libertad, Pampaneira
☎ 958 76 31 27; www.nevadensis.com
✉ Rustic Blue (private), Bubión
☎ 958 76 33 81; www.rusticblue.com

Casa Tradicional Alpujarreña
✉ Plaza Iglesia, Bubión ☎ 958 76 30 32
🕐 Mon–Fri 11–2; Sat, Sun and public hols 11–2, 5–7

㉑ Almería

According to an old saying, "When Almería was Almería, Granada was but a farmstead", an expression of pride justified, not least, by the city's dramatically sited Moorish fortress. The city's Moorish name al-Mariy-ya translates as "mirror of the sea". Below it, the older, western part of the city, characterised by narrow streets and crumbling buildings, lies side by side with the busy shopping streets and recently refurbished boulevards of the modern city. In Almería you move easily between Moorish and medieval Andalucía and the busy world of 21st-century Spain.

In the southeast of Andalucía, the wide open Gulf of Almería attracts visitors with its long beaches and its provincial capital's mix of modern flair and historic allure. The town's touristic highlight is the very beautifully restored Alcazaba, the largest Moorish fortress in Andalucía.

From the 8th century, Almería was the chief port of al-Andalus and grew rich on two-way trade with North Africa and the eastern Mediterranean. The city fell to the Christians in 1490, and the break with North Africa led to a decline exacerbated by destructive earthquakes in the 16th century. By the 19th century Almería was beginning to prosper once more. Today *plasticultura*, greenhouse farming, and increased tourism, have brought much development to the rather unspectacular but convivial and lively city.

The Alcazaba
The Alcazaba's 10th-century builders took advantage of the craggy edges of their hilltop site, and even today the restored walls and towers of the fortress look like natural extensions of the encircling cliffs. The approach ramp to the **Alcazaba** complex winds steeply up to the **Puerta de la Justicia** (Justice Gate), a perfect example of a Moorish entrance archway. The double horseshoe arch has a staggered inner gate that was designed to disorientate an

View from Cerro de San Cristóbal, the peak near Alcazaba, on Almería

attacker. Beyond is the **Primer Recinto** (First Precinct), the lowest level of the Alcazaba, used as a camp by the Moorish garrison and as a refuge for citizens during sieges. It has been transformed into a series of terraced gardens. From here you climb gently to a cool oasis of trees that shades the high wall of the **Segundo Recinto** (Second Precinct), a large area filled with the poignant ruins of the sumptuous living quarters that reflected the wealth and importance of Almería in the 10th and 11th centuries, first under the Córdoban Caliphate, then as an independent principality, and later as part of Muslim Granada. The **Tercer Recinto** (Third Precinct) contains the formidable inner fortress built by the Christian conquerors after 1492 on the site of a previous keep. From its walls there are breathtaking views to the sea. Immediately below the fortress of Alcazaba lies the **Barrio de Chanca**, Almería's old cave district with the often brightly painted façades of the flat-roofed houses and of the **cave dwellings** that punctuate the rocky escarpments above them. The houses, and a few of the caves, are occupied by the poorest citizens of Almería.

Other Sights

The city's **cathedral** is a typical fortified church with four imposing corner towers, tower-like apses and battlements. Diego de Siloé built it after the earthquake of 1522 between 1524 and 1543 in place of the Friday Mosque. Less overbearing are the main entrance and the Puerta de los Perdones, both by Juan de Orea, with twin pillars, richly decorated with sculptural figures and crowned with the coat of arms of Carlos I. The exquisite choir stalls of carved walnut are also by de Orea (1558).

The **Museo Arqueológico** (Archaeological Museum) exhibits items from the Los Millares pre-Bronze Age site (Insider Info, ► 102), along with material from the Roman and Moorish periods. The **Centro de Artes** (Art Gallery), a bone-white rotunda near the station exhibits traditional and contemporary art. Central Almería is divided by the Rambla de Belén, a wide boulevard that slopes down towards the harbour and

Granada and Almería

is dotted with palm trees and fountains. To the west is the city's main street, the sleekly refurbished Paseo de Almería lined with shops, restaurants and café-bars. At its north end is Puerta de Purchena, a busy junction, groaning and fuming with traffic, its pavements thronged with voluble Almeríans. The pedestrianised Plaza Manuel Pérez García leads from the western end of **Puerta de Purchena** into the attractive shopping street of Calle de las Tiendas.

Fountain in Almería's Alcazaba

TAKING A BREAK

For great *jamón* and fish *tapas* and meals, and a terrific selection of sherries, don't miss **Bodega las Botas** (Calle Fructuosa Pérez 3), a high-roofed bar with traditional upturned sherry barrels for tables.

✠ 201 E2 🖩 Tourist Information; www.turismodealmeria.org ✉ Parque Nicolás Salmerón s/n ☎ 950 17 52 20 ✉ Plaza de la Constitución ☎ 950 21 05 38

Parking: There are underground car parks midway along the Rambla de Belén and off the main roundabout at the Rambla's southern end.

Alcazaba
✉ Almanzor s/n ☎ 950 27 16 17 🕔 Sun 10–5, Tue–Sat Mid-Sep–March 9–6:30, April–May 9–8, June–mid-Sep 9–3:30, 6:30–10 ♿ Free to EU passport holders

Catedral
✉ Plaza de la Catedral 🕔 Mon–Fri 10–1:30, 4–5, Sat 10–1:30

Museo Arqueológico
✉ Calle de Ronda 91 ☎ 950 17 55 10 🕔 Tue 2–8:30, Wed–Sat 6–8:30, Sun 9–2:30 🕔 €1.50 (free to EU passport holders)

Centro de Artes (Museo Almería)
✉ Plaza Barcelona s/n ☎ 950 26 96 80 🕔 Mon 6pm–9pm, Tue–Sat 11–2, 6–9, Sun 11–2 ♿ Free

INSIDER INFO

- The sun can be blisteringly hot here, so **use sunscreen and wear a hat**, especially when visiting the Alcazaba where there is not much shelter.
- Try to take in Almería's lively **morning market.** It's held in Calle Aguilar de Campo, an alleyway reached from halfway down Paseo de Almería.
- The 17th-century **Plaza Vieja** (Old Square) is a tranquil place to relax. Palm trees encircle a white monument, which commemorates the execution in 1824 of Almerians who defied the repressive rule of King Fernando VII.
- The **Cerro de San Cristobal**, a barren hill crowned by a giant statue of Christ and the ruin of a church, lies north of the Alcazaba. It is best viewed from the Alcazaba rather than struggling up its rubbly slopes. However, rather unimposing, it is definitely not a must see.

At Your Leisure

🟥 Cabo de Gata

This peninsula on the eastern side of the Gulf of Almería is believed to be the driest and possibly the hottest place in Europe, a landscape of long empty beaches, salt pans and raw volcanic hills. On the southern tip of the peninsula, at the actual cape (*cabo*), stands a lonely lighthouse from where there are dramatic views of rugged cliffs and offshore pinnacles. Cabo de Gata's attractions lie in its often empty beaches, its plant and bird life and the remoteness of

NATURE AT ITS BEST

The **Parque Natural de Cabo de Gata-Níjar** is an area of special protection for plants and birds. Plants that can cope with the desert-like conditions include the Zizyphus, or jujube, a shrub whose thorny leaves and branches form an umbrella over the soil to preserve moisture, and Europe's only indigenous palm, the dwarf fan palm. Behind the village of San Miguel de Cabo de Gata lies **Las Salinas**, a large area of salt marshes, where you may spot flamingos, avocets, storks and egrets among the many resident and migrant birds.

Centro de Información Parque Natural Cabo de Gata: Avenida de San José 27, Níjar, tel. 950 38 02 99, www.cabodegata-nijar.com; daily 10–2, 5–8, (in winter Sun only 10–2).

Centro de Visitantes de Las Amoladeras: between Almería and Cabo de Gata, Km 7, Paraje de las Amoladeras

the cliffs and lonely coves of the wild coast to the northeast of the cape. The most accessible beaches lie on the shores of the Gulf of Almería alongside the road between the village of San Miguel de Cabo de Gata and the lighthouse. They are marred only by the occasional winds that blow up by midday. Just before the lighthouse, a narrow road, signed *Acceso Sendero Vela Blanca*, leads off north for a few kilometres to a final headland crowned by a radio station and by the old Moorish watchtower of Vela Blanca. Beyond here a dirt track winds along the side of wild mountain slopes and gives access on foot to some small, secluded beaches.

🔶 201 E2

🍴 La Gallineta (€€–€€€) ✉ Ctra. El Pozo de los Frailes, El Pozo de los Frailes ☎ 950 38 05 01

Tourist Information ➤ panel, left

🟥 Níjar

The village of Níjar, centre of a ceramics industry dating from Moorish times, sits in the foothills of the Sierra de Alhamilla 30km (19mi) northeast of Almeria. Below is the arid plain of the Campo de Níjar, carpeted with the glistening sheets of *plasticultura* greenhouses. Níjar's potters specialise in vivid colours created from mineral dyes; you can buy their wares in the pottery and craft shops in main street,

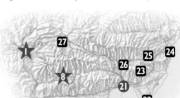

Granada and Almería

OFF THE BEATEN TRACK

For a rewarding experience head for **Los Millares**, about 12km (7.5mi) north of Almería and remote hills (🛡 197 E2, Wed–Sun 10–2; free). Always check first with one of the Almería tourist offices that the site is open, or phone 677 90 34 04). This internationally important pre-Bronze Age site contains the remains of walls, stone huts and beehive-shaped tombs (one has been reconstructed). There is also some interesting decorated pottery and, in one larger building, evidence of copper smelting. It is a 1km (0.75mi) walk from the roadside entrance and the heat in summer can be savage. Cover up and take water. Los Millares is best reached by car.

Avenida García Lorca. However, the main workshops and show-room are in the adjoining **Barrio Alfarero**, which leads off from the top of García Lorca. The craft shops also sell brightly coloured carpets and blankets. Beyond Avenida García Lorca is the Old Town with tree-lined **Plaza la Glorieta** and the 16th-century church of Santa María de la Anunciación, noted for its *mudéjar*

The white houses of Mojácar Pueblo picturesquely enthroned on a hill

ceiling. Continue beyond the church to the **Plaza del Mercado** with its huge central tree and blue-tiled public fountain. For excellent Níjar ceramics look for La Tienda de los Milagros (➤ 107) in Calle Pocico 9.

🛡 201 E2

🛈 Tourist Information: ✉ Plaza Glorieta (town hall) ☎ 950 36 00 12; www.nijar.es

🌃 Mojácar

Mojácar is the main beach resort in Almería province and can become extremely busy in high season. If you want easily accessible beaches with modern conveniences, how-ever, this is the place to find them. There are two Mojácars. The long, straggling coastal resort of **Mojácar Playa** makes the most of a narrow stretch of excellent beach along-side the rather busy main road. Beachfront development runs for several kilometres and there are numerous hotels, shops, cafés, restaurants and lively bars. Just 2km (1.25mi) inland is old Mojácar, known as **Mojácar Pueblo**, a settle-ment clustered round a rocky hill-top. The village can still charm in spite of the crowds of summer visitors who throng the souvenir shops.

🛡 201 F2

🛈 Tourist Information: ✉ Plaza del Frontón, Mojácar ☎ 902 57 51 30; www.mojacar.es

🞮 Sorbas

The village of Sorbas, 40km (25mi) northeast of Almería, is noted for its pottery and you can visit workshops and salerooms in its Barrio Alfarero (► 108). Signposted to the south of the village are the 🞮 **Cuevas de Sorbas**, at the heart of the limestone hills. You can take two-hour guided trips through the cave systems. These are mildly adventurous, but even young children can cope with the occasional scrambling and clambering. Helmets and headlamps are supplied, but be prepared to get muddy.

➕ 201 E2 🛈 Tourist Information:
✉ Plaza de la Constitución 1 (town hall)
☎ 950 36 47 01; www.sorbas.es

Cuevas de Sorbas

➕ 201 F2 ☎ 950 36 47 04; www.cuevasde sorbas.com. Booking a day ahead is advised.
🕐 Summer daily every hour on the hour 10–8, winter 10–1, 3–6
🐾 From €15 (depending on the route)

🞮 🎎 Mini Hollywood (Oasys)

The extraordinary Arizona-style "Badlands" of Tabernas to the north of Almería city is where such Western classics as *The Magnificent Seven*, *A Fistful of Dollars* and *The Good, the Bad and the Ugly* were filmed. The mock Wild West towns that were built for these movies amid drystone gulches and treeless wastes remain as tourist attractions. Mini Hollywood is the largest and the best managed. It lies – as part of the "Oasys Theme Park" (Safari park, zoo and water park) – just off the Carretera Nacional, about 10km (6 miles) west of the village of Tabernas. Special cowboy shows are staged at set times outside the sheriff's office, with energetic jail breaks, gunfights and hangings. Youngsters love it, but adults may groan at the staginess of it all. Adjoining the town is the Reserva Zoológica, a well-kept zoo with big cats and a range of animals including bison, hippos, zebra …

➕ 201 E2 ☎ 902 53 35 32; www.oasys parquetematico.com 🕐 July–Aug 10–9, otherwise shorter (often closed in winter)
🍴 Restaurant and café (€/€€)
🐾 €22 (dogs are not admitted)

🞮 Guadix

The bustling country town of Guadix, 60km (37mi) east of Granada, contains a remarkable "suburb" of cave dwellings that have been carved out of soft sandstone rock.he caves here comprise entire dwellings with all the modern conveniences, and the windowless rooms maintain a constantly equable temperature. Many caves have whitewashed extensions and well-tended gardens. In the **Cueva Museo** (Cave Museum), which can be reached by road train from the town centre, a series of domestic rooms have been beautifully preserved and furnished in traditional manner. The main town of Guadix is dominated by a magnificent Renaissance cathedral in rich red sandstone. Opposite its main door is an archway that leads to the attractive Renaissance square of Plaza de la Constitución, known also as Plaza Mayor. From the square, cobbled alleyways lead to a clutch of handsome Renaissance buildings in the upper town.

➕ 200 C3
🛈 Tourist Information:
✉ Plaza de la Catedral
☎ 670 95 70 25; www.turismoguadix.es

Cueva Museo

✉ Plaza del Padre Poveda ☎ 958 66 55 69
🕐 Mon–Fri 10–12, 4–6, Sat 10–2 🐾 €2.60

Where to...
Stay

Prices
Expect to pay per double room per night

€ up to €60 €€ €60–€90 €€€ €90–€140 €€€€ over €140

GRANADA

Casa del Aljarife €€€
The views of the Alhambra from this pension, set in a tiny square at the heart of the Albaicín, are splendid. The 17th-century house has been sensitively restored, and has a delightful shady central courtyard and rooftop terrace typical of the area. The rooms (there are just four) are small but have plenty of character with interesting angles and use of space.

✚ 205 D3
✉ Placeta de la Cruz Verde 2, Albaicín
☎ 958 22 24 25; www.casadelaljarife.com

Hostal Britz €€
The Britz, just within walking distance of the Alhambra, offers great value. Rooms are basic but comfortable, and some have terraces and brightly tiled ensuite bathrooms. The location on the bustling Plaza Nueva means it can be noisy, but also that a choice of pavement cafés is just a short stroll away.

✚ 204 C2
✉ Cuesta de Gomérez 1 ☎ 958 22 36 52

Hotel Los Tilos €€
This good-value, no-frills hotel has a comfortable, modern interior, and is about as central as you can get, overlooking a pleasant square where there is a daily flower market. Best of all is the fourth-floor terrace where you can sip a drink, read a book or just enjoy a fabulous panoramic view of the city skyline.

Insider Tip

✚ 204 A2 ✉ Plaza Bib-Rambla 4
☎ 958 26 67 12; www.hotellostilos.com

LAS ALPUJARRAS

Hotel Catifalarga €€
This restored old farmhouse, just outside Capileira, is surrounded by terraced orchards. The rustic-style rooms have wooden shutters and beams; several have private terraces. The views are stunning and activities can be organised.

✚ 196 C2
✉ Carretera de Sierra Nevada, Capileira
☎ 958 34 33 57; www.catifalarga.com

Las Terrazas €/€€€
There's a delightful homey feel to the *hostal* with mountain bikes to borrow and very helpful hosts. Rooms are simple, with locally woven bedspreads, and breakfast is included. Also apartments to rent.

✚ 200 C2 ✉ Plaza del Sol 7, Bubión
☎ 958 76 30 34; www.terrazasalpujarra.com
🕐 Closed Jan

ALMERÍA

Hotel La Perla €/€€
The oldest hotel in town and still family-run, La Perla was favoured by the stars in Almería's "spaghetti western" days. It has been expanded to several more floors but still exudes a certain old-world charm. The rooms are pleasant – ask for one overlooking the plaza – and the facilities, including air conditioning, satellite TV and parking, are good.

✚ 201 E2 ✉ Plaza del Carmen 7
☎ 950 23 88 77; www.hotellaperla.es

Where to...
Eat and Drink

Prices
Expect to pay per person for a meal, including wine and service
€ up to €15   €€ €15–€40   €€€ over €40

GRANADA

Cunini €€/€€€
This is one of the city's most famous restaurants with fish and seafood the specialities. Expect impeccable service and commendable food. Dishes include *caldereta de arroz*, *pescado y marisco* (rice, fish and seafood stew) and *pescaditos fritos* (fried fish). Located around the corner from the cathedral, there is an attractive outside terrace.
✚ 204 A2 ✉ Calle Pescadería 14
☎ 958 25 07 77; www.marisqueriacunini.es
Ⓒ Closed Sun and Mon evenings

La Gran Taberna €/€€
The interior of this town-centre *tapas* bar is typical, with stools around barrels, and hams, strings of garlic and red peppers hanging above the bar. If you want a quiet drink, forget it, especially if it's a football night when the TV will be blaring. The *tapas* here are terrific. You can choose from a vast selection, including trout with cottage cheese, Roquefort with beets and goat's cheese canapés as well as the more standard selection.
✚ 204 C2 ✉ Plaza Nueva 12
☎ 958 22 88 46 Ⓒ Daily 9–3, 7–midnight

Taberna Tendido 1 €
Situated right under the Plaza de Toros, it's no surprise that *rabo de toro estofado al vino tinto* (bull's tail cooked in red wine) is on the menu here, along with a choice of lighter bites, including salads, cheeses and smoked fish. There are also fixed-price menus available. The brick-clad interior is cosy and inviting and the place is usually buzzing with a lively young crowd.
✚ 204, northwest of B5 ✉ Calle Dr Olóriz 25
☎ 958 27 23 02; www.tendido1.com

San Nicolás €€€
Head straight for a table by the window if you want to enjoy the fabulous views of the Alhambra (particularly recommended at sunset). The restaurant's décor is sumptuous and elegant, with exquisite marble, pale pistachio-coloured walls and linen-clad tables. The menu includes such nouvelle-Andaluz dishes as leg of pork filled with lavender and honey, and there's an outside terrace for alfresco lunches and a little candlelit romance.
✚ 203 D3 ✉ Calle San Nicolás 3, Albaicín
☎ 958 27 28 42; www.restaurantesannicolas.com
Ⓒ Tue–Sat noon–11, Sun noon–4

Via Colon €€
This entertaining café-bar stands between busy Gran Via de Colón and the quieter environs of Granada's cathedral. It's a bustling spot, especially at lunchtime, but there's a quieter outside terrace right under the cathedral walls. Inside, pride of place goes to a remarkable full-size harp and arty angel that grace the end of the bar with some style. To eat, you'll find a range of tasty *tapas* and specialities such as *pastel de puerros* (leek tart), as well as a mouth-watering crêpes.
✚ 204 B3 ✉ Gran Via de Colón
☎ 958 22 07 52; www.restauranteviacolon.com
Ⓒ Daily 8am–midnight

Granada and Almería

Restaurante Ibero-Fusión €€

This family-run business near the church offers inexpensive regional dishes but also more exotic choices such as curry, dhal and couscous as well as plenty of vegetarian dishes. The atmosphere is lively and informal with swift and efficient service. Good wine selection.

➕ 200 C2 ✉ Calle Parra 1, Capileira
☎ 653 93 50 56; www.casaibero.com
🕐 Daily 7–11

La Fragua €€

You can enjoy blissful views over the rooftops to the valley beyond from the pine-clad dining room in this old village house. Pork specialities are served here, as are excellent lamb dishes. Or you could try the delicious locally cured ham or pork loin with mixed herbs. There's wonderful bread from the local baker and the puddings are superb. A couple of doors away is the hotel of the same name.

➕ 200 C2 ✉ Calle San Antonio 4, Trevélez
☎ 958 85 86 26; hotellafragua.com
🕐 1–4, 8–10:30

Insider Tip

Restaurant Ruta de Las Nieves €€

The setting is rustic, with a traditionally furnished beamed dining room. Step out onto the terrace for a great valley view. There are good-value *raciones*, such as spicy chicken (*pollo en salsa*), ham and chicken croquettes (*croquetas*), as well as a well-priced daily menu including trout, ham and a traditional fry-up of local sausages, ham and eggs with *patatas pobres* (fried potatoes with onion and garlic) on the side. Several popular hikes start from Capileira, so you can expect to see plenty of walkers fuelling up here before they set off.

➕ 200 C2
✉ Carretera de la Sierra s/n, Capileira
☎ 958 76 31 06
🕐 Daily 1:30–4, 8:30–10:30

Torreluz Mediterráneo €€€

One of the city's most sophisticated restaurants, with elaborate brocade chairs, light brick walls and plenty of stained glass and gilt. The service is discreet and attentive, the ingredients fresh, and the dishes flavourful. Specialities include suckling pig (*cochinillo*) slowly roasted in a wood-burning oven, grilled meats, and fresh fish.

➕ 201 E2 ✉ Plaza Flores 1
☎ 950 28 14 25; www.torreluz.com/restaurante-mediterraneo
🕐 Mon–Sat 1:30–4, 8:30–midnight

El Alcázar €/€€

This *marisquera* (seafood restaurant) is one of many in the street, but is clearly the most popular with locals. The food is simple but exceptionally fresh, and the choice is excellent. Try the *gambas pil pil* if you like your prawns with a chilli kick, or the *sopa de pescado* (fish soup), another speciality. There are a few tables inside, but most spill out onto the pavement. Or you can get your seafood to go.

➕ 201 E2 ✉ Calle Tenor Iribarne 2
☎ 950 23 89 95
🕐 Mon–Sat noon–4:30, 7–midnight

Restaurante Valentín €€€

Valentín is one of Almería's best known restaurants, and one of several good places to eat located on this street. The speciality here is seafood with dishes like *cazuela de rape* (monkfish baked in a sauce of almonds and pine nuts) and *langosta* (lobster). The atmosphere is intimate and the interior typically Andalucían with dark wood, exposed brickwork and white paintwork. If you are celebrating then push the boat out with the excellent *menu degustación*.

➕ 201 E2 ✉ Calle Tenor Iribarne 19
☎ 950 26 44 75; www.restaurantevalentin.es
🕐 Closed Mon and Sep

Where to...
Shop

Both Granada and Almería provinces have rich craftwork traditions, ranging from Granada's inlaid woodwork to the vividly coloured pottery of Níjar and the textiles and clothing of Las Alpujarras.

GRANADA CITY

Granada city's main shopping area is the streets between the arms of its two main thoroughfares, Calle Reyes Católicos and Gran Vía de Colón. In **Reyes Católicos** are a number of small, but very stylish fashion shops. A few metres in from here is the **Alcaicería**, a mock-Arab souk or arcade, crammed with souvenir shops full of Granadine crafts including brass and copperwork, embossed leather and pottery. Nearby is the narrow, pedestrianised **Zacatín** with a good range of clothes and gift shops. A Granada speciality is *taracea* (marquetry), and there are several shops selling it in **Cuesta de Gomérez**, the narrow street leading steeply uphill from Plaza Nueva to the Alhambra. One of the best is **González Ramos Taller de Taracea** (Cuesta Gomérez 16, tel: 958 22 70 62). The street also contains plenty of souvenir shops, as well as some of the best guitar-makers in Andalucía. Try **Casa Ferrer** (Cuesta de Gomérez 30, tel: 958 22 18 32), a highly rated music shop, founded in the late 19th-century by a member of the same family that still runs it.

For the full range of shopping there's the department store **El Corte Inglés** in Acero del Darro, the broad continuation of Reyes Católicos. One of the best food and drink shops in the city is the well-stocked **Mantequería Castellano**

Insider Tip

(Calle Almireceros 6, tel: 958 22 48 40) just off Gran Vía de Colón and opposite the cathedral. In nearby **Calderería Vieja and Calderería Nueva**, in the heart of the Albaicín, there are a number of shops selling "Arabic" spices, perfumes, food and souvenirs. One of the best for leatherwork is **Artesenía Albaicín** (Calle del Agua 19, tel: 958 27 90 56), which has a good selection of tooled leather goods, including bags, purses, wallets and coasters.

LAS ALPUJARRAS

In the High Alpujarras, shops in villages such as Pampaneira (➤ 94) sell souvenirs, pottery and traditional *jarapas* (rugs and bedcovers). Worth seeking out in Pampaneira is **Bodega La Moralea** (Calle Verónica 12, tel: 958 76 32 25), which carries a vast stock of local food products and artefacts. In Bubión (➤ 95) follow signs for **Taller del Telar** (Calle Trinidad, tel: 958 76 31 71, www.tallerdeltelar.com) for textiles and fabrics. For the *jamón serrano*, the cured ham of the region, Trevélez (➤ 96) is the best bet.

ALMERÍA CITY AND PROVINCE

Almería city's main shopping area is **Calle de las Tiendas** and its surrounding alleyways. The morning **market** in Calle Aguilar de Campo, off Paseo de Almería, is lively and colourful.

For fine pottery, head for **Níjar** (➤ 101), where you can also buy brightly coloured *jarapas*. Look for **La Tienda de los Milagros** (Callejón *Insider Tip* del Artesano 1, tel: 950 36 03 59) for an imaginative approach to pottery. Another good source of ceramics is **Sorbas** (➤ 103), where workshops in the Barrio Alfarero (the Potter's Quarter) produce more functional wares than those of Níjar in such family-run workshops as **Alfarería Juan Simón** (San Roque 21, tel: 950 36 40 83).

Where to...
Go Out

Ask at tourist offices in Granada city for *Guía de Granada* (it costs €1), a monthly listings guide. The city's daily newspaper *Ideal* also has a useful entertainment section in Spanish.

NIGHTLIFE

Many of the clubs and music bars in Granada cater to the city's lively student population. These inexpensive places are situated between the streets of Martinez de la Rosa and Pedro Antonio de Alarcon. If you are looking for something a little more sophisticated, try **Granada 10** (Cárcel Baja, tel: 958 22 40 01) just off Gran Vía de Colón near the cathedral. This doubles as a cinema, but the music starts about midnight. It attracts a smarter set, and is consequently more expensive than many other places in the city.

The mainstream **El Camborio** (Camino del Sacromonte) is a less expensive alternative. Here you'll find several dance floors and a garden terrace with views of the Alhambra. Again, midnight is the earliest time for things to start happening.

Almería has some lively music bars in the Calle San Pedro area, and during the summer months **disco-marquees** are set up on the Paseo Marítimo to the east of the seaward end of the Rambla de Belén. These venues can be fairly noisy and youth-orientated, but Spanish youngsters are not ageist, so, whatever your age, you can do it.

DANCE

Granada's **Teatro Alhambra** (Calle de Molinos 56, tel: 958 02 80 00)

stages flamenco, ballet and modern dance, as well as Spanish-language plays.

There are a number of flamenco venues in Granada city. One of the most popular is **Jardines Neptuno** (Calle Arabial, tel: 958 52 25 33), though the show is more cabaret than pure flamenco and organised as part of an all-in-one restaurant experience.

Something closer to the real thing can be seen at **Peña de la Platería** (Placeta de Toqueros 7, tel: 958 21 06 50) and **Tarantos** (Camino del Sacromonte 9, tel: 958 22 45 25).

OUTDOOR ACTIVITIES

The Sierra Nevada and Las Alpujarras have much to offer outdoor enthusiasts. Las Alpujarras offers ideal **walking** conditions and, if you are experienced and well equipped, there's high-level walking on the Sierra Nevada peaks. Enquire about maps and guide books at **Nevadensis** (Plaza de la Libertad, Pampaneira, tel: 958 76 31 27), the friendly and helpful Parque Natural Sierra Nevada information office.

For **horse riding**, contact **Dallas Love** (Bubión, tel: 608 45 38 02) or **Cabalgar Rutas Alternativas** (Bubión, tel: 958 76 31 35, http:// ridingAndalucía.com), who organise anything from a few hours' riding to nine-day treks, plus day-long four-wheel-drive tours through the mountains.

For adventure activities such as riding, rock climbing and paragliding, contact Nevadensis (see above) or **Rustic Blue** (Barrio la Ermita, Bubión, tel: 958 76 33 81, www.rusticblue.com).

For **water sports** enthusiasts there is diving in the Cabo de Gata area (► 101). For information, contact Puerto Deportivo de San José, San José, tel: 950 38 00 41).

Córdoba and Jaén

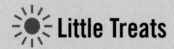 **Little Treats**

Cool, classic Gazpacho

The cold vegetable soup tastes out of this world in **El Churrasco in Córdoba** (➤ 135), where guests are served white Gazpacho with pine nuts.

Vía Verde del Aceite

Two tunnels, nine bridges, 55km (34mi). You need half a day on the bike on the disused railway line from Jaén to the lake **Laguna del Conde** (www.viasverdes.com).

For Early Birds

A mass takes place every morning in the **Mezquita of Córdoba** (➤ 115). It is worth getting up early for: the morning light conjures up a totally unique atmosphere!

Córdoba and Jaén

Getting Your Bearings

Art or nature? Ideally both, as can be seen here in the north of the country. No other place in Andalucía has as many Renaissance buildings as Úbeda and Baeza in the Jaén province. And there is nowhere else in the world with as many olive trees. The mountains in the northeast are wonderful havens for nature. Córdoba in the neighbouring province of the same name to the west was deemed the richest and largest town of the Middle Ages.

Today, the Mezquita – Europe's oldest mosque – and the remains of the ancient city of Medina provide evidence of the area's glamorous past. Yet Córdoba also has many other attractions: quiet squares, flowering *patios* and a hinterland full of baroque glory.

The province of Jaén, less accessible and less immediately rewarding than its neighbour, also contains treasures.

Sierra Morena

Baños de la Encina 34

Linares

35 **Montoro** · Andújar

Medina Azahara 31

2 **Córdoba**

· Porcuna

33 **Jaén**

· Castro del Rio

· Martos

· Montilla · Baena

32 **Zuheros**

0   30 km

0   15 mi

· Cabra

28 **Priego de Córdoba**

· Iznájar

In Bedmar, there is one row of white houses after another. Villages like these provide conspicuous milestones in the mountainscape of the Jaén province

110

Getting Your Bearings

TOP 10

⭐ Córdoba ➤ 114
⭐ Úbeda ➤ 122

Don't Miss

28 Priego de Córdoba ➤ 124
29 Baeza ➤ 126
30 Parque Natural de Cazorla y Segura ➤ 128

At Your Leisure

31 Medina Azahara ➤ 130
32 Zuheros ➤ 130
33 Jaén ➤ 131
34 Baños de la Encina ➤ 132
35 Montoro ➤ 132

Jaén city has a monumental cathedral and a bustling commercial and social life but is surpassed for overall charm by its smaller neighbours, Baeza and Úbeda. Both developed in the 16th century, Spain's golden age and became models for Renaissance art in Spain and Latin America. Like the Old Town of Córdoba, Úbeda and Baeza are both UNESCO heritage sites. For lovers of the outdoors, there are the magnificent mountains of the Sierra de Cazorla on Jaén's eastern border, ideal for the peace and quiet of woodland walks or for visits to isolated villages.

Úbeda
29 Baeza
Parque Natural de Cazorla y Segura 30
Cazorla
Jódar
Pozo Alcón
Guadahortuna

Córdoba's Alcázar, a haven of peace and quietness

Five Perfect Days

Explore Moorish Córdoba, then drive through wine country to the baroque treasures of Priego de Córdoba. Move on through the olive groves of Jaén province to Renaissance Baeza and Úbeda, taking in the mountain landscapes of the Sierra de Cazorla. For more information see the main entries (► 114–132).

Day One

Morning
Visit ⭐ Córdoba's Mezquita (right, ► 115), then stroll round the streets of the **Judería** (► 119), visiting the old **synagogue** (► 119) on the way. Lunch in the bar of Pepé de la Judería or of El Rincón de Carmen, both in Calle Romero.

Afternoon
Visit the palace and gardens of the **Alcázar de los Reyes Cristianos** (► 120), then enjoy a short siesta. Take an early *tapas* tour followed by a late evening meal before rounding off the day with a feast of classical flamenco at the Tablao Cardenal (► 138) opposite the Mezquita.

Day Two

Morning
Explore the quieter streets to the east of the Mezquita, or visit one of Córdoba's lesser-known attractions, such as the **Museo Arqueológico** (► 120) or the **Palacio Museo de Viana** (► 121).

Afternoon
Head southeast through the Montilla wine-producing country to ㉘ **Priego de Córdoba** (► 124), perhaps visiting the charming hill village of ㉜ **Zuheros** (left, ► 130) on the way. Stay overnight in Priego and enjoy the town's baroque churches and fountains and its charming old quarter, the Barrio de la Villa, in the mellow light of the early evening.

Day Three

Morning
Take the scenic road north from Priego, then follow the A316 east, calling in at **33 Jaén** (➤ 131), if you have time, to see the cathedral (left) and the Arab baths. Continue to **29 Baeza** (➤ 126).

Afternoon
After exploring Baeza's Renaissance buildings, such as the **Palacio de Jabalquinto** and the **cathedral**, take in the evening scene in the central Paseo de la Constitución. Stay overnight.

Day Four

Morning
Enjoy breakfast with the locals at the Bar Cafetería Mercantil on the corner of Plaza de España. Then drive some 50km (31mi) to **Cazorla** (➤ 128), on the western edge of the Sierra de Cazorla, for an overnight stay.

Afternoon
Make for the nearby mountains after lunch for a scenic drive, or a stroll amid the pinewoods of the **30 Parque Natural de Cazorla y Segura** (➤ 128).

Day Five

Morning
Head west to **5 Úbeda** (➤ 122) and visit the remarkable buildings that enclose the Plaza de Vázquez de Molina. Make time to visit the Museo de Alfarería (Pottery Museum) and, if possible, Calle de Valencia (➤ 137), where Úbeda's potters produce some of the finest ceramics in Spain.

Afternoon
After lunch, set off back to Córdoba. On the way, if there's time, visit the hilltop village of **34 Baños de la Encina** and its magnificent Moorish castle.

⭐2 Córdoba

Andalucía's most important town after Seville sits perched on the gentle slopes of Sierra de Córdoba by the Rio Guadalquivir. With its narrow, winding streets, small squares and whitewashed houses, often with the pretty patios so typical of the area, Córdoba can boast to having one of the largest historic centres of all the Spanish provincial towns and, on top of that, the fantastic Mezquita.

Even during the Old Iberian period, there was a settlement here in the bend of the Betis (Guadalquivir), which provided the Carthaginian Hannibal with mercenaries for his military campaign across the Alps. Under the Romans, the town then called Colonia Patricia was elected capital of the province Hispania Ulterior Baetica in 152 BC and eventually came under the Byzantine rule that ended the rampages of the Vandals. Occupied by the Moors in the 8th century, the city became the capital of Muslim Spain, and for 200 years a succession of gifted rulers turned it into a glittering rival to Baghdad and Damascus. In 1236, Córdoba fell to the Christians who, through neglect, made the city a byword for decay. It was only in the 20th century that the city revived becoming a centre for light industry, agriculture and tourism.

The Mezquita dominates Córdoba's skyline

✚ 199 E4

Tourist Information
✉ Campo Santo de los Mártires (opposite Alcázar), Plaza de las Tendillas, Calle Rey Heredia, by the train station ☎ 902 20 17 74; www. turismodecordoba.org

The Mezquita

Much of Islamic Córdoba survives and nowhere more triumphantly than in the Mezquita. The main body of the Mezquita dates from between the 8th and 12th centuries, but what makes it remarkable is the presence of a cathedral choir and high altar at the heart of the mosque, added in the 16th century after the Christian Reconquest.

The blank, massive exterior walls of the Mezquita are typical of Moorish style; external decoration was of little importance to Islam and public buildings were always constructed with potential defence in mind. Only the splendid carvings on the arched entrance gateways hint at the marvels within.

Go through the Puerto del Perdón, beside the Torre del Alminar, into the **Patio de los Naranjos** (Courtyard of the Orange Trees), where Muslim worshippers once carried out their ritual ablutions. A stall in the back wall of the courtyard sells entrance tickets to the mosque, which you enter through the modest doors of the Puerta de las Palmas (directly opposite the Puerta del Perdón). Once inside, thickets of pillars stretch away in all directions. Over 1,000 pillars – some plain, others multicoloured columns of marble, jasper and onyx – support semicircular and horseshoe arches composed of alternating stripes of red brick and white stone. The impression created is of great depth, intimacy and mysteriousness.

In Moorish times, light would have flooded in from the Patio de los Naranjos through open doorways at prayer time; these doors are now permanently closed.

The famous clustered arches of the Mezquita

Once the Main Mosque ...

... of western Islam – one of the world's largest mosques, and now a cathedral (Mezquita Cathedral) is the most important example of Moorish religious architecture in Spain. While the exterior is fairly plain, the interior impresses with a "forest" of over 850 columns of jaspis, onyx, marble and granite, which are arranged in double arcades and two-coloured horseshoe arches.

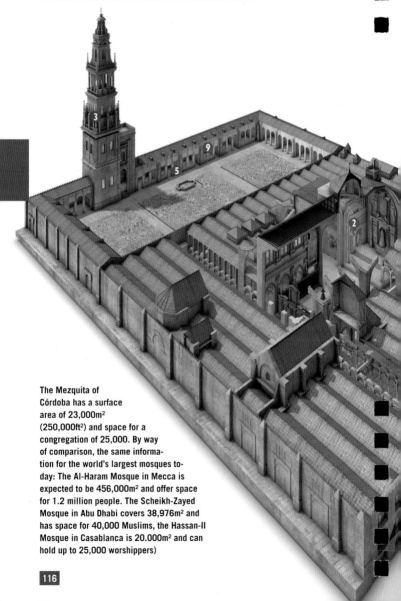

The Mezquita of Córdoba has a surface area of 23,000m² (250,000ft²) and space for a congregation of 25,000. By way of comparison, the same information for the world's largest mosques today: The Al-Haram Mosque in Mecca is expected to be 456,000m² and offer space for 1.2 million people. The Scheikh-Zayed Mosque in Abu Dhabi covers 38,976m² and has space for 40,000 Muslims, the Hassan-II Mosque in Casablanca is 20.000m² and can hold up to 25,000 worshippers)

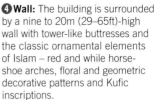

❶ Maksûra: Originally the area where the caliphs prayed

❷ Cathedral: Bishop Alonso Manrique decided to erect a large cathedral in the centre of the Islamic prayer room in 1523. The mixture of Gothic and Renaissance styles look completely out of place in this architectural setting.

❸ Campanario (belfry): After the completion of the cathedral around 1588, work started on transforming the minaret into a bell tower. The tower crowns a statue of the archangel Raphael, the town's patron saint.

❹ Wall: The building is surrounded by a nine to 20m (29–65ft)-high wall with tower-like buttresses and the classic ornamental elements of Islam – red and while horse-shoe arches, floral and geometric decorative patterns and Kufic inscriptions.

❺ Water basins: The large basins, not all of which have survived the course of time, were used for ritual washing before entering the court-yard to the public prayer hall.

❻ Muslim prayer room: More than 850 columns bear the arches with the alternating stripes of red and white arch bricks made of lime-stone and brick. In the Mezquita, there are no prescribed routes or directions; every position is its central point: For devout Muslims, Allah is near wherever he prays. At the time, daylight would have shone through the now walled entrances and thousands of burning oil lamps were used to illuminate the room as well.

❼ Mihrâb Nuevo (New Mihrâb): Unsurpassed: the prayer niche of the Imam. Interestingly, the inner sanctum of the mosque does not point in the traditional east-south-east direction of Mecca, but actually faces south. The dome is made of marble and decorated with floral and geometric patterns, Koran verses and mosaics that are the work of Byzantine artists.

❽ Capilla del Cardenal: This is where the church treasure is kept: The most valuable pieces include a silver monstrance (1510–1516) and a processional cross from Enrique de Arfe, nine statues of saints, an ivory crucifix by Alonso Cano as well as Arabic manuscripts (9th/10th century).

❾ Arcades: Under the arcades on the north side, student and teachers met to expostulate On the west of the bell tower, doctors provided advice, and on the east the qadi dispensed justice.

Córdoba and Jaén

The finest example of Islamic design is on the far side of the building. At the end of the widest aisle is the *maksura* (the area where the ruling caliphs prayed), with the *mihrab* (prayer niche, which normally indicates the direction of Mecca). Far more than a simple niche, the Mezquita's *mihrab* is a distinct chamber, its entrance framed by a beautiful horseshoe arch. Even from behind the barrier that keeps the public at a respectful distance you are aware of the brilliant light that reflects off the coloured mosaics cladding the walls and roof.

The central dome in front of the *mihrab* is supported by intersecting ribs that form a star shape, a design new for its time that was copied by later Christian architects in churches throughout Europe. It was this remarkable merging of structural forms with decorativeness that distinguished Muslim architecture and that is seen so superbly in the Mezquita.

At the centre of the Mezquita, implanted within the mosque in 1523 by the Christian rulers of Córdoba, is the open-sided **cathedral** *coro* (choir) and *capilla mayor* (high altar chapel). The intrusion of the cathedral into the Mezquita was condemned by the Emperor Carlos V; he had supported the idea initially, but was horrified when he saw what had been done and accused the Archbishop of Córdoba of having "destroyed what was unique in the world". Although they are undoubtedly ill-judged intrusions in terms of the Mezquita as a whole, choir and chapel have no enclosing walls and are masked in part by the Islamic columns that crowd round them. Looked at in isolation, their Gothic and Renaissance elements, the superbly carved choir stalls and slim, twisted pillars, are of great beauty. More fitting post-Muslim additions are the **Capilla Real** of 1258 and the 14th-century **Capilla de Villaviciosa,** the latter incorporating a *mihrab* of the early 9th century. Both chapels display the glazed panels and elegant arches typical of the *mudéjar* style (➤ 12).

Floral patterns as opposed to images of worship adorn the walls of the mihrâb in the Mezquita

✚ 202/203 D2
✉ Calle Torrijos 10 ☎ 957 47 05 12
🕐 March–Oct Mon–Sat 10–7, Sun and public hols 8:30–11:30, 3–7; Nov–Feb Mon–Sat 10–5, Sun and public hols 8–10 and 2–5 💶 €8

Mass is celebrated in the cathedral each morning (Mon–Sat 9:30, Sun 10 and 11), when entrance to the rest of the Mezquita is free. Entry to the cathedral is forbidden unless you stay for the duration of the service.

The Judería and Alcázar

To the north of the Mezquita is the Judería, the old Jewish quarter. Narrow cobbled streets, whitewashed houses, plant-filled courtyards, and quiet, secluded squares create a unique atmosphere, which is best enjoyed well away from the tourist area directly adjoining the Mezquita.

Close to the Mezquita, the streets of the Judería are awash with souvenir shops, but you can still find some enchanting corners such as the Callejón de las Flores, a narrow cul-desac bursting with flowers, and with walls that neatly frame the Mezquita's belfry. At the heart of the Judería, in Plaza Maimónides, you come to the **Museo Taurino** (Museum of Bullfighting, currently closed for renovation work), all bulls' heads and gloomy bravado.

In Córdoba's Judería there are beautiful patios between the souvenir shops and restaurants

To the left of the Museo Taurino is Calle Judíos, where there is an impressive statue of Moses Maimonides, the great 12th-century Jewish philosopher and theologian, who was born in Córdoba. Further up the street is the small, well-preserved 14th-century **synagogue**, sole Andalucían survivor of the Jewish expulsion in 1492. Nearby is a modern reconstruction of a **Zoco**, an Arab souk or market; craft

Alcázar de los Reyes Cristianos
✚ 202 C2 ✉ Plaza Campo Santo de los Mártires ☎ 957 42 01 51
🕐 Tue–Sat 8:30–3; Sun 8:30–2:30
🖐 €4.50 (combined ticket with Museo Julio Romero)

Capilla Mudéjar de San Bartolomé
✚ 203 C3 ✉ Averroes ☎ 957 21 88 31 🕐 Daily 10–2 🖐 €2

Sinagoga (Synagogue)
✚ 202 C2 ✉ Calle Judíos 20 ☎ 957 20 29 28
🕐 Daily 9–2:45 🖐 €1.50 (free with EU passport)

Córdoba and Jaén

shops and a bar overlook a charming patio. Calle Judíos
leads to the **Puerta de Almodóvar**, a 14th-century gateway
in Córdoba's ancient walls.

Beyond the Judería, on the banks of the river, stands
the **Alcázar de los Reyes Cristianos** (Palace of the Christian
Kings). It was built in the late 13th century by the Christian
conquerors of Al-Andalus as a replacement for a Moorish
Alcázar that stood alongside the Mezquita. For many
years it was the headquarters of the Inquisition and
became a prison in the 19th century, though today its
glorious gardens, filled with colourful flowers and shrubs
and shimmering pools and fountains, barely hint at its
grim past. The surviving buildings are somewhat stark,
but contain superb Roman mosaics recovered from various
parts of the city.

Other Sights

North of the Mezquita, in an area of narrow streets far
less visited than the Judería (➤ 119), is Córdoba's
Museo Arqueológico
(Archaeological
Museum) in a
Renaissance man-
sion, the Palacio
de los Páez, on
tree-shaded Plaza
Jerónimo Páez. The
palace has coffered
ceilings and elegant
staircases, and
displays prehistoric,
Roman and Moorish
exhibits. Highlights
include Roman
mosaics and an
exquisite miniature
of a bronze stag,
found at the ruined
10th-century palace-
city of Medina
Azahara 6km (4mi)
west of Córdoba
(➤ 130).

Just inland from
the river is **Plaza del
Potro** (Square of the Colt), with a statue of a rearing
horse on the central fountain. The plaza was once a
livestock market surrounded by medieval brothels and
drinking dens, the haunt of such Cordoban characters
as the celebrated poet Luis de Góngora (1561–1627).
On the plaza's western side is the old Posada del Potro
Inn, mentioned in Cervantes's *Don Quijote*, and now a
Casa del Flamenco. Opposite is the Hospital de la Caridad,
housing the **Museo de Bellas Artes** (Museum of Fine Arts).

**If you leave
the labyrinth
of little streets
in Córdoba's
Jewish quarter,
you will
immediately
find the next
attraction
awaiting you,
such as the
Alcázar seen
here**

The decorated ceilings of the ground-floor rooms are as fine as some of the paintings; the collection includes work by Zurbarán, Goya and Murillo. On the other side of the central patio is a museum dedicated to Córdoban artist **Julio Romero de Torres**, most of whose paintings feature sultry nudes.

The heart of the modern city is **Plaza de las Tendillas**, where fountains spout sparkling jets of water from ground level – irresistible to local youngsters in hot weather. As you relax at a café table, you may hear the plaza's clock chiming flamenco phrases. From Plaza de las Tendillas, you can walk west down the shopping street of Conde de Gondomar to the pedestrianised Avenida del Gran Capitán, scene of Córdoba's evening *paseo*.

TAKING A BREAK

Begin your evening with a sherry in the popular bar or cool leafy patio of **El Caballo Rojo** (Calle Cardenal Herrero 28), reputed to be the oldest restaurant in Córdoba.

INSIDER INFO

- Alcázar and Museo Taurino: **free entry** Wed–Fri 8:30–10:30 (except for public holidays).
- **Opening times** of Córdoba's sights and museums change frequently. Check the information on the internet before your trip: **www.turismodecordoba.org** (left bar: Horarios monumentos y museos).
- Córdoba stages a **Fiesta de los Patios** (Festival of the Patios) during the first week of May each year, when flower-filled patios normally hidden within private houses are open for visits, often to the accompaniment of music, including flamenco.
- The 14th-century **Palacio Museo de Viana** (Plaza de Don Gome 2, tel: 957 49 67 41, admission €8) has 12 patios, each with it's a fountain and with roses, jasmine, wisteria and bougainvillaea woven together with geraniums. Be warned, though, the Spanish-language guided tours of the palace's rooms are rather overcrowded.
- The bar **Casa Pepe "De la Judería"** (€€) conjures up high-class *tapas*, and this level is matched in the high-quality regional dishes served in the restaurant. An added bonus: the beautiful view from the roof terrace.
- Although the **Torre de Calahorra** on the opposite side of the Puente Romano looks very impressive, you don't really need to bother visiting the museum inside. It presents an overly romanticised picture of the coexistence of Christians, Muslims and Jews in the Córdoba during the Middle Ages.

Insider Tip

Museo Arqueológico
✚ 202 D3
✉ Plaza Jerónimo Páez ☎ 957 35 55 17
◷ Tue–Sat 9–3:30 (winter 10–8:30), Sun 10–5
€ €1.50 (free with EU passport)

Museo de Bellas Artes
✚ 203 E3
✉ Plaza del Potro 1 ☎ 957 10 36 59

◷ Tue–Sat 9–3:30 (winter 10–8:30), Sun 10–5
€ €1.50 (free with EU passport)

Museo Julio Romero de Torres
✚ 203 E3
✉ Plaza del Potro 1
☎ 957 47 03 56
◷ Tue–Sat 8:30–3, Sun 8:30–2:30
€ €4.50 (combined ticket with Alcázar)

★5 Úbeda

In medieval times Úbeda became synonymous with absentminded-ness and the phrase "wandering across the hills of Úbeda" is still used to describe those who are forgetful. Its origins lie in a romantic tale. A young Christian knight missed a crucial battle because he was with his lover, a beautiful Muslim girl. When asked by King Fernando III where he had been, he replied, "Sire. On those hills...".

Úbeda hides an architectural treasure at its heart. Plaza de Vázquez de Molina is an enclave of exquisite Renaissance buildings, claimed to be the finest such complex in Spain. The plaza was created by medieval Úbeda's leading families, the Cobos and the Molinas, who acquired great wealth from a 16th-century boom in textile production. Both families employed the best architects and artists to immortalise their names in stone, among them Andrés de Vandelvira and Alfonso Ruiz, who in the first half of the 16th century designed a masterpiece of Renaissance architecture, the single nave **Sacra Capilla del Salvador** (Chapel of the Holy Saviour) based on the plans of architect Diego de Siloé. The benefactor was the secretary of King Carlos I, Francisco de los Cobos, who is interred in the crypt. The chapel's main façade is decorated with relief work and flanked by two small round towers. In the arch above the entrance,

The most important event in the church year is the Semana Santa, the week before Easter. As here in Úbeda, it is often started with large processions

you can see allegorical presentations of belief and justice as well as the coat of arms of the Los Cobos and the Molinas. Enthroned above them is Christ the Saviour with Saint Peter and Saint Paul standing either side of him. In the chancel, behind an exquisite choir screen, the altarpiece bears a representation of the Christ figure. It is all that remains of the "Transfiguration of Christ" work by Alonso de Berruguete which was damaged by fire during the civil war in 1936. Vandelvira is behind the magnificently designed sacristy which contains some of the church silver. Other notable buildings in the plaza include the **Palacio de las**

Cadenas (Palace of the Chains) designed with an elegant classical façade for Juan Vázquez de Molina by Vandelvira, and now Úbeda's town hall. The **Museo de Alfarería** (Pottery Museum) in the cellars of the palace displays many examples of the green-glaze pottery for which Úbeda is noted. Directly opposite is the church of **Santa María de las Reales Alcázares**, whose Gothic cloister stands on the foundations of the mosque of Islamic Úbeda.

Just north of the plaza is the old market square, **Plaza del Primero de Mayo**, scene of bullfights and horrifying *autos da fé* (trials by fire) during the Inquisition. It contains the Old Town hall with elegant arcades, and the church of **San Pablo** with a fine Gothic portal and balcony. Narrow lanes lead

The apse of the Sacra Capilla del Salvador is magnificently decorated

off north through a splendid 13th-century gateway, the Puerta de Losal. Beyond here is Calle de Valencia and the workshops of potters still making Úbeda's distinctive ceramics (➤ 137).

TAKING A BREAK

Take a step back in time and stop off for coffee at Úbeda's 16th-century *parador* on Plaza de Vázquez de Molina (➤ 136).

✚ 200 C4

Tourist Information
✉ Palacio del Contadero, Calle Baja del Marqués
☎ 953 77 92 05; http://turismodeubeda.com

Sacra Capilla del Salvador
✉ Plaza de Vázquez de Molina 🕐 Mon–Sat 9:30–10, Sun 6–7 🎟 €5

Museo San Juan de la Cruz
✉ Carmen 13 ☎ 953 75 06 15 🕐 Tue–Sun 11–1, 5–7 🎟 €3.50

INSIDER INFO

- You will have to find your way through Úbeda's everyday streets to reach **Plaza de Vázquez de Molina**. Look for signs that read *Zona Monumental*. **Calle Real**, the long narrow street between the main square, Plaza de Andalucía, and Plaza de Vázquez de Molina, has craft shops selling the **esparto grass artefacts** traditional to Úbeda.
- Walk down the right-hand side of the Capilla del Salvador to reach **Plaza de Santa Lucía** and a viewpoint that looks out over olive groves to the hazy mountain wall of the Sierra de Cazorla.

㉘ Priego de Córdoba

The quiet provincial town – a centre of the textile trade and olive oil production – is located in a breathtaking mountain landscape near the Sierra Subbética nature reserve. During the 17th and 18th century, silk manufacture brought affluence to the region, enabling the erection of lavishly decorated baroque churches and beautiful fountains. In the Moorish quarter, the Barrio de la Villa, alleyways wind between whitewashed houses decked with flowers.

The town dates from at least Roman times and was fought over by Moorish and Christian forces during the 13th and 14th centuries. At the centre of Priego is the busy **Plaza de Andalucía** and adjoining **Plaza de la Constitución**, where the life of the town is gossiped over each morning. Historic Priego lies to the east of Plaza de Andalucía. Here, among other fine buildings, is the **Iglesia de la Asunción** (Church of the Ascension), Priego's most famous monument. A highlight of the church, which is plain white on the outside, is the Sagrario (Chapel of the Sanctuary), which you enter through the side aisle. Francisco Javier Pedrejas, 1772–1784, used effusive stucco ornamentation to decorate this octagonal-shaped chapel with Biblical scenes. Apostle figures adorn the pillars, and in the centre are representations of church leaders.

From Plaza de Santa Anna, alongside the church, the Calle Real leads into the **Barrio de la Villa**, where the white walls of the houses are hung with baskets of geraniums and draped with bougainvillaea. The quarter is free of cars, but unfortunately not of scooters and motorcycles. At the barrio's eastern edge is the **Paseo de Adarve**, a promenade giving great views of the surrounding countryside. Northwest of the barrio is the **Iglesia de San Pedro** (Church of St Peter), with a splendidly painted main altar.

The Calle del Río runs past the Iglesia del Carmen to a magnificent fountain. The older part, the **Fuente de la Salud** (Fountain of Health) in the top part of the complex was created by Francisco del Castillo in the 16th century and consists of a mannerist-style façade with a stone lattice-work in the centre of which is a small niche with the Virgen de la Salud. The new fountain in the lower section, the white **Fuente del Rey** (King's Fountain), first built in the 19th century, displays a monumental style with playful details that are reminiscent of a baroque garden. Water pours from the marble mouths of 139 gargoyles into the fountain's main basin and in the middle the chariot of Neptune and his wife Amphitrite surges through the waves.

TAKING A BREAK

After you've ogled the lavish confection of white stucco in the Iglesia de la Asunción, enjoy a glass of wine at **El Aljibe** (► 136) across the square.

✚ 200 B3

Tourist Information
✉ Plaza de la Constitución 3
☎ 957 70 06 25; www.turismodepriego.com

Parking: Car park in Plaza Palenque, at the west end of Carrera de las Monjas. Busy in the mornings.

The Fuente del Rey is reminiscent of a baroque garden

Iglesia de la Asunción
✉ Plaza de Abad Palomino
⏱ Tue–Sat 9:30–1:30, Sun 10:30–1:30

INSIDER INFO

- The tourist office can organise **tours of Priego's finest sights** – a good idea if your time is short. You should make a prior arrangement for such a tour.
- Priego's **churches** are usually open 11–1, and are often open for services in the mornings.
- The **Carnicerías Reales** (near San Pedro Church) is a 16th-century slaughterhouse and market, now shorn of its original associations and preserved for its architectural value. The arcaded and cobbled patio of the old market, with its spiral stone staircase, exudes a special flair. The mullioned windows provide a wonderful view of the olive groves, and the setting is perfect for the occasional exhibitions staged here by local artists.

㉙ Baeza

Surrounded by olive groves, wheatfields and vineyards, and perched high above the Río Guadalquivir valley, Baeza is an architectural pearl of the Renaissance with little modern encroachment on its historic buildings.

The best place to begin your exploration is in the **Plaza del Pópulo**. This exquisite Renaissance square, known also as Plaza de los Leones because of the ancient stone lions adorning its weatherworn fountain, is enclosed by the handsome façade of an old slaughterhouse and the twin archways of the Moorish Puerta de Jaén and the 16th-century Arco de Villalar. At the top end of the square is the elegant Casa de Pópulo, once a courthouse and now Baeza's tourist office.

Baeza stands on a lofty escarpment overlooking the great central plain of Jaén province

To the left of the tourist office, a flight of steps, the Escalerillas de la Audiencia, leads to a narrow lane, Calle Romanones, that takes you to Plaza Santa Cruz and the **Palacio de Jabalquinto**, whose Gothic façade is studded with diamond-shaped bosses. The interior courtyard of the palace is being restored. It has a fountain and is surrounded by a double tier of arcades from which a fine baroque staircase leads to the upper floor. Directly opposite the palace is the little Romanesque **Iglesia de Santa Cruz** with traces of Visigothic arches and of the mosque the church replaced.

Just up from Plaza Santa Cruz is quiet Plaza de Santa María with its central fountain in the form of a triumphal arch. The square is dominated by Baeza's **Catedral de Santa María**, which has a spacious Renaissance nave designed by Andrés de Vandelvira, the architect

INSIDER INFO

- Make sure you have change when you **visit the cathedral**. At the west end of the church is an uninteresting painting of St Peter, but pop a coin in a slot and the painting rumbles aside to reveal, to musical accompaniment, the **silver monstrance** used in Baeza's holy processions.

- **Don't be alarmed** by the number of uniformed **Civil Guards** strolling around Baeza in the evening. Most of them are students from the nearby Academia de Guardias de la Guardia Civil.

- From Plaza de Pópulo, with its famous fountain, go through the imposing Puerta de Jaén arch and follow the road beyond for 250m (275yds) to reach the **Paseo de las Murallas**. This road and walkway leads along the edge of the escarpment towards the Catedral de Santa Maria, with **fine views** across the surrounding countryside.

of many of Úbeda's buildings (➤ 122). The main altar has an exuberant altarpiece and there are a number of splendid *rejas* – wrought-iron grilles that screen side chapels. The cathedral was built on the site of a mosque and some remains of the earlier building have been uncovered in the Gothic cloister.

On low ground below Baeza's historical quarter is the town centre, busy Plaza de España and tree-lined Paseo de la Constitución, where youngsters play football and cycle madly around the central concourse. The Paseo is lined by arcaded buildings and numerous bars and cafés. Stroll west from here for a look at the ornate 16th-century façade of the town hall in Calle Benavides.

TAKING A BREAK

Join the locals at the friendly **La Méson Góndola** (➤ 136), one of Baeza's most atmospheric bars, and indulge in their delicious *patatas baezanas* (fried potatoes with mushrooms).

🕂 200 C4

Tourist Information
✉ Plaza del Pópulo (Plaza de los Leones)
☎ 953 77 99 82; turismo.baeza.net

Parking: There is convenient parking round the Paseo de la Constitución.

In Baeza's historic centre, visit the Plaza de Santa Maria and admire the well-preserved fountain by Ginés Martínez in front of the cathedral

Palacio de Jabalquinto
✉ Plaza Santa Cruz 🕘 Mon–Fri 9–2 💲 Free

Iglesia de Santa Cruz
✉ Plaza Santa Cruz 🕘 Mon–Sun 11–1 💲 Free

Catedral de Santa María
✉ Plaza de Santa María 🕘 Mon–Fri 10:30–2, 4–7, Sat 10:30–7, Sun 10:30–6 💲 Guided tours: €4

㉚ Parque Natural de Cazorla y Segura

In the far northeast of Andalucía the Sierra de Cazorla and the Sierra de Segura rise up out of the wheatfields and olive groves on the hill slopes of Jaén province. They are separated by the headwater of the Guadalquivir river. It is here that the watershed runs between the Mediterranean, into which the Río Segura flows, and the Atlantic, which is the destination of the Guadalquivir.

In the Parque Natural de Cazorla y Segura, rugged mountains rise to over 2,000m (6,562ft), with deep rocky gorges and thickly forested valleys, and tiny hilltop villages scattered throughout. The gateway to the park and the main settlement is the attractive town of Cazorla. **Cazorla** stands at the western edge of the Sierra de Cazorla directly below the great cliff faces of the mountain of Peña de los Halcones (Crag of the Falcons). The town straggles along the base of the mountain beginning at its busy main square, Plaza Constitución, from where the main street, Calle Dr Muñoz, leads to the far older Plaza de la Corredera, a lively square lined by cafés and shops. Beyond here, winding lanes take you past a lookout point, **Balcón del Pintor Zabaletato**, with glorious views of the ruined church of Santa María and the partially ruined castle, **La Yedra** that rises above. Below the church and castle is the heart of local life, Plaza Santa María.

Waterfalls are one of the natural beauties of Sierra de Cazorla

The Natural Park

The Sierras de Cazorla y Segura, together with lesser ranges, make up the largest natural park in Andalucía. The mountains of the park support forests of evergreen oaks and pines as well as native species such as elder, maple and juniper. There are over 1,200 species of plants, and the animals of the Sierras include red deer, fox, wild cat, Spanish ibex and wild boar. You may also see some of the birds of prey that congregate in the Sierras, including griffon vultures, golden eagles and peregrine falcons (sometimes visible from roadside vantage points). A network of good roads makes driving within the park area a pleasure. There is good walking in the area around Cazorla, but deeper into the mountains there are only a few waymarked paths. Local companies organise day walks, horse riding, mountain biking and four-wheel-drive trips into more remote areas (► 138). You can book such activities at agencies in Cazorla town.

Insider Tip

INSIDER INFO

- For exploring the Parque Natural de Cazorla the **best maps** are Editorial Alpina's 1:40,000 series, Sierra de Cazorla and Sierra de Segura editions (www.editorial alpina.com). Walking and biking trails are marked and described in these booklets.
- If you set off along an **unwaymarked path** or track in the heart of the Sierras, make a note of any junctions so that you can retrace your steps.
- Cazorla has a daily **market** in Plaza del Mercado, between the car park and the main shopping street, with local produce and crafts.
- The restored tower of the castle of La Yedra in Cazorla houses a **folklore museum** displaying farming artefacts, olive-oil presses and reconstructions of traditional rural life (Camino del Castillo, Cazorla, Tue–Sat 9–3:30 (winter 10–8:30), Sun 10–5; €1.50, free with EU passport).

You enter the park about 2km (1.25mi) east of Cazorla, just beyond the village of **Iruela** with its tiny castle perched on a pinnacle of rock. A 34km (21mi) drive northeast through the mountains will take you from Cazorla to the Centro de Interpretación Torre del Vinagre. The interpretation centre can be very busy in summer but it has excellent displays outlining the park's ecology. Nearby is a botanical garden with specimens of Sierra plant life.

The battlements of the La Yedra Fortress tower above Cazorla

➕ 201 D4 ℹ️ Cazorla Tourist Information: ✉️ Paseo del Santo Cristo 17 ☎ 953 96 91 91; www.turismoencazorla.com

Parking: There is a car park in Plaza del Mercado, just down from the Plaza de la Constitución.

At Your Leisure

The ruins of Medina Azahara still give a good impression of its former glory

31 Medina Azahara

The ruins of the 10th-century palace-city of Medina Azahara lie about 7km (4.25mi) west from Córdoba. The complex was begun in 936 and in its heyday reflected some of the most sumptuous architecture and design of Moorish al-Andalus. The main attraction is the superb Hall of Abd al-Rahman III, where the lavish marble carvings have been carefully restored. Medina Azahara is best reached by car. The visit begins in the new research centre. Every half an hour a bus shuttles visitors from the car park to a drop-off point just above the excavation site. There is a bus service from Córdoba leaving twice a day (Tue–Sun). Departure point: Paseo de la Victoria (Glorieta Hospital Cruz Roja) and Paseo de la Victoria (opposite the Mausoleo Romano). On some Saturdays, the bus travels out to the site three times. Tickets are available at the tourist information centre In Córdoba.

⊞ 199 E4 ⊠ 7km (4.5mi) west of Córdoba
⏰ Sun 10–5; Mid-Sep–March Tue–Sat 9–6:30, April–May Tue–Sat 9–8, June–mid-Sep Tue–Sat 9–3:30 ⚙ Free with EU passport

32 Zuheros

The narrow streets of Zuheros are a delight to explore; their charm reflects the village's situation on a rocky hillside amid the Sierra Subbética hills near Priego de Córdoba. Built into the rocks above the houses are the remains of a Moorish castle. In Plaza de la Paz are the handsome 18th-century **Iglesia de la Virgen de los Remedios** and the village **museum** displaying artefacts from the prehistoric, Roman and Moorish periods. Zuheros is noted for its cheeses and olive oil, which you can buy from the tourist centre at the entrance to the village. The **Cueva del Cerro de los Murciélagos** (Cave of the Bats), with fascinating rock formations, lies about 4km (east of Zuheros. Archaeological finds here during the mid-19th century included mummified bodies and wall paintings that indicate habitation by neolithic people.

✚ 199 F4
ℹ Tourist Information
✉ Plaza de la Paz 1 (Zuheros Museum) ☎ 957 69 45 45; www.turismodezuheros.es

Zuheros Museum
✉ Plaza de la Paz 1 ☎ 957 69 45 45
🕐 Daily 10–2 and 4–7

Cueva del Cerro de los Murciélagos
✚ 199 F4 ☎ 957 69 45 45 🕐 Guided tours mid-April to mid-Sep Mon–Fri 12:30 and 5:30, Sat, Sun and public hols 11, 12:30, 2, 5, 6:30 (phoning ahead advised) 🖐 €4.60

🗒 Jaén

The town of Jaén is worth visiting for its majestic cathedral, fine museums, restored Arab baths and its old quarter. The **cathedral**, on Plaza de Santa María, was erected over a period of 250 years from the mid-16th century. The huge west façade is a dramatic display of elegant Corinthian columns and statuary, the whole framed by soaring twin towers. The cavernous interior has clusters of Corinthian columns on a monumental scale, and the choir has exquisite carvings. The cathedral contains the Santo Rostro

The magnificent façade of Jaén cathedral towers above the roofs of the city

(Holy Face) claimed to be the cloth used by St Veronica to wipe Christ's brow on the way to his crucifixion. It is on public display every Friday.

Jaén's restored Arab baths, the **Baños Árabes**, lie beneath the 16th-century Palacio de Villadompardo (housing an arts and customs museum and a museum of native art). The splendid brickwork ceilings are pierced by star-shaped lights and supported by typically Moorish columns and horseshoe arches. A glass floor reveals Roman remains. The **Museo de Jaén** has Phoenician, Roman and Moorish artefacts and, in a building adjoining the main museum, a display of outstanding 5th-century BC stone sculptures. Moorish character survives in Jaén's labyrinthine quarters of **La Magdalena** and **San Juan** on the northeastern slopes of the scrub-covered hill of Santa Catalina, itself crowned by a ruined Moorish castle.

✚ 200 B3
ℹ Tourist Information:
✉ Calle de la Maestra ☎ 953 31 32 81

Catedral
✉ Plaza de Santa María 🕐 Mon–Fri 10–2, 5–8, Sat 10–2, 5–7, Sun 10–noon 🖐 €5

Baños Árabes
✉ Plaza de Santa Luisa de Marillac
☎ 953 24 80 68 🕐 Sat 9–2:30, 4–9:30, Sun 9–2:30 🖐 Free with EU passport

Museo de Jaén
✉ Paseo de la Estación 29 ☎ 953 10 13 66
🕐 Tue–Sat 9–3:30 (winter 10–8:30), Sun 10–5
🖐 Free with EU passport

Córdoba and Jaén

🔢 Montoro

The town stands on a spur of land within a loop of the Río Guadalquivir that is spanned by a handsome 15th-century bridge. The ochre and whitewashed houses blend in well with the reddish colour of the hill on which Montoro is situated. Towering over the houses descending in terraces down to the river is the baroque tower of the Iglesia de San Bartolomé. The long main street, Calle Corredera, leads to the central square, Plaza de España, and the three-tiered tower of the Iglesia de San Bartolomé. Opposite the church is the old ducal palace, now the town hall. North of the plaza, narrow alleyways lead into an older district, where you'll find the church of Santa María de la Mota, now a small museum of mineralogy and archaeology.

✚ 200 A4 🛈 Tourist Information:
✉ Corredera 19 ☎ 957 16 00 89

Santa María de la Mota
✉ Plaza de Santa María 🕐 Sat 6–8, Sun 11–1

🔢 Baños de la Encina

Baños de la Encina has one of the finest hilltop castles in Spain. The 14 towers and massive keep of this Moorish fortress dominate the tiny village below. The castle was built between 967 and 986 by the Córdoban Emirate as an outlying defence against belligerent clans in the nearby Sierra Morena and Sierra de Cazorla (► 128). To visit the castle, ask for the key at the tourist information office, or at the town hall in Plaza de la Constitución. The interior of the castle is now a gaunt empty space, but you can climb the great keep, the Tower of Homage, from which there are sweeping views. Climb with care: the stairways are unlit and roosting pigeons tend to fly suddenly from the gloom. The castle's narrow, unprotected parapet encircles the inner walls, but is best avoided.

✚ 200 B4
🛈 Tourist Information:
✉ Callejón del Castillo 1
✉ 953 61 32 29; www.bdelaencina.com

Skyline view of the village of Baños de la Encina

OFF THE BEATEN TRACK

Just 20km (12.5mi) south of Priego de Córdoba is a large lake, the **Embalse de Iznájar**, where you can go sailing. In the far northeast of Jaén province is **Segura de la Sierra**. Approached by a seemingly endless series of hairpin bends, this wonderful hilltop village has an old Moorish castle, restored Arab baths, a Renaissance church and a fountain with its own shoal of fish.

Where to…
Stay

Prices
Expect to pay per double room per night
€ up to €60   €€ €60–€90   €€€ €90–€140   €€€€ over €140

CÓRDOBA

Hotel Exe Conquistador €€€
The hotel is directly opposite the Mezquita, which is visible from the restaurant and some of the rooms. The air-conditioned rooms are relatively big. The restaurant serves international food as well as regional Andalucían dishes. On warm days, breakfast, lunch and dinner are in the pretty courtyard otherwise reserved for aperitifs.
➕ 203 E3
✉ Magistral González Francés 3–5
☎ 957 48 11 02; www.execonquistador.com

Hotel y Hostal Maestre €/€€
Aside from price, there is not much difference between the hotel and *hostal*, tucked down a quiet side street one block back from the river. The hotel rooms look onto a gracious inner courtyard framed by arches, which means plenty of light; the Castilian-style furniture, gleaming marble and quality oil paintings add a touch of class. Rooms in the *hostal* are smaller, but the entrance patio is pure Córdoba with pots, plants, plates – even a canary in a cage.
➕ 203 E3
✉ Calle Romero Barros 4 & 6
☎ 957 47 24 10; www.hotelmaestre.com

Lola €€/€€€
At this former 19th-century palace, the owner, Lola, has decorated the rooms with decorative flair and superb attention to detail.

The hotel is furnished with antiques, woven rugs, original beams and art deco pieces. The marble bathrooms are large and modern and there's a roof terrace with Mezquita tower views. The hotel is in an ideal location for sightseeing and it is within walking distance of shops and restaurants.
➕ 202 C2
✉ Romero 3
☎ 957 20 03 05; www.hotellola.es

Hotel Mezquita €€
This was the 16th-century palace of the renowned Córdoban painter Julio Romero de Torres, and the hotel has retained an evocative historical ambience with paintings and antiques. There are original columns and stonework, plus a gracious central patio used for dining during the summer. The rooms have modern facilities and are furnished in a suitably regal fashion with satin drapes and ornate furniture. The location is ideal for sightseeing – right opposite the main entrance to the Mezquita.
➕ 203 D3 ✉ Plaza Santa Catalina 1
☎ 957 47 55 85; www.hotelmezquita.com

Los Omeyas €€/€€€€   **Insider Tip**
Located amid the tangle of back streets in Córdoba's former Jewish quarter, Los Omeyas has been refurbished to reflect the city's Andaluz heritage with Mezquita-style arches, white marble and latticework. A central patio provides access to comfortable, tastefully

decorated rooms with air con
ditioning. Try for one on the top
floor for a view of the ancient tower
of the great Mezquita, although
tour groups tend to fill the place.
Breakfast is a reasonable extra.

✚ 203 D3 ✉ Calle Encarnación 17
☎ 957 49 22 67; www.hotel-losomeyas.com

PRIEGO DE CÓRDOBA

Hostal Rafi €

One of very few small *hostals* in
town, the Rafi is right in the centre,
with shops and the best-known
baroque churches all nearby.
Rooms are fairly ordinary but the
baths are full-size and modern.
A door from the lobby leads to
the adjacent bar, which is usually
packed with locals who've come
to enjoy the good choice of *tapas*
and light meals.

✚ 203 B3 ✉ Isabel La Católica 4
☎ 957 54 04 49; www.hostalrafi.net

JAÉN

Insider Tip

Parador Castillo de Santa Catalina €€€€

This is one of the most spectacular
paradores in Spain, situated on the
dramatic Cerro de Santa Catalina
mountain amid the towers of a
medieval Moorish castle. The
rooms have luxurious canopied
beds and balconies for marvelling
at the view. The décor throughout is magnificent: a successful
interplay of high-vaulted ceilings,
baronial spaces and Islamic decorative touches. The restaurant,
serving typical Jaén dishes, is also
recommended.

✚ 200 B3
✉ El Castillo de Santa Catalina, Jaén
☎ 953 23 00 00; www.parador.es

BAEZA

Hotel Fuentenueva €€

The stone walls are all that remain
of the original house (1812); the
interior displays a lavish overhaul
with salmon-coloured, marble floors,
modern furnishings and bubbling
fountains. From the Japanese roof
garden with a pool, you can enjoy
the wonderful view of Baeza's city
centre.

✚ 200 C4 ✉ Calle Carmen 15
☎ 953 74 31 00; www.fuentenueva.com

Hostal El Patio €

Housed in the 16th-century
palace of the Marqués Cuentacilla,
on a cobbled side street leading
to an old church, this *hostal* has
homey appeal. The name is ap-
propriate: the central space is vast
and filled with overstuffed, heavily
brocaded furniture, interspersed
with original columns. The rooms
are basically furnished but comfortable enough, and the location
is wonderfully quiet and convenient
to the centre of town. No credit
cards.

✚ 200 C4 ✉ Calle Conde Romanones 13
☎ 953 74 02 00

ÚBEDA

María de Molina €€€

The hotel is located on the historical
central plaza in a 16th-century
palace. Many of the original
elements remain, such as the
columned central patio, wall-hung
tapestries and a magnificent stone
fountain. Wicker furniture, ochre
walls and plenty of palms and
plants set the mood in the lobby
and restaurant, while the rooms,
solidly decorated with dark wood,
have walk-in wardrobes and
balconies overlooking Úbeda's
grandest square.

✚ 200 C4 ✉ Plaza del Ayuntamiento s/n
☎ 953 79 53 56; www.hotelmaria demolina.es

Nueve Leyendas €/€€

Convivial hotel in the historic centre
with library, lounge and tastefully
furnished rooms (room 203 is
particularly lovely)

✚ 200 C4 ✉ Plaza López de Almagro 3
☎ 953 79 22 97; www.hotelnueveleyendas.com

Where to...
Eat and Drink

Prices
Expect to pay per person for a meal, including wine and service
€ up to €15   €€ €15–€40   €€€ over €40

CÓRDOBA

El Burlaero €€

This restaurant is well known among Spaniards, who come to enjoy game dishes of wild boar, pigeon, partridge, rabbit and Iberian pig. The bar is a cosy clutter with a backdrop of guitars, matador capes, hams, barrels and photos. The restaurant is spread over several rooms with low, beamed ceilings and typical Córdoban patio. Be bold and start your meal with the delicious local speciality *el salmonerejo*, a thick cold soup of tomato, garlic and egg.

✚ 202 C3 ✉ Calleja de la Hoguera 5
☎ 957 47 27 19; www.restauranteburlaero.com
⏰ Daily 11–4:30, 7:30–11

El Churrasco €€

Situated in the heart of the Judería, this excellent restaurant specialises in meaty dishes including its namesake *churrasco* (grilled meat in a spicy sauce), as well as fish. If you feel like *tapas*, head for the adjacent bar and order a *media ración* of *berenjenas crujientes con salmorejo* (crispy fried eggplant slices with thick gazpacho) There's a charming interior patio and several dining rooms with beams, exposed brick and evocative art work.

✚ 202 C3 ✉ Calle Romero 16
☎ 957 29 08 19; www.elchurrasco.com
⏰ Closed Aug

Almudaina €€€

One of the best addresses in Córdoba, situated in an historic building with seven rooms and an exquisite patio facing the Alcázar. Meals are served in the glass-covered courtyard. Dishes include excellent regional dishes and the service is very courteous. The prices won't make you smile with pleasure, but everything else will.

✚ 202 C2 ✉ Campo Santos de los Mártires 1
☎ 957 47 43 42; www.restaurante almudaina. com ⏰ Closed Sun dinner

El Rincón de Carmen €€/€€€

A romantic-dinner-for-two kind of place, this 18th-century house in the heart of the Jewish quarter has a patio filled with fragrant jasmine. The menu is extensive, with an emphasis on rice dishes, including black rice (coloured by squid ink) and several Valencian paella favourites. In the adjacent café you can enjoy drinks and snacks relaxing in the comfort of cushioned cane chairs.

✚ 202 C3 ✉ Calle Romero 4 ☎ 957 29 10 55
⏰ Daily noon–4, 8–11:30

Taberna Plateros €/€€

This place dates from the 17th century. A large patio restaurant leads to more rooms and the traditional marbled bar where blue collar workers and businessmen meet. Photographs of late local bullfighter Manolete line the walls, and the patio is decorated with giddily patterned tiles and bricks. There is a great selection of *tapas* and the starters a meal in themselves.

✚ 203 D3 ✉ San Franciso 6
☎ 957 47 00 42; www.tabernaplateros.com
⏰ Tue–Sat 8–4, 7:30–midnight

Córdoba and Jaén

PRIEGO DE CÓRDOBA

El Aljibe €/€€

This is right on the corner of the main plaza. Dark wood, brick and terracotta tile make for cosy informality and the *tapas* choice is good, with some unusual local specialities like dates stuffed with bacon. If you're hungry, head for the restaurant downstairs where a three-course *menú del día* will cost you less than a round of drinks back home.

✚ 202 B3 ⌧ Calle Abad Palomino 7
☎ 957 70 18 56; www.restaurante-elaljibe.com
🕐 Daily 12:30–midnight. Closed Easter week and mid-Sep for the local *feria*

BAEZA

Casa Juanito €€

The owners love to introduce ancient local recipes into their menu, so the dishes are tasty and unusual. Extra virgin olive oil is a standard ingredient, made from their own press. Other specialities include partridge salad, fillet of beef with tomatoes and peppers, and *alcachofas Luisa* (artichoke hearts with tomatoes and garlic).

✚ 200 C4 ⌧ Puche Pardo 57
☎ 953 74 00 40; www.juanitobaeza.com
🕐 Tue–Sat 1:30–3, 8:30–11:30. Closed 24 and 31 Dec

La Méson Góndola €

Old men in flat caps prop up the bar while local families hog the tables. During the winter, there is a roaring fire behind the bar and the low-beamed ceiling and brick-and-tile combo make this a particularly hospitable bar and restaurant. Try the *patatas baezanas* starter, the tasty house speciality of sautéed potatoes topped with fried mushrooms, parsley and garlic.

✚ 200 C4
⌧ Portales Carbonería 13
☎ 953 74 29 84; www.asadorlagondola.com
🕐 Daily 8am–midnight

CAZORLA

La Sarga €€/€€€

This restaurant in the town centre has a fine reputation for its excellent regional dishes. Totally ecological dishes can be ordered here. The service is, like the facilities: friendly formal.

✚ 201 D4 ⌧ Plaza de Andalucía
☎ 953 72 15 07
🕐 Closed Tue and two weeks Sep, Jan

ÚBEDA

Parador Restaurante Nacional del Condestable Dávalos €€/€€€

Stylishly refurbished, the parador restaurant has an excellent reputation for quality, serving market-fresh produce in imaginative, traditional recipes which have been handed down for generations. Once those belonging to a 16th-century palace, the surrounds are suitably sumptuous, while the service is formal and attentive. Be sure to have a peek at the wine cellar with its original stone arches, simple wooden tables and giant kegs of wine.

✚ 200 C4
⌧ Plaza de Vázquez de Molina
☎ 953 75 03 45
🕐 Daily noon–4, 7–midnight

Restaurante El Marqués €€

A welcome addition to the centre of town, this hotel has an excellent restaurant, elegantly decorated in warm hues of ochre and cream with subtle lighting, modern furnishings and a sophisticated feel. It's a great place to sip an espresso, enjoy a light lunch or get serious with the three-course *menú del día* celebrating local cuisine with an imaginative nouvelle twist.

✚ 200 C4 ⌧ María Molina Hotel, Plaza del Ayuntamiento s/n
☎ 953 75 72 55
🕐 Daily noon–4, 8–midnight

Where to...
Shop

Córdoba's long-established leather and filigree silver workshops produce exquisite goods. South of the city is the wine- and olive oil-producing area around Priego de Córdoba, with local produce of the finest quality, while some of the best pottery in Andalucía is made by artisans in the town of Úbeda in Jaén province.

CÓRDOBA PROVINCE

For fashion and general shopping in Córdoba city, head for the streets in the area between Plaza de las Tendillas (➤ 121) and the pedestrianised Avenida del Gran Capitán, especially Conde de Gondomar which links the two, and where you'll find chic dress shops, among them **Modas Pilar Morales** (Conde de Gondomar 2, tel: 957 47 12 54).

Córdoba's **El Corte Inglés** department store is at the junction of Avenida del Gran Capitán and Avenida Ronda de los Tejares. The souvenir scrum round the Mezquita (➤ 115) is fine for everyday gifts and postcards, but for some of Córdoba's celebrated leather crafts, a better bet is such leading workshop/outlets as **Meryan** (Calleja de las Flores 2/Encarnación 12, tel: 957 47 59 02), which sell a good range of pottery, leather goods and other artefacts.

Artesanía La Corredera (Calle Rodríguez Marín, tel: 957 48 97 16) and **Meryan** (Calleja de las Flores 2) Moorish-abstract decorated leatherware and ceramic products.

In the **Zoco** craft market (➤ 119), there are several shops selling filigree silverware. There is also a highly entertaining **market** in Plaza de la Corredera trading clothes, craftwork and oddments every day, but with a big and lively turnout on Saturday mornings.

As you head south towards Priego de Córdoba you enter olive oil and Montilla wine country. These sherry-like wines (though with no added alcohol) come under the denomination of Moriles, after the main wine-producing town in the area. Priego de Córdoba is also a centre of olive oil production: around 80 percent of Spain's olive oil is produced in Andalucía.

JAÉN PROVINCE

Úbeda (➤ 122) is noted for its fine pottery, which is distinguished by its beautiful dark green glaze. Calle de Valencia is the town's "potters' quarter", where there are several top potter's workshops such as the **Alfarería Paco Tito** (Calle Valencia 22, tel: 953 75 14 96) and nearby **Cerámica Alameda** (Cno. El Cementerio).

In Calle Real, Úbeda's old main street, there are one or two shops that still sell goods made from esparto grass, a long-established craft in the area. Try **Acuario** (Calle Real 61, tel: 953 75 40 14) which also has good ceramic tiles. **Alfarería Góngora** (Cuesta de la Merced 32, tel: 953 75 46 05), is also good for high-quality ceramics and craftwork.

In the **Sierra de Cazorla** browse round the stalls in **Cazorla's daily market** in Plaza del Mercado and then look at the typical village shops in Calle Dr Muñoz, with their local goods and food products.

For Sierra crafts and gifts, the natural park's information centre, the **Centro de Interpretación** at Torre del Vinagre (tel: 953 71 30 17), has plenty to choose from.

Insider Tip

Where to...
Go Out

In Córdoba city, ask at the tourist office for a free copy of the monthly listings guides *Qué Hacer en Córdoba?* and *Welcome & Olé!* There is also a useful guide to *tapas* bars in the city. The daily Spanish-language newspaper is *Córdoba*. A good source of local information on the best entertainment hot spots is the young tourist guides of Cicerones de Córdoba. You will find them at the Alcázar, Puerta de Almodóvar, Plaza de las Tendillas and Palacio de Viana.

NIGHTLIFE

You'll find lively dance and music bars on Calle Cruz Conde just north of Plaza de las Tendillas.

FLAMENCO

One of the best venues for "classical" flamenco in **Córdoba** city is the **Tablao Cardenal** (Calle Torrijos 10, tel: 957 48 33 20), right opposite the Mezquita. The show is staged in a delightful patio with an authentic ambience. There is a bar and restaurant service, and flamenco sessions start at 10:30pm. Reservations are advised.

Another good Córdoban flamenco venue is **La Bulería** (Calle Pedro López 3, tel: 957 48 38 39) near Plaza de la Corredera.

In Baeza, **Peña Flamenco** (Conde de Romanones 11) stages occasional flamenco. Ask at the tourist information office for details.

A similar club in Úbeda is **Peña Flamenco El Quejío** (Alfareros 4); again you should enquire at the tourist information centre.

THEATRE

Córdoba has a fine theatre in its **Gran Teatro** (Avenida del Gran Capitán 3, tel: 957 48 02 37, www.teatrocordoba.org) staging excellent music, dance and drama presentations. You can get a monthly programme of events from the theatre or tourist office.

BULLFIGHTING

Córdoba's bullring (Avenida Gran Vía Parque, tel: 957 23 25 07) stages fights throughout the summer. Ask at the tourist office for details and dates. For bullrings and scheduled fights in provincial towns and villages, check with relevant tourist offices or at the relevant bullring.

LEISURE AND SPORTS

Córdoba's **Hammam Baños Árabes** (Calle Corregidor Luís de la Cerda, tel: 957 48 47 46, www.hammam alandalus.com) are traditional Moorish-style steam baths with hot and cold water and massages. There is also a *tetería* (tearoom) where you can relax afterwards.

For outdoors enthusiasts, there is plenty of adventure in the mountainous Parque Natural de Cazorla y Segura (➤ 128). The **Quercus** team (Calle Juan Domingo, tel: 953 72 01 15) in Cazorla town organise four-wheel-drive tours into the remoter areas, as well as horse treks and mountain biking.

The **Centro de Interpretacíon** at Torre del Vinagre (tel: 953 71 30 17) can also arrange four-wheel-drive tours of the park as well as horse treks and mountain biking.

Try **Tierraventura Cazorla** (Calle Ximinez 17, tel: 953 71 00 73, www.tierraventuracazorla.com) for a whole range of outdoor activities.

Insider Tip

Sevilla and Huelva

 **Little Treats**

Learn how to dance the flamenco

Why not complement the Spanish lessons with a flamenco course? In Seville (➤ 144), **dance schools** also offer courses for tourists (i. a. www.tallerflamenco.com).

Cycle tour through Seville

Pedal your way through Seville (➤ 144)! The town has 142km (88mi) of cycle paths, and there are eight beautiful routes through the **metropolis** (www.sevillaenbici.com).

Through the Parque Nacional Coto de Doñana

Enjoy an exciting boat trip through the national park (➤ 160) on the "Real Fernando" from **Sanlúcar de Barrameda** (www.visitasdonana.com).

Getting Your Bearings

The city of Seville is the essence of all things Andalucían, a city of enduring excitement and spontaneity, of orange trees and flamenco; a city where the jingle of horse-drawn carriages is still heard in quiet streets and flower-filled parks and where modernistic buildings blend happily with Moorish palaces, majestic churches and medieval streets. It is where you find the best tapas bars in Spain and where a hint of pleasurable expectancy is always in the air.

A bird's-eye-view of Seville's Reales Alcázares, a treasure house of mudéjar architecture

Seville is also one of the hottest places on mainland Europe. Thus, it is no wonder that the town does not wake up until a lot of other people are going to bed – nights in Seville have a lot to offer. Out in the larger province beyond the city are lesser-known but fascinating places to visit such as the old Roman city of Itálica, the walled town of Carmona, with its Moorish streets and Roman necropolis, and historic Écija.

Even further afield is Huelva province. The city of Huelva, an industrialised port that has no great monuments in its otherwise pleasant old centre, has little to offer the visitor, but the northern part of Huelva province has the peaceful, wooded hills of the Sierra Morena, which it shares with neighbouring Seville province. Here you will find the friendly hill town of Aracena, famous for its limestone caverns, the Gruta de las Maravillas, while a network of winding roads lead to serene villages amid forests of cork oak, where you can stretch your legs and breathe pure mountain air. Huelva's southernmost coastline, the Costa de la Luz, has one of the longest and most remote beaches in Andalucía. Behind the coast lies the huge delta of the Río Guadalquivir and the Parque Nacional de Doñana, a vast area of wetlands, sand dunes and wooded scrubland that is a wildlife site of world importance.

Aracena & Gruta de las Maravillas ㊱

Minas de Ríotinto

㊴ **Río Tinto**

Valverde del Camino

0   30 km
0   15 mi

Carmona ⑥

Écija ㊲

Itálica ㊳
Sevilla ✈

Alcalá de Guadaira

Huelva

㊶ **El Rocío**

Utrera

Morón de la Frontera

Costa de la Luz ㊵
Matalascañas

⑨ **Parque Nacional de Doñana**

Jerez de la Frontera

Well looked after: wild horses in the Parque Nacional Coto de Doñana

Perfect Days in...

Four Perfect Days

Soak up the magic of Seville, then take in the Old Town of Carmona and the spectacular limestone caverns of Aracena, before unwinding on Huelva's quiet Costa de la Luz and exploring Spains most important marshland, the Parque Nacional de Doñana. For more information see the main entries (➤ 144–166).

Day One

Morning
Visit ⭐ **Seville's cathedral** and the **Giralda** tower as early as possible, then take a stroll through the streets and plazas of the **Barrio de Santa Cruz** (➤ 152).

Afternoon
See the **Reales Alcázares** (➤ 150) and spend a restful hour or two in the shaded grounds of the **Parque de María Luisa** (➤ 155) before wandering back through the **Plaza de España** (➤ 156). Enjoy a *tapas* tour of **Barrio de Santa Cruz**, followed by a late meal at one of the area's many restaurants (➤ 168); or join the locals in the busy shopping streets of **Sierpes** and **Tetuán** (➤ 170), sampling *tapas* bars in the adjoining streets and plazas.

Day Two

Morning
Head for the **Museo de Bellas Artes** (➤ 152) for a view of some of the finest paintings in Spain; or visit the exquisite **Casa de Pilatos** (➤ 155), which reflects the glory of 15th-century *mudéjar* decorative art.

Afternoon
Take the Córdoba road, the A4, to ⭐ **Carmona**. Visit the atmospheric **Necrópolis Romana** (➤ 159), then explore the narrow streets of the old walled town, including the impressive church of **Santa María la Mayor**. Stay overnight.

Day Three

Morning
Set off towards Seville, then go north onto the N630 and visit the Roman city ruins of **Itálica** (➤ 164). Continue north into the Sierra Morena hills for a night's stay at **36 Aracena** (➤ 162).

Afternoon
Visit Aracena's famous caverns, the **36 Gruta de las Maravillas** (➤ 162), then climb (gently) through cobbled streets to the hilltop Moorish castle and its adjoining church.

Day Four

Morning
Make an early start and drive south to the **40 Costa de la Luz** (➤ 166) and spend an hour or two on the quiet beaches or go for a walk along the **Playa Cuesta de Maneli** boardwalk (➤ 166) through sand dunes covered with aromatic trees and shrubs. Bring something for a picnic as there are no bars or cafés within miles.

Afternoon
Head for the Centro de Recepción del Acebuche, the main reception centre of the **9 Parque Nacional de Doñana** (➤ 160). If you don't have time for a pre-booked tour of parkland sites (➤ 172), be sure to visit the bird hides near the centre, or visit the centre at **Las Rocinas** (➤ 160), where there is an enjoyable circular walk through a wetland area. Then it's back to Seville for another bout of lively Sevillian nightlife.

Aracena & Gruta
36 de las Maravillas

39 Río Tinto

Itálica **38**

3 Sevilla

6 Carmona

37 Écija

Costa de
la Luz
40

41 El Rocío

9 Parque Nacional
de Doñana

★3 Sevilla

Sevilla (Seville), bestriding the broad Río Guadalquivir, is Andalucía at its most stylish. It is an exciting and theatrical place, scene of Spain's most exuberant festival, the Feria de Abril, while the everyday life of the Sevillanos is played out with equal verve in the bars, fine restaurants and fashionable shopping streets.

An inscription on the Puerta de Jerez reads: "Hercules built me; Julius Caesar surrounded me with walls and high towers; the Holy King conquered me". It remains questionable whether Hercules really founded Seville on his way to the Atlantic coast near Cadiz to steal the giant Geryon's herd of cattle. What is fact though, is that when the Romans arrived in around 206 BC and drove out the Carthaginians, there was a settlement there called Hispalis, which under the new name of Colonia Iulia Romula became both a harbour town as well as an important post against Caesar's rival Pompeius, to whom Córdoba was loyal. In 712, the Moors ended the rule of the Visigoths They called the town Ichbilîja, but paid little attention to their conquest. Under the Christians in the 16th century, Seville experienced a boom as Spain's most important port of departure to America. In the 17th century, this golden age ended owing to the silting of the Guadalquivir. In 1929, the Iberoamericana Exhibition took place here, and many of the beautiful public buildings dating from this occasion have been preserved. In the heart of the town three buildings created an ensemble now listed as a UNESCO world heritage site: the Admiralty Hall of the Alcázar where overseas expeditions were organised, the cathedral containing the tomb of Christopher Columbus, and the Archivo General de Indias with its important documents regarding colonial history.

Sevilla exudes charm and joie de vivre

Tourist Information
✛ 198 C3 ✉ Plaza del Triunfo 1 ☎ 954 21 00 05; www.visitasevilla.es

Parking: There is out-of-centre parking near Santa Justa railway station, at Calle Luis de Morales, just off Avenida de Luis Montoro (the approach road from the Costa del Sol, Málaga and Granada). Car parks are signed at various points on Seville's inner ring road.

La Catedral & La Giralda

Seville's Cathedral of Santa María de la Sede is the largest Gothic church in the world, a treasure house of monumental architecture and great sculptures, paintings and decorative craftwork.

After Seville was wrested from the Moors by Fernando III in 1248, the city's mosque was used for Christian worship until the early 1400s, when plans for a new cathedral were launched. Most of the mosque was demolished and within 100 years the main body of the cathedral was completed.

The Giralda towers above the piers and pinnacles of the cathedral

The Giralda

The exterior focus of the cathedral is the **Giralda tower** built by the Moorish Almohad rulers of Seville between 1184 and 1198: The *Sevillanos* revere the 97m (318ft) high tower as the emblem of the town, although they tend to leave climbing it to the tourists. The original minaret was remodelled into a belfry in the 16th century by the Spanish. It was crowned by a statue representing Faith, in the form of a weathervane, a *giraldillo*, from which the tower's name derives. It is the Moorish section of the tower that is its great glory, however, a masterpiece of cool and subtle stonework, of geometric tracery that reflects changing patterns as the angle of the light alters. Instead of steps, the tower has 35 ramps, wide enough to allow two mounted guards to pass each other when they were on duty. The entrance to the Giralda is in the northeast corner of the cathedral, immediately to the left as you enter the building through the Puerta de la Concepción. At the top of the tower, the barred window offers a rather restricted view of the adjacent cathedral roofs, many spires and horizontal buttresses. Kestrels soar above and you can see exactly how many swimming pools there are on the roof terraces of Seville.

INSIDER INFO

Seeing Seville from a 🚏 **horse-drawn carriage** is still a popular, though expensive, treat for many visitors. The beautifully maintained carriages wait for custom in Plaza Virgen de los Reyes alongside the cathedral. It costs about €50 for an hour's tour for up to four passengers.

The Cathedral

The enormous Gothic cathedral was built in just over 100 years (1402 to 1506). Constructed on the foundations of the former Great Mosque, it is entered through the **Puerta del Perdón** (Gate of Absolution). Beyond it lies the **Patio de los Naranjos** (Patio of the Orange Trees), where worshippers carried out ritual ablutions before entering the mosque. Towering above the patio is the intricate façade of the **Puerta de la Concepción**, the doorway through which you enter the cathedral proper. Take some time to appreciate the size of the building's cavernous interior. At the heart of the huge central nave are the **Capilla Mayor**, the main chapel, with the **Coro** (Choir) to its right. The gilded and painted *retablo* (altarpiece) of the Capilla Mayor is one of the cathedral's treasures. The vast screen

Columbus' tomb in the cathedral: four heralds (symbolising the four king-doms...

is composed of 45 carved panels depicting scenes from the life of Christ and featuring over 1,000 biblical figures. The focus of this awesome Gothic masterpiece is a silver-plated cedar statue of the Virgen de la Sede (the Virgin of the Chair). The choir has 117 stalls, each one intricately carved.

Behind the Capilla Mayor, the east wall of the cathedral is lined with chapels, including the centrally placed **Capilla Real** (Royal Chapel), which has an imposing *retablo* in stone. Moving towards the south side of the cathedral takes you to the **Sacristía Mayor**, a beautiful domed chamber by Diego de Riaño and Diego de Siloé. To the left of the Sacristía Mayor is the oval **Sala Capitular** (Chapter House), which has a superb domed ceiling and a decorated marble floor. Murillo's beautiful *La Immaculada* (The Inmaculate Conception) is one of the fine paintings here. Apart from the Sacristía Mayor, of particular interest in the **Sacristía de los Cálices**, built in 1529, are the many paintings, which include Goya's *Las santas Justa y Rufina* and Valdés Leal's *San Lázaro con Santa Marta y María Magdalena*.

Adjoining the Sacristía de los Cálices is a striking **monument to Christopher Columbus** depicting the great sailor's coffin. For a long time, it was a controversial point as to whether the seafarer's remains were actually inside, since the corpse had been on a real odyssey before it arrived there. After Columbus' death in 1506, he was buried in Seville, but in 1596 transported to Santo Domingo on Haiti and from there to Havana, Cuba, where Arturo Mélida sculpted a tomb which was installed in the cathedral (1892). When Cuba "was lost" in the Spanish-American war of 1898, Columbus was returned to Seville. A DNA test carried out in 2006 by Spanish scientists that compared samples from the tomb with DNA from family members finally confirmed that the remains in the coffin really were those of Christopher Columbus.

TAKING A BREAK

Stop for drink at the appropriately named **Cervecería Giralda** at Calle Mateos Gago 1 and enjoy just about the best view of the cathedral at the same time.

...León, Castilla, Navarra and Aragón) carry the stone sarcophagus

Catedral Santa María de la Sede and Giralda

✚ 206 B2 ✉ Plaza Virgen de los Reyes

☎ 954 21 49 71 🕐 Mon 11–3:30, Tue–Sat 11–5 (summer until 4), Sun 2:30–6

🚊 C1, C2, C3, C4 💶 €8

INSIDER INFO

■ At almost any time of year, queues can build up for the cathedral from late morning onwards, especially once tour groups begin to assemble. Thus it is better to come **very early or in the afternoon**, unless you are happy to wait. Last entry is one hour before closing.

Catedral de Santa María de la Sede

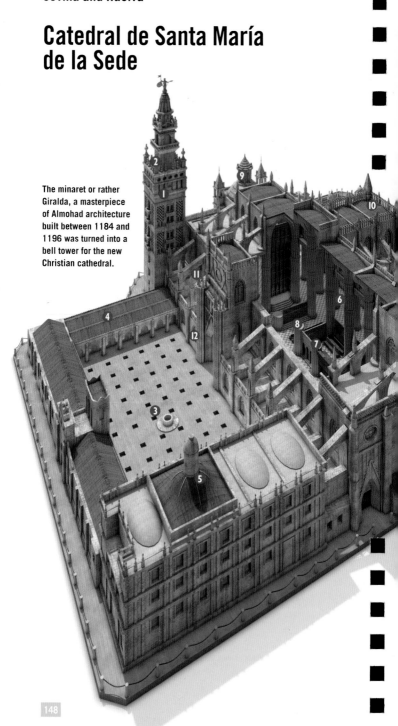

The minaret or rather Giralda, a masterpiece of Almohad architecture built between 1184 and 1196 was turned into a bell tower for the new Christian cathedral.

According to traditional accounts, the members of the cathedral chapter said, "Let us build a church so beautiful and so grand that those who see it finished will think we are mad." Their wish was fulfilled. At a length of 115m (377ft), 74m (242ft) wide and a height of 40m (131ft), it is the largest Gothic church in the world.

On the tympanum of the enormous Gothic portal complex, eventually completed in 1833, there is a stone relief depicting the ascension of the Virgin Mary.

❶ Giralda: The tower was originally conceived as a minaret for the main mosque.

❷ Gallery: The viewing gallery is at a height of 70m (229ft).

❸ Fountain: The octagonal-shaped fountain is the remains of the Muslim *midhâ*, the basin used for ritual cleansing.

❹ Library: The library of the cathedral chapter founded in the 13th century possesses i.a. handwritten papers by Columbus and the Bible of Alfonso X.

❺ Sagrario: This baroque building contains a *retablo* (altarpiece) with Pedro Roldán's *Descent from the Cross.*

❻ Nave: "Notre Dame de Paris could walk without bending her head down the central nave." (Théophile Gautier).

❼ Choir: The choir is separated off by a grille: the choir stool is Gothic. The Capilla de la Concepción Chica on the south wall contains the *La Cieguecita, a* wooden sculpture of the Virgin Mary.

❽ Capilla Mayor: The *retablo* is the dominant piece here: at 23m (75ft) in height and 20m (65ft) in width, it is the largest altarpiece in the world.

❾ Capilla Real: Fernando III's body rests in the silver shrine made in 1729 that can be seen in front of the *retablo* with the picture of the *Virgen de los Reyes* (13th century). To the left lies his son Alfonso X, and to the right his wife Beatrix von Schwaben.

❿ Sacristía Mayor: It contains art objects, including the key of Seville (1248), a reliquary of Alfonso X in the shape of a triptychon (*Tablas Alfonsinas*), a reliquary of the Cross found by Saint Helena, the bronze candelabra "Tenebrario" by Bartolomé Morel and Pedro de Campana's painting *Descent from the Cross.*

⓫ Capilla de San Antonio: Here you will find *The Baptism of Christ* and *The Vision of St Anthony by* Murillo.

⓬ Capilla de Santiago: contains a picture of St James at the Battle of Cavijo by Juan de Roelas and a painting by Valdés Leal *(San Lorenzo).*

Reales Alcázares

The Alcázar located immediately opposite the cathedral was originally the fortress-palace of the Moorish rulers who worked on it from the 9th century onwards.

The layout of the palaces reflects classic Islamic architecture, with central courtyards from which individual halls and chambers lead off to all sides. Great use is made of painted stucco and of tiles known as *azulejos* (► 12), which form a dazzling kaleidoscope of geometric patterns. Not the least of the Alcázar's delights are the beautifully kept gardens.

Seville's original Reales Alcázar was begun in the early 8th century on the ruins of Roman and Visigothic fortifications. The interior of the building dates almost wholly from the later Christian era. After the conquest of Seville by

Fernando III, the Christian kings moved in here. Pedro I, commonly called Pedro the Cruel (reigned from 1350 to 1369) decided to build his mistress María de Padilla a regal residence. He had Moorish architects and craftsmen brought in from the allied Granada and Toledo, who built the palace section named after him and with it one of the most beautiful examples of Moorish architecture in Spain. The Catholic kings altered quite a few of the rooms; under Carlos V a new extension was added.

Visiting the Reales Alcázares

At the busiest times, visitors are only are allowed through the admissions control at 30-minute intervals, so you may have to queue. Beyond the entrance vestibule is the **Patio del León** (Court of the Lion) and, beyond that, the larger **Patio de la Montería** (Hunting Court). To the right of the latter is the **Salón del Almirante** (Admiralty Hall), established in 1503 by Isabel I de Castilla as a suite of rooms in which to plan

Visitors enter the walled Alcázar from the Plaza del Triunfo through the Puerta del León and find themselves in ...

The gardens of Alcázar bring together Islamic and Renaissance design

voyages to the Americas. The finest room is the **Sala de Audiencias** (Audience Hall) with an *artesonado* ceiling, a fine model of Columbus's vessel the *Santa María*, and a 16th-century *in situ* altarpiece, *The Virgin of the Navigators*, portraying Columbus, Amerigo Vespucci and other voyagers.

You next enter the true Palace of Pedro I. In the central courtyard, the **Patio de las Doncellas** (Court of the Maidens), a space rich with multi-lobed arches and beautiful lattices of stone, a frieze of *azulejos* clads the lower walls and a

central fountain sends a slim column of water into the air. The patio is encircled by richly decorated rooms leading one into the other through narrow doorways. At their heart lies the **Patio de las Muñecas** (Court of the Dolls), so called because of the tiny heads set into its walls. The two-storey **Salón de los Embajadores** (Room of the Ambassadors), next to it, is the oldest and most beautiful room in Alcázar. It is crowned with a magnificent stalactite dome (1420) made of cedarwood.

... the Patio del León, planted with orange trees and flowers, whose walled quad dates back to the Almohad period

A stairway in the corner of the Patio de las Doncellas leads to the gloomy 17th-century **Salones de Carlos V**. From near the Estanque del Mercurio, a passageway leads you past a cafeteria into a covered coach hall, the Apeadero, and then to the exit.

🕂 206 C2 ✉ Plaza del Triunfo
☎ 954 50 23 4; www.alcazarsevilla.org 🕐 Daily 9:30–7 (winter until 5)
🍴 Café 🚇 C1, C2, C3, C4 💶 €8.75 (children under 16 free)

Sevilla and Huelva

Barrio de Santa Cruz

Right: Bar in Barrio de Santa Cruz

Alongside the cathedral and Reales Alcázares are the narrow streets and plazas of Barrio de Santa Cruz, a welcome antidote to the traffic-jammed main streets of the city. Santa Cruz was the *aljama*, or Jewish quarter, of medieval Seville. Much of the original *barrio* was destroyed after a vicious pogrom in 1492, and despite rebuilding work at the beginning of the 20th century some of the style of the original survives. As you wander through the streets, you will catch tantalising glimpses of lovely central patios through wrought-iron grilles.

A peaceful little enclave that many visitors seem to miss is **Plaza de Santa Cruz;** the wrought-iron cross at its centre symbolises the original Iglesia de Santa Cruz, destroyed by Napoleonic troops. Another pretty square is Plaza Doña Elvira with its central fountain and dappled shade. The **Hospital de los Venerables Sacerdotes,** a one-time hospice for retired priests in Plaza de los Venerables, now houses a gallery containing paintings and sculptures by leading Spanish artists. The building has a delectable patio. On the *barrio's* eastern boundary are the pleasantly shady **Jardines de Murillo** (Murillo Gardens), and everywhere you turn there are bars and cafés.

Museo de Bellas Artes

One of Spain's major art galleries, the Museo de Bellas Artes (Fine Arts Museum) is located in the former **Convento de la**

The El Rinconcillo (Quiet Corner) tavern-restaurant is in a building that dates back to 1670

Hospital de los Venerables Sacerdotes
✠ 206 C2
✉ Plaza de los Venerables 8 ☎ 954 56 26 96
🕐 10–2, 4–8 (guided tours)
💶 €5.50

Museo de Bellas Artes
✠ 206 A3 ✉ Plaza del Museo ☎ 955 54 29 31
🕐 Tue–Sat 10–8:30 (summer 9–3:30), Sun 10–5
🍴 C1, C2, C3, C4
💶 €1.50 (free with EU passport)

INSIDER INFO

- **Seville by Bus:** The Sevirama company (Paseo de Colón 18; tel: 954 56 06 93; www.busturistico.com) runs open-top bus tours (expensive). Buses leave every half hour from just north of the Torre del Oro (➤ 156) from 10am, visiting the Plaza de España (➤ 156), Triana (➤ 157) and the Isla Mágica (➤ 157). Headphones offer commentary in different languages. You can get on and off at will with the all-day ticket.
- **Seville by Boat:** Hour-long river cruises leave every 30 minutes from 10am to 11pm from the quayside in front of the Torre del Oro (➤ 157), where there is a booking office (Cruceros Turísticos Torre del Oro; tel: 954 56 16 92; www.crucerostorredeloro.com). The trip along the Guadalquivir River is a relaxing way to catch some of the main sights.

Sevilla and Huelva

Merced Calzada, a short walk northwest of the cathedral.
With its hushed galleries and peaceful central patio, this
lovely building is a pleasure in itself and an ideal repository
for examples of the finest of Spanish painting from the early
medieval period to the 20th century.

The permanent collection is displayed in 14 of the
convent's rooms. The highlight of any visit must be **Room V**,
the one-time chapel of the convent. As you enter from the
side, you come face to face with the *Apotheosis of St Thomas
Aquinas*, arguably the finest work of the 17th-century painter Francisco de Zurbarán. Turning to your right, you'll see
the room in its full glory; even the dome of the chapel is
aglow with restored paintings. On the wall of the original
apse is a celebration of the work of the Seville-born painter
Bartolomé Esteban Murillo, including the *Inmaculate
Conception* and the haunting *Santa Justa and Santa Rufina*.
In a small chamber round to the right is Murillo's ravishing
Virgin and Child, known as *La Virgen de la Servilleta* because
it is said to be painted on a dinner napkin. There are more
Murillos in **Room VII**, while **Room X** is devoted to Zurbarán.
Other artists represented at the art gallery include the
painters Goya, Velázquez, El Greco and Murillo's Sevillian
contemporary Juan de Valdés de Leal, and sculptors such as
the 15th-century Sevillian Pedro Millán, whose compelling
Entombment of Christ is on display in **Room I**.

Rooms XII and XIV show 19th- and 20th-century art.
In Room XII look for Gonzalo Bilbao's sentimental but
persuasive evocation of the world of *Carmen* and the
Seville Tobacco Factory (➤ 15), *Las Cigarreras. Noche
de Verano en Sevilla*, by the Impressionist painter born in
the Andalucían capital can also be seen here. Other gems

Insider Tip

The central
courtyard of
Casa de Pilatos
is a two-storey
arcaded struc-
ture; the round
arches are
adorned with
Moorish motifs.
In the middle of
the courtyard
is a fountain
with dolphin
designs and a
Janus head

here are José García Ramos's dancers in *Bulerías* and his painting of a man drinking in *Hasta Verte Cristo Mío*.

Casa de Pilatos (Pilate's House)

About 500m (546yd) east of the San Salvador church is the Casa de Pilatos on the square of the same name. This palace which now belongs to the Duke of Medinaceli combines Moorish, Gothic and Renaissance elements in such a winning way that the result is almost on a par with the Alcázar. Construction started in 1492 and was completed around 1520. Since the master of the works had travelled to Palestine the year before, it was generally assumed that the building was a copy of the house of Pontius Pilate in Jerusalem. The house is laid out around a spectacular patio, which is entered through an entrance modelled on a triumphant arch and made of Carrara marble; the work is by the Genoese artist d'Aprile in 1532. Much work since the mid-20th century has restored the house to its original splendour. A conducted tour takes you through a succession of chambers and salons exquisitely decorated and furnished. The small interior gardens include Italianate loggias and Roman statuary, amid palm trees and flowers.

Plaza de España & Parque de María Luisa

Of Seville's parks and open spaces, the Plaza de España and Parque de María Luisa are the finest. Both were created as showpieces for Seville's 1929 Iberoamericana Exhibition. Leafy **Parque de María Luisa** is just the place to linger for an hour or two during the heat of mid-afternoon, an oasis of tree-filled gardens, resplendent with colourful ceramics, ornamental bridges and follies, and in summer

bright with geraniums and bougainvillaea. At its east end is
the handsome Plaza de América, flanked by the **Museo
Arqueológico** (Archaeological Museum), whose collections
range from prehistory to the Moors, and the **Museo de Artes
y Costumbres Populares** (Museum of Folk Art), which displays
artefacts and costumes from the 18th and 19th centuries.
Both were built as part of the 1929 Exhibition. **Plaza de
España** lies just north of Parque de María Luisa across the
broad Avenida de Isabel la Católica. It is a huge crescent of
arcaded redbrick building with curving staircases. At ground
level, a series of brightly coloured tile mosaics display the
coats of arms of Spain's main provinces. In front of the
crescent is a canal-style lake, criss-crossed by ornamental
bridges, where people drift sedately in little rowing boats.

The crescent-shaped Plaza de España

Plaza de San Francisco & Calle Sierpes

To the north of the cathedral at the end of broad and busy
Avenida de la Constitución are two adjoining squares. **Plaza
Nueva** has little architectural appeal but buzzes with life in
the evenings. Equally busy, **Plaza de San Francisco** has been
at the heart of Sevillian life since the 16th century. Political
meetings and other major events are staged between the
16th-century Ayuntamiento (city hall) with its Renaissance
façade and the 19th-century balconied buildings opposite.
From here, stroll along **Calle Sierpes**, Seville's great shopping
street, crammed with shops of every kind, its side streets
alive with *tapas* bars or sheltering beautiful baroque
churches. At the far end of Sierpes you come to the **Campaña**
where you can browse through a colourful craft market, then
eat pastries at a pavement table of the popular coffee shop
and *pastelería*, Confitería La Campaña.

Torre del Oro, Plaza de Toros de la Maestranza, Triana

Seville is greatly enhanced by its river setting, and both
banks repay exploration. On the east side, bordering the
older part of the city, is the **Torre del Oro,** a 12th-century
Moorish tower that now houses a small maritime museum.
Further north along the Paseo de Cristóbal Colón is
Seville's huge baroque bullring, **La Maestranza** (➤ 172).

INSIDER INFO

- The most convenient **bus services for central Seville** are Nos C1 and C3, which operate a clockwise route, and C2 and C4, which operate in the reverse direction. Ask for a bus company route map at tourist offices (➤ 144) or at the office of Transportes Urbanos de Seville (TUSSAM) at Avenida de Andalucía 11.

- A good place to escape the afternoon heat is the **Museo de Bellas Artes** (➤ 152), one of the few places to remain open during the mid-afternoon siesta period.

- A few metres down Calle Jovellanos, a narrow street off busy Calle Sierpes (on the left from Plaza San Francisco), is the **Capilla de San José** (St Joseph's Chapel). Its late baroque altar is one of the finest in Andalucía.

- **Isla de La Cartuja**, an island formed by two arms of the Río Guadalquivir, was the focus of Seville's Expo 92. The Carthusian monastery which gave the island its name, has an exhibition centre for contemporary art (CAAC, tel: 955 03 70 70, Tue–Sat 11–9, Sun 11–3; €3). Also on the island is the entertainment park, 🎡 **Isla Mágica** (May–Sep daily 11–7 or midnight; www.islamagica.es).

Claimed as the finest bullring in the world, it dates from the late 18th century. A little further south, you can cross the Guadalquivir on the Puente de Isabel II to reach the district of **Triana**, once Seville's gypsy quarter, home of flamenco and of ceramic production. Most of the gypsy families have been rehoused outside the city and the *barrio* has been gentrified, but a stroll through its streets will take you to some fine churches, *tapas* bars and cafés, and ceramics outlets.

La Maestranza, Seville's 18th-century bullring

Casa de Pilatos
🔲 206 C3 ✉ Plaza de Pilatos 1
☎ 954 22 52 98 🕐 May–Sep 9–7, Oct–April 9–6 🚌 C1, C2, C3, C4 (for Plaza San Agustín) 💶 €6

Plaza de España & Parque de María Luisa
🔲 206 C1 ✉ Avenida de Isabel la Católica
🚌 C1, C2, C3, C4 💶 Free

Museo Arqueológico
🔲 206 south of C1 ✉ Plaza de América
☎ 955 12 06 32 🕐 Sun 10–5 Mid-Sep–May Tue–Sat 10–8:30, June–mid-Sep 9–3:30
💶 €1.50 (free with EU passport)

Museo de Artes y Costumbres Populares
🔲 206 south of C1 ✉ Plaza de América
☎ 954 71 23 98 🕐 Tue–Sat 9–8:30, Sun and holidays 9–2:30 💶 Free

⭐6 Carmona

Carmona sits enthroned on a bare hill ridge in the middle of the Vega de Corbones, one of the most fertile stretches of land in Andalucía. The historic centre ranks it among the most exquisite little towns in Andalucía, only surpassed by Baeza and Úbeda. Carmona also possesses a first-class cultural landmark in the form of an extensive Roman burial ground.

There are about 1,000 tombs in Carmona's **Necrópolis Romana** dating from about 2 BC to AD 4, about 250 of which have been uncovered. There are conducted tours of the site, but you can easily find your own way around. The site museum has displays of mosaics, gravestones and funerary pottery.

The main town of Carmona is entered by an impressive Roman gateway, the **Puerta de Sevilla**. You can reach the upper walls and battlements of the gateway through the tourist office. Across busy Plaza Blas Infante from the Puerta de Sevilla, outside the walls, is the 15th-century **Iglesia de San Pedro**, its tower built in the form of Seville's Giralda. On one corner of Carmona's palm-fringed central square, Plaza de San Fernando, stands the **Casa de Cabildo,** the old town hall. East of the plaza, Calle Martín López de Córdoba takes you to the Gothic **Iglesia de Santa María la Mayor**; look for a column with a Visigothic calendar inscribed in the stone. At the eastern end of the town is the refurbished Roman gateway, the **Puerta de Córdoba**.

Carmona at dusk with the towering tower of Iglesia San Bartolomé in the background

TAKING A BREAK

Enjoy a drink, even as a non-resident, at Carmona's exclusive **Parador Nacional** hotel in the renovated Alcázar del Rey Pedro, the remains of a Moorish fortified palace standing high above the town. Many people consider it one of the most magnificent hotels in Spain. If you're feeling flush, stop off for lunch or dinner.

INSIDER INFO

- Protect yourself from the sun at the **Necrópolis Romana**, and don't forget to have a look at the nearby Roman ampitheatre if you have time.
- Visit Carmona's morning **market**, held in the arcaded patio of a 17th-century convent, just south of Plaza de San Fernando.
- Carmona's *ayuntamiento* (town hall) is a splendid **Renaissance building**. A Roman mosaic of the **head of Medusa** is displayed in its patio (Mon–Fri 8–3; free).

Insider
Tip

🔲 199 D3 🛈 Tourist Information:
✉ Alcázar de la Puerta de Sevilla
☎ 954 19 09 55; www.turismo.carmona.org

Parking: There is limited parking just inside the Puerta de Sevilla and random parking in the streets around Plaza de San Fernando.

Necrópolis Romana
✉ Avenida de Jorge Bonsor 9
☎ 600 14 36 32

🕐 Tue–Fri 9–3:30, Sat 10–3:30, Sun 10–5
🎫 Free

Iglesia de San Pedro
✉ Calle San Pedro
🕐 Tue–Sat 9:30–2. Closed Aug 🎫 €1.20

Iglesia de Santa María la Mayor
✉ Calle Martín López de Córdoba
🕐 Mon–Fri 9–2, 5–7, Sat 11–2, Sun 9–11:30
🎫 €3 (incl. museum)

★⁹ Parque Nacional Coto de Doñana

The wilderness of the Doñana National Park forms Spain's largest wildlife reserve. The park is one of the most important wetland sites in the world, a sanctuary for resident and migratory birds and an exciting range of mammals including the Spanish lynx, wild boar and otters.

The park covers an area of more than 500km² (193mi²) around the delta of the Río Guadalquivir, which borders it on the east. To the south, it stretches to the estuary of the river opposite Sanlúcar de Barrameda, in the west to the Atlantic and in the north to the A483 from Matalascañas to El Rocío. This region has always been sparsely populated – the climate of the marshes *(marismas) being too hostile for comfort*, with malaria rampant there until the mid 20th century. Thus, the area was originally used almost exclusively for hunting purposes (span. *coto* = revier) and otherwise left more or less to its own devices.

Deer like this red stag wander in Doñana National Park

One of the first people to go hunting here was Alfonso X in the 13th century. He was followed by the Dukes of Medina Sidonia, to whom the land was bequeathed. In 1595, the 7th Duke of this family, Alfonso Pérez de Guzmán, Commander of the Spanish Armada defeated in 1588, erected a palace for his wife Doña Ana there. This palace, situated in the middle of the park, is now a research

INSIDER INFO

- All the Doñana **information centres** are closed during the week of the pilgrimage to El Rocío (► 166). It's wise to stay away from the area during this time in late May or early June when things get hectic.
- If you don't have your own, there are **binoculars** for hire at the main Centro de Recepción del Acebuche.
- It can become **very hot** during the morning Land Ranger Tour from Centro de Recepción del Acebuche. The evening tour is more likely to produce sightings of the park's larger animals, though for keen birdwatchers there is less chance of seeing the park's rare birds.
- From Las Rocinas you can reach a handsome old hunting lodge, **Palacio del Acebrón**, where there is an exhibition on traditional life in the marshes, and a nature trail too.

Insider Tip

Numerous migrant birds spend the winter here, or take a break on their way to Africa and socialise with the species resident here

centre. Over a period of time, the name "Coto de Doña Ana" became "Coto de Doñana". In 1897, the dukes sold the area to the sherry baron William Garvey. Around this time, the Brits Abel Chapman and Walter Buck started to draw attention to the natural treasures of the Coto. Yet it was not until the 1960s that conservationists started to lobby for the creation of a national park, which ultimately resulted in the establishment of the "Parque Nacional Coto de Doñana" in 1969 originally covering an area of 370km² (143mi²); in 1978, this was extended to 500km² (193mi²) to protect 265km² (102mi²) in the surrounding area.

Since 1994, the park has been a **UNESCO biosphere reserve**. Around 300,000 birds, representing 300 species, migrate from northern Europe to the Doñana *marismas* in October each year, then head north again in March. Winter is thus the best time for dedicated birdwatchers to visit. In summer you still have a good chance of spotting a variety of birds including flamingos, storks, grebes, hoopoes and large raptors such as eagles, vultures, kites and marsh harriers.

Several visitor centres manage entrance to the Donaña. The **Centro de Recepción del Acebuche** (➤ below) is the main information centre, offering exhibitions, audiovisual media, souvenirs and a café. Tours can be arranged here in all-terrain vehicles (about 80km/50mi, 3–4 hours). Reservation necessary.

TAKING A BREAK

Coto de Doñana is a great picnic area, so stop off at a delicatessen and pick up some fresh bread, Manchego cheese, *jamón serrano* and a couple of bottles of Rioja.

✚ 194 B2

Visitor Centres
✉ Centro de Recepción del Acebuche (off A483, 5km/3 mi north of Matalascañas, ☎ 959 43 04 32; www.donanavisitas.es ⏰ Mid-Sep–April 8:30–3, May–Sep 8:30–5, closed Sun) 🎫 Guided tours €29.50

✉ Centro Recepción Las Rocinas (off A483, on southern outskirts of El Rocío ☎ 959 43 95 69 ⏰ June–Sep 10–3, 4–6, Oct–May 9–7

36 Aracena & Gruta de las Maravillas

The main attraction of the cheerful country town of Aracena is a complex of spectacular limestone caverns that riddle the hillside on which the town stands. Above ground, Aracena's roughly cobbled streets are romantically overlooked by a ruined medieval castle and a 13th-century Gothic church.

Aracena lies at the heart of the Sierra de Aracena, an area of smooth-browed hills covered with cork oak and eucalyptus trees. It is the 🚻 **Gruta de las Maravillas** (Grotto of Marvels) that brings visitors to the town. The section open to the public extends for about 1.2km (0.75mi) through galleries and passageways that bristle with fantastic stalactites and stalagmites. Paved walkways and staircases lead through the complex past a series of small lakes. Lighting and piped music add to the theatrical effect. The guide's commentary is in Spanish, but many of the features speak for themselves. And it is well worth giving your own imagination free rein. Highlights include the **Sala de los Culos** (Room of the Backsides), where certain deposits of calcium carbonate resemble well-rounded parts of the human anatomy.

Back on the surface, it's pleasant to stroll around Aracena's cobbled streets and its busy main square, Plaza Marqués de Aracena. On the hilltop above the town, beyond a 16th-century brick gateway, are the ruins of a Moorish castle along with the adjoining Nuestra Señora de los

The Gruta de las Maravillas is said to have been discovered by a 19th-century shepherd seeking lost sheep

HEAVENLY HAM: EXPENSIVE AND GOOD

Aracena in the Sierra Morena is the centre of **Jamón Ibério** – the finest but also most expensive ham in the world. Numerous shops sell this traditionally cured delicacy, which you can also try in one of the bars down towards the end of town. The area's main *jamon*-producing village is nearby Jabugo (see Drive ►188). Basically, a distinction is made between the Jamón Serrano that comes from the white domestic pig and Jamón Ibério. The latter is only made from the typically black pasture pigs, an old endemic race on the Iberian peninsula whose breeding and rearing in their natural environment cost far more than for a domestic pig.

Dolores, an impressive medieval church with ornamented tower. Although you can take a "road train" of open-sided carriages (a somewhat out-of-character tourist facility) to the castle and church, or go by car, the steep walk through the older part of town, taking in attractive **Plaza Alta**, is the best option. The near-deserted plaza was the central square of old Aracena before the modern town developed round Plaza Marqués de Aracena below. Located in the old town hall in Plaza Alta is the information centre for the surrounding natural park.

✚ 198 B4
ℹ Tourist Information:
✉ Calle Pozo de la Nieve, Plaza San Pedro (also ticket office for the Gruta de las Maravillas) ☎ 663 93 78 76; www.aracena.es

Parking: There is a car park in Plaza San Pedro at the entrance to the town from the N433. Pay the fee to the attendant.

Gruta de las Maravillas
✉ Off Plaza San Pedro ☎ 959 12 82 06/12 83 55
🕓 Daily 10:30–1:30, 3–6. Guided tours Mon–Fri every hour, Sat, Sun every half hour. Tickets from tourist centre opposite entrance to caves. Tours limited to 35 people at a time; waits of an hour or two at busy periods.
💶 €8.50

INSIDER INFO

- It can feel very **chilly** inside the Gruta de las Maravillas, even on the hottest days; take an extra top layer of clothing.
- If you **don't understand Spanish**, it's best to stay at the back during the guided tour of the caves, and admire the surroundings at leisure. But don't linger too long: the lights in each section switch off automatically.
- A flash photography unit may be stationed at the midway point of the Gruta de las Maravillas – you can buy **photographs** of yourself after the tour. If you don't want your picture taken, be ready to raise your hand to your face.
- Attached to the ticket office of the Gruta de las Maravillas is a small **geology museum**. Unless you have a special interest in geology, give the collection a miss.

At Your Leisure

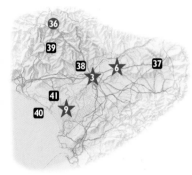

⁊⁊ Écija

Écija's 11 churches, their baroque towers steepled and domed and gleaming with coloured tiles, give the town its dramatic skyline. There is a fine central square, Plaza Mayor or Plaza de España, surrounded by arcades and dotted with palm trees. Écija's remarkable secular buildings include **Palacio de Peñaflor**, the long elegant curve of its balconied façade painted with colourful frescos, and the interior rich with plasterwork and marble. **Palacio de Benamejí** houses the small **Museo Histórico Municipal** providing excellent background to the town's history.

✚ 199 E4
ℹ Tourist Information: ✉ Elvira 1
☎ 955 90 29 33; www.turismoecija.com

Palacio de Peñaflor
✉ Calle Castellar ⊙ currently closed
⚲ Free

Museo Histórico Municipal
✉ Palacio de Benamejí, Plaza de la Constitución 1 ⊙ June–Sep Tue–Fri 10–2:30, Sat 10–2, 8–10, Sun and public hols 10–3, Oct–May Tue–Fri 10–1:30, 4:30–6:30, Sat 10–2, 5:30–8, Sun and public hols 10–3 ⚲ Free

⁊⁊ Itálica

The remains of one of the most important cities of the Roman Empire lie 9km (5.5 mi) north of Seville. Itálica was established in 205 BC alongside the Río Guadalquivir as a port and an administrative centre of Roman Spain. It was the birthplace of the emperors Hadrian and Trajan. In time, the river changed course, Itálica lost its trading links, and the city's artefacts, mosaics and magnificent stonework were plundered. Much of the vast amphitheatre has survived and foundations of villas and streets have been uncovered, along with mosaics, including a Neptune motif and another with 33 species of birds.

✚ 198 C3
✉ Avenida de Extremadura 2, Santiponce
☎ 955 12 38 47
⊙ Sun 10–5, Tue–Sat 9–6:30 (mid-Sep–March), 9–8 (April, May), 9–3:30 (June–mid-Sep)
⚲ €1.50 (free with EU passport)

Écija is dubbed Ciudad de las Torres, the "City of Towers"

The evocative ruins of Itálica, the first Roman town in Spain

39 Río Tinto

Thousands of years of opencast mining have left huge scars on the Río Tinto landscape. Vivid colours – rust red, emerald green and ochre – stain the ground where iron, copper and silver have been mined since Phoenician and Roman times. In the late 19th century the mines were sold to British and German banks; they formed the Río Tinto Mining Company and began to excavate on a massive scale. Today the mines are again under Spanish control, although produc-tion has declined. The village of Minas de Ríotinto is unattractive, but its 🏛 Museo Minero (Mining Museum) tells a dramatic story through its excellent displays on geology, archaeology and social history. You can join a tour taking in underground workings and a huge 330m (1,083ft) deep open-cast pit. Or you can ride through dramatic mining country in a train whose restored carriages are 100 years old. You can find out about train trips and special tours at the museum; phone ahead

Insider Tip

for up-to-date information about timetables.

✚ 198 B4

Museo Minero

✉ Plaza del Museo ☎ 959 59 00 25; www.parquemineroderiotinto.com

🕓 Daily 10:30–3, 4–7 (mid-July–Sep until 8)

🎫 Museum: €4. Mining tours: €8. Train trips: €10. Combined ticket: €17

40 Costa de la Luz (Huelva)

Travel a few kilometres southeast of the estuary of the Río Tinto and Río Odiel, with its factories and refineries, and you reach a largely uninhabited coastline and a beach of golden sand that runs for 25km (15.5mi) between the resorts of Mazagón and Matalascañas. The beach, backed by pine-covered sand dunes, is accessible from only a few places on the coast road, behind which lies the Parque Nacional Coto de Doñana (➤ 160). The most con-venient beach access points are at Mazagón and Matalascañas. Both resorts get very busy in summer, and **Mazagón** may be too close to the estuary mouth for some. A few kilometres southeast of Mazagón is the hotel complex of **Parador Cristóbal Colón** where there is public parking above a popular section of beach. About 8km (5mi) further down the road there is a roadside

---

car park from where you can take a pleasant stroll along a boardwalk, through pine and juniper-covered dunes, to the remote midway point of the **Playa Cuesta de Maneli** 🏷️ Insider Tip beach. At **Matalascañas** the beach is backed by a soulless resort.

✚ 198 B2

41 El Rocío

To the first-time visitor, El Rocío, a village on the western edge of Doñana National Park, resembles a Wild West town. The empty wide streets and broad squares are unsurfaced, and the rows of two-storeyed wooden buildings with

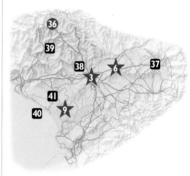

railed verandas add to the im-pression. El Rocío is the centre of an extraordinary pilgrimage, the Romería del Rocío (➤ 23). Each Whitsun, up to half a million *romeros* (pilgrims) from all over Spain and some from other coun-tries descend on the town of El Rocíos and its about 800 remaining residents to pay boisterous homage to Nuestra Señora del Rocío (Our Lady of the Dew), aka La Blanca Paloma (The White Dove), whose revered image is kept in El Rocío's enormous white-painted church. Most of the buildings in El Rocío are owned by *hermandades,* broth-erhoods of devotees, who often stage minor celebrations here on weekends throughout the year.

✚ 198 B3

👶 TIPS FOR KIDS

- **Gruta de las Maravillas** caverns at Aracena (➤ 162)
- The train rides at the **Minas de Ríotinto** (➤ 165)
- **El Castillo de las Guardas Nature Park** (on A476 Río Tinto road from the A66 Seville–Aracena road, tel: 955 95 25 68; daily 10:30–5; €22.50): you can take an 8km (5-mile) tour in your own vehicle of a reserve where you can spot elephants, giraffes and zebras and other exotic species. There is also a popular snake house.

Where to...
Stay

Prices

Expect to pay per double room per night

€ up to €60   €€ €60–€90   €€€ €90–€140   €€€€ over €140

SEVILLE & SURROUNDING AREA

Las Casas de la Judería €€€€

This is one of the prettiest hotels in Seville, tucked down an alleyway on the edge of the Barrio de Santa Cruz, but close to the shops and commercial centre. The individually decorated and appropriately palatial bedrooms are around three classic courtyards, once incorporated into three palaces.

✚ 206 C2
✉ Calle Santa María la Blanca 5, Sevilla
☎ 954 41 51 50; www.casasypalacios.com

Hotel Londres €

This simple but comfortable place is located near the Museo de Bellas Artes and the main shopping district. There are plenty of bars, cafés and restaurants within the vicinity and the cathedral is a mere 10-minute walk away. The rooms here are old fashioned but comfortable and there are some with balconies. Look for the plaque to Manuel Machado (fellow poet and brother of the more famous Antonio) which is across from the door of the hotel.

✚ 206 A4 ✉ San Pedro Mártir 1, El Arenal
☎ 954 21 28 96; www.londreshotel.com

La Hospedería €€

Around 80km (50mi) to the north-east of Seville, the hotel doubles as a Centre for Contemporary Culture; it boasts its own art gallery and displays original artwork in all the rooms. The magnificent stone building is a restored 15th-century Carthusian monastery set in beauti-ful grounds. Just right if you are seeking some out-of-town peace.

✚ 206 A3 ✉ Carretera Cazalla–Constantina A455, Km 2.5, Cazalla de la Sierra, Seville
☎ 954 88 45 16; www.cartujadecazalla.com
◷ Closed 24–26 Dec

Hostería del Laurel €€   *Insider Tip*

This 21-room hotel is in an unbeatable position, on a small tree-lined square in the heart of the Barrio de Santa Cruz. It is better known for its *bodega*, which is mentioned in Zorilla's 19th-century play *Don Juan Tenorio*, as well as for the adjoining restaurant. The rooms, spread between two floors, are spotlessly clean and simply furnished.

✚ 206 C2
✉ Plaza de los Venerables 5, Seville
☎ 954 22 02 95; www.hosteriadellaurel.com

Hotel Alfonso XIII €€€€

Seriously luxurious at prices to match, this five-storey rococo building was built during the 1929 Expo in the *mudéjar*/Andalucían revival style. Even if you can't afford to stay a night, sip a sherry overlooking the plant-filled central patio, surrounded by antique furniture, hand-painted tiles, crystal chandeliers and acres of marble and mahogany. The rooms are predictably sumptuous and the service professional and efficient. This is where the members of the Spanish royal family stay when they visit Seville.

✚ 206 B1 ✉ San Fernando 2, Seville
☎ 954 91 70 00;
www.hotel-alfonsoxiii-sevilla.com

CARMONA

El Comercio €

This *pension* is incorporated into the ancient city walls at the Puerta de Sevilla. There are no mod cons, but the pretty central patio is the perfect place to relax away from the noise of the street. The rooms are simple with comfortable beds, and guests always get a good welcome.

✚ 199 D3 ✉ Calle Torre del Oro 56
☎ 954 14 00 18

Parador de Carmona €€€€

A stunning clifftop location, with sweeping views across the flat plain of the River Corbones. The public rooms surround a central Moorish-style patio, and the bedrooms are large and luxuriously furnished; all look out either onto the inner court-yard or the valley. If you can't afford a room, have a drink at the bar or check out the excellent restaurant (➤ 170).

✚ 199 D3 ✉ Alcázar s/n
☎ 954 14 10 10; www.parador.es

ARACENA

Los Castaños €€

Los Castaños is just a few minutes' walk from the caves, and has plenty of shops, restaurants and bars on the doorstep. The rooms are modern and spacious with balconies. The best view is from the dining room.

✚ 198 B4 ✉ Avenida Huelva 5
☎ 959 12 63 00; www.loscastanoshotel.com

Insider Tip

👥 Finca Valbono €€€

In a nature reserve surrounded by rolling hills, and with a choice of self-contained cabins or hotel rooms, Finca Valbono is the perfect place for a family to stay. There are horse-riding facilities, as well as a large pool and wonderful walks. The restaurant specialises in cordon bleu cuisine with a few down-to-earth choices for children.

✚ 199 B4 ✉ Carretera de Carboneras, Km 1
☎ 959 12 77 11; www.fincavalbono.com

Where to...
Eat and
Drink

SEVILLE

Taberna del Alabardero €€€

This elegant restaurant, located in a magnificent townhouse not far from the La Maestranza bullring is a culinary landmark. Market-fresh seasonal dishes are served in the grand, tile-decorated interior. The menu of the day is good and not expensive.

✚ 206 B3
✉ Zaragoza 20
☎ 954 50 27 21; www.tabernadelalabardero.es
🕐 Daily1:30–4:30, 8:30–midnight. Closed Aug

Casa Robles €€

On a pretty cobbled street near Calle Sierpes, this traditional restaurant specialises in seafood with more than a dozen types of shellfish served daily. Juan Robles conjures up the dishes in the kitchen of his family business, founded in 1954. There are three small dining rooms and a *tapas* bar serving all the usual favourites, plus some interesting *revuelto* (scrambled egg) combinations.

✚ 206 B2
✉ Calle Álvarez Quintero 58
☎ 954 21 31 50; www.casa-robles.com
🕐 Daily 1–4:30, 8–1. Closed 24 Dec for dinner

Habanita €€

Insider Tip

Habanita, one of Seville's few vegetarian restaurants, is tucked down a side street in the buzzing Alfalfa *barrio*, within easy walking distance north of the city centre. The reasonable prices here attract students and travellers alike and the menu is vast, with an emphasis on Cuban and Mediterranean dishes. There are some real one-offs like yucca with garlic, plus black beans, tamales and strict vegan fare. They are not too pious to serve alcohol and sugar-laden desserts though!

🔂 206 C3 ⊠ Calle Golfo 3
☎ 606 71 64 56 (mobile); www.habanita.es
🕚 Mon–Sat noon–4:30, 8:30–late

El Corral del Agua €€

In one of the prettiest situations in the heart of the Barrio de Santa Cruz, this restaurant is housed in a former 18th-century palace and has a lovely patio filled with brilliant red geraniums. The food here is traditional and reliably good with dishes including squid in garlic and honey-glazed lamb featuring on the menu.

🔂 206 C2 ⊠ Callejón del Agua 6
☎ 954 22 48 41; www.corraldelagua.es
🕚 Closed Sun and Jan–Feb

Patio San Eloy €

In this famous bar there's enough tilework for a mini *alcázar*, with *azulejo* steps providing additional seating. Popular with students, shoppers and business people alike, the *tapas* menu includes a vast range of multi-tiered sand-wiches with interesting fillings plus the usual *tortilla* (omelette), *jamón* and olives, best washed down with an ice-cold *fino* direct from the barrel.

🔂 206 B3 ⊠ San Eloy 9e
☎ 954 50 10 70 🕚 Daily 11:30–11:30

Pizzería San Marco €€

Not your usual fast-food Italian, this one is housed in an authentic Muslim bathhouse, giving it a great atmosphere – rather like sitting inside your own private mosque. The menu has a good range of typical pizza and pasta dishes, and the place is usually packed. Enjoy a glass of house Rioja while you wait at San Marco's very own Harry's Bar, not quite as grand as the prototype in Venice, but fun.

🔂 206 C2 ⊠ Calle Mesón del Moro 6
☎ 954 21 43 90; www.sanmarco.es
🕚 Tue–Sun 1:30–4:30, 8:30–12:30

Restaurant La Cueva €€

This restaurant is a picture-postcard sort of place, with a cool green patio for dining al fresco. Ochre walls, cobbles and columns com-plete the look, while the indoor dining room is hung with all the matador paraphernalia – including the bull (his stuffed head, that is). The food here is surprisingly rea-sonable, including the three-course *menú del día*, and the dishes are solidly Andaluz with a selection of good fish choices and an above-average paella.

🔂 206 C2 ⊠ Rodrigo Caro 18
☎ 954 21 31 43
🕚 Tue–Sat 12:30–3:30, 7:30–11:30

CARMONA

Molino de la Romera €€/€€€

This 15th-century mill has retained much of its original character with ancient cobbled floors, arches and patio. The bar does a brisk evening trade in drinks and *tapas* for a predominantly student crowd, while the restaurant has a typical Andalucían menu with *gazpacho*, salads and soups, *tortilla*, fried fish, grilled meat and various seafood dishes. For something more formal, there is also a fabulous *mesón* (period-décor restaurant), open at weekends only, located in an evocative, church-like space with its own bar and fireplace.

🔂 199 D3 ⊠ Sor Ángela de la Cruz 8
☎ 954 14 20 00; www.molinodelaromera.com
🕚 Bar: Mon–Fri 1–11. Restaurant: Mon–Fri 7:30–11pm. Closed 24 and 31 Dec

Insider Tip

Restaurante Parador de Carmona €€€

A former Moorish fortress provides a superb setting, and the dining room with its vaulted ceiling, chandeliers and clifftop views makes this restaurant a winner for special occasions. The menu is select with an emphasis on game, particularly partridge and venison; the house wine is excellent and a reasonable price.

🚹 199 D3 ✉ Calle Alcázar s/n
☎ 954 14 10 10; www.parador.es
🕐 1:30–4, 8:30–11. Closed July and 24 Dec

ARACENA

Restaurante Casas €€

There's not much wall space left at this typical Sierra Morena restaurant specialising in the region's famous ham and pork. A mixture of mirrors, plates, religious pictures, and various pots and pans are the backdrop to the cosy beamed dining room. The food represents honest, home-style cooking at its best – although the choice is rather limited – with dishes prepared according to what is in season.

🚹 198 B4 ✉ Calle del Pozo de la Nieve
☎ 959 12 80 44; www.restaurantecasas.es
🕐 Daily noon–5

Montecruz €€

Hams hang above the bar in this colourful, bright bar/restaurant. There's a stunning view of the castle from the formal dining room upstairs, which is packed out with Spanish families at weekends. The décor is upbeat with colourful tiles, blue and yellow paintwork and pine furnishings; you can eat on an outdoor terrace in summer. Starters include such local specialities such as *migas* (fried breadcrumbs) with sardines, and spinach and chickpeas, available in either *tapa* or *ración* portions.

🚹 198 B4 ✉ Plaza de San Pedro
☎ 959 12 60 13; www.restaurantemontecruz.com
🕐 Daily 10–4, 9–11:30

Where to...
Shop

The city of Seville encourages chic fashion, but there are top-quality gift and jewellery shops too, as well as shops specialising in ceramics and traditional crafts. Huelva cannot match Seville for general shopping, but you can buy some of the finest jamón serrano and other food products that you'll ever taste.

SEVILLE CITY

Seville's main shopping area lies between the bustling Plaza Nueva (► 156) and adjacent Plaza de San Francisco (► 156) and, to their north, the Plaza del Duque de la Victoria. Central to it all is the pedestrianised **Calle Sierpes** (► 156) which, together with its neighbouring streets of Velázquez, Tetuán, Méndez Nuñez and their interconnecting alleyways, has a vast range of shops selling clothes, shoes, leatherwear, children's wear and ceramics.

For the ultimate in style, **Max Mara** (Plaza Nueva 3, tel: 954 21 48 25) has up-to-the-minute fashions, as does top Spanish style house **Zara** (Plaza del Duque de la Victoria, tel: 954 21 48 75). For American fashion try **Nicole Miller** (Albareda 16, tel: 954 56 36 14), and for Spanish with a touch of Italian couture there's **Vittoria & Lucchino** (Calle Sierpes, tel: 954 22 79 51).

For something quintessentially Spanish, Sierpes has a number of splendid shops selling flamenco scarves and veils, shawls and shoes, including **Molina** (Sierpes 11, tel: 954 22 92 54) and **María Rosa** (Calle Cuna 13, tel: 954 22 24 87) on parallel Calle Cuna.

Away from Sierpes, try **Artesanía Textil** (García de Vinuesa, tel: 954 56 28 40), just east of the cathedral, where you can buy place mats, wall hangings and tablecloths in the finest Andalucían styles. And check out **Sombrería Maquedano** (Sierpes 40, tel: 954 56 47 71) for stylish hats and impeccable service.

For jewellery of the highest quality, try **Joyería Abrines** (Calle Sierpes 47, tel: 954 22 84 55) and **Casa Ruiz** (O'Donnell 14, tel: 954 22 21 37 and Sierpes 68, tel: 954 22 77 80).

Near the north end of Sierpes is a branch of the department store **El Corte Inglés** (Plaza del Duque de la Victoria). For something less mainstream, have a look round the **jewellery and clothes market**, staged every Thursday, Friday and Saturday in Plaza del Duque de la Victoria itself. And to see what gets Sevillanos really excited as the Feria de Abril (➤ 22) approaches, look into **Arcab** (Paseo de Cristóbal Colón 8, tel: 954 56 14 11) for all things equestrian.

La Campaña (tel: 954 22 35 70), at the north end of Calle Sierpes, has a superb selection of cakes and pastries.

Horno San Buenaventura (Avenida de la Constitución/Calle G Vinuesa, tel: 954 22 18 19), directly opposite the cathedral, has a café-restaurant with a mouth-watering selection of sweets, chocolates, ice-cream, cakes and pastries.

Other good shopping areas include the narrow Calle Hernando Colón that leads from Alemanes, opposite the main entrance to the cathedral, to Plaza de San Francisco, and is packed with gift, clothes and souvenir shops.

In Barrio de Santa Cruz (➤ 152), in with the souvenir shops are some classy shops. One such is **Agua de Sevilla** (Rodrigo Caro 16, tel: 954 21 06 54), a very stylish perfumery and accessories shop near the Reales Alcázares (➤ 150),

where you can buy exquisite jasmine-scented cologne.

For ceramics try **Martian Ceramics** (Calle Sierpes 74, tel: 954 21 34 13), **El Postigo** (Arfe, tel: 954 56 00 13), **Cerámicas Antonio del Rey** (Feria 15), or across the river in the Triana district, **Azulejos Santa Isabel** (Alfarería 12, tel: 954 33 36 18).

CARMONA

For excellent pottery look in Taller de Cerámica at **María Jurado Pérez** (Urb. El Socorro 229; www.mariajurado.es). For typical rural goods, visit Carmona's morning **market** just off Calle Domínguez de Aposanto.

HUELVA PROVINCE

The shopping paradise of Huelva can be found in the multiple-storey **Centro Comercial Aqualón**. You can enjoy a lovely view of the river from the top floor (Glorieta Norte; www.ccaqualon.com). The choice includes a wide range of shops, cinemas, restaurants and bars.

Aracena's **Jamones y Embutidos Ibéricos, La Trastienda** (Plaza San Pedro 2, tel: 959 12 71 58) sells all manner of cured and cooked meats, but the widest (though priciest) choice is in the village of **Jabugo** (➤ 188).

Enticing selections of *jamón*, *chorizo* (spicy sausage) and *salchichón* (salami) are all on sale at top outlets such as **La Cañada de Jabugo** (Carretera San Juan del Puerto-Cáceres 2, tel: 959 12 12 07).

Down on Huelva's Costa de la Luz there are few out-of-the-ordinary shopping options, but the main information centre of the Parque Nacional de Doñana, the **Centro de Recepción del Acebuche** (➤ 161), has a useful gift shop that sells craftwork from the area.

Where to...
Go Out

Seville's monthly listings magazine *El Giraldillo* (www.elegirhoy.com) can be bought at kiosks, or is sometimes available free at tourist offices, as is the magazine Sevilla Welcome & Olé.

NIGHTLIFE

There are plenty of music bars in the Plaza de la Alfalfa area, a few streets east of Calle Sierpes. On the west bank of the Río Guadalquivir is Calle del Betis where there are a number of lively music bars fronting the Triana district.

FLAMENCO

Seville is big on flamenco and there are any number of "spontaneous" venues. There are also some fairly phoney shows, but a good compromise is **El Arenal** (Calle Rodo 7, tel: 954 21 64 92), a long-established venue with twice-nightly *tablaos* (➤ 21) and optional dinner.

At the heart of the Barrio de Santa Cruz (➤ 152) are **Los Gallos** (Plaza de Santa Cruz 11, tel: 954 21 69 81) and **El Tamboril** (Plaza de Santa Cruz).

The popular **La Carbonería** (Calle Levíes 18, tel: 954 21 44 60) often has flamenco on Thursday and Monday nights, and at other times, but rarely before 10pm. Calle Levíes is reached off Calle San José, which is a few streets northeast of Calle Mateos Gago in Barrio de Santa Cruz.

THEATRE

Seville's **Teatro de la Maestranza** (Paseo de Cristóbal Colón 22,

tel: 954 22 33 44; www.teatro delamaestranza.es), near the bullring, stages outstanding productions of opera, classical music and jazz. **Teatro Lope de Vega** (Avenida María Luisa, tel: 954 47 28 28) also puts on a programme of theatre, music and dance.

BULLFIGHTING

At Seville's magnificent 18th-century bullring, **La Maestranza** (Paseo de Cristóbal Colón, tel: 954 22 45 77), top *corridas* are always packed out, and to get a ticket, even for the sunny side, you need to book well ahead.

The season runs from Easter Sunday to October, with big names fighting during June and July and novices taking up the rest of the calendar. Fights are on Sunday evenings and on every evening during the Feria de Abril (➤ 24). It is always best to try to buy tickets direct from the box office at the ring.

OUTDOOR ACTIVITIES

The Aracena area of the **Sierra Morena** has numerous opportunities for walking and it's worth checking at Aracena's tourist office for information on guided walks and cycle trips. They can usually provide maps of the trails.

On Huelva's Costa de la Luz (➤ 166) there are opportunities within **Coto de Doñana National Park** (➤ 160) for more intensive birdwatching trips.

You can also take part in a car tour of the park (contact the Centro de Recepción del Acebuche, tel: 959 43 04 32).

Equestrian fans can even birdwatch from horseback on day-long rides through the Doñana marshland (contact **Doñana Ecuestre**, El Rocío, tel: 674 21 95 68; www.donanaecuestre.com). Don't forget the insect repellent!

Walks & Tours

1 GRANADA'S ALBAICÍN
Walk

DISTANCE 3km (2mi)
TIME 2–3 hours
START/END POINT Plaza Nueva ✚ 204 C2

Granada's picturesque old Moorish quarter, the Albaicín, is explored on this circular walk that offers stunning views of the Alhambra and the Sierra Nevada on the way. The route climbs the Albaicín hill along narrow alleyways, past historic churches and through the bustling heart of the quarter to the magnificent viewpoint of the Mirador de San Nicolás.

❶–❷

From Plaza Nueva walk through Plaza Santa Ana past a church, the Iglesia de Santa Ana y San Gil, and along the narrow Carrera del Darro, keeping a close lookout for traffic. Down on your right the minuscule Río Darro filters its way through water weed. As you walk along the street you pass first the old Moorish bridge, the Puente de Cabrera, and then the Puente de Espinosa, both rising at an angle as they span the river. From here you can see the walls of the Alhambra looming high above. On the opposite bank of the stream, just beyond the second bridge, are the ruins of an 11th-century gateway, the Puerta de los Tableros, and of an old bridge, the Puente del Cadí. Look left for the alleyway called Bañuelo with, just left of the entrance, the 11th-century **Baños Árabes** (▶89).

❷–❸

Continue along Carrera del Darro, passing the **Convento de Santa Catalina de Zafra** (open daily)

where you can buy delicious almond cakes from the nuns, **Insider Tip** and the **Museo Arqueológico** (▶89) on your left. Keep on past the wide terrace of Paseo del Padre Manjón, known also as Paseo de los Tristes because priests once publicly prayed here; today it is crammed with café tables served from the long line of bars along the street front. The Alhambra towers above.

❸–❹

Just past the Café Bar La Fuente, turn left up narrow, pebbled Calle Horno del Oro. Go up steps at the top of the alley, then

turn right up some more steps. Cross a lane and continue up roughly pebbled Calle Valenzuela.

The inner courtyard of the Alhambra

4–5

Follow the lane round to the right and keep on, past a junction on the left. Pass the Aljibe de Bibalbonud, a brick-built Moorish well, and Convento Santo Tomasas de Villanueva. Continue through the tree-lined Placeta del Abad and go alongside the wall of the church of **San Salvador**. Turn left to reach the entrance to the church. The church was built on the site of a 13th-century mosque, and the original patio, complete with arcades and pointed horseshoe arches, still survives.

5–6

Leave the church and turn left, and then left again into Calle Panaderos. Pass another old well, the Aljibe de Polo, and continue past small local shops and characterful bars to reach pleasant, tree-shaded Plaza Larga, lined with more bars and shops and filled with fruit and flower stalls in the mornings. Cross the plaza to its opposite corner and go under the **Puerta de la Pesas** (Gate of the Weights), an arched gateway in the old walls of the Albaicín's original Moorish castle, its Alcazaba.

6–7

Beyond the arch, climb some steps into Placeta de las Minas, turn left along Callejón San Cecilio

At its top go up more steps, bear left, then turn right at a junction. In 20m (22yd) go sharply left, then uphill and round to the right. At a junction with Carril de San Agustín, go sharply left and up the pebbled lane. There are fine views of the Alhambra to your left.

Reinvigorating for tired hikers: a break in the Arab baths

and follow the lane round right to reach Plaza del Cementerio de San Nicolás and the 16th-century church, Iglesia San Nicolás. To the right of the church is a Moorish cistern, its faucets still spouting water. Immediately in front of the church is the **Mirador de San Nicolás**, Granada's most famous viewpoint. Keep a strong grip on your belongings here.

7–8

Go down the right-hand side of the Mirador, keep downhill, then go right along Nuevo de San Nicolás. At a crossing, turn left onto narrow Cuesta María de la Miel, then at a T-junction turn right along Algibe del Gato. In a few metres, go down left and then round right and into **Placeta Nevot**. On the right-hand side of the square is an Arabic-style building with a fine arched doorway.

8–9

Keep going downhill and on through **Placeta de la Cruz Verde** (from where you'll get a fleeting glimpse of the

Alhambra). Continue down San Gregorio, then along Calderería Nueva passing Granada's fast-growing modern "Arab quarter", with its Islamic food shops, tea houses and craft galleries. Reach a T-junction with Calle de Elvira, and turn left to return to Plaza Nueva.

TAKING A BREAK

In Plaza del Cementerio de San Nicolás just before the Mirador de San Nicolás are two bar-restaurants with outside seating, **Café-Bar El Mirador** and **Café-Bar Kiki San Nicolás**.

WHEN?

Mid-morning is a good time for this walk. The area is full of the morning sun and the plazas and busier streets are full of life.

PLACES TO VISIT

Iglesia de San Salvador

🕐 Mon–Sat 10–1, 4–6:30

2 HIDDEN CORNERS OF CÓRDOBA
Walk

DISTANCE 4km (2.5mi)
TIME 2–3 hours
START/END POINT The Mezquita ✚ 203 D3

Escape from the crowds round the Mezquita by heading off to explore a Córdoba where there are no souvenir shops but instead fascinating old buildings, hidden corners, and engaging local bars and cafés.

❶–❷

Start outside the north corner of the Mezquita where Magistral González Francés meets the narrow Calle Encarnación. Go up Encarnación passing the patio entrance to **Meryan**, one of Córdoba's finest leathercraft shops. At a T-junction alongside the Iglesia de la Encarnación turn right down Calle del Rey Heredia. Embedded in the corner of the church is a Roman column, one of numerous relics of pre-Muslim Córdoba found all over the city. In 20m (22yd), turn left along Horno del Cristo, then bear left into Plaza Jerónimo Paez. Beyond the square's screens of palm trees, cypresses and orange trees stands the ornate Renaissance façade of the **Museo Arqueológico** (➤ 120).

❷–❸

Follow narrow Marqués del Villar to the right of the museum. The street twists to left and right, and leads past a splendid baroque entranceway with spiral columns and a studded door. At a T-junction, turn right down Ambrosio de Morales to reach **Plaza Seneca** with its broken statue and Roman capitals, reminders of one of Córdoba's famous sons, the philosopher Seneca the Elder, born there in 55 BC. Here too is the **Taberna Sociedad Plateros** bar, one of several bars owned by the city's venerable Society of Silverworkers. The bar's beamed ceiling is supported by old stone columns.

❸–❹

Carry on in the same direction along San Eulogio and Calle

Insider Tip

Moorish building on Roman foundations: Córdoba's Puente Romano

Walks & Tours

Cabezas past Hostal Portillo, named after the **Arco de Portillo**, a Moorish gateway seen down to the left. Just beyond yet another Roman column incorporated into a wall is the imposing, though decaying façade of a Renaissance palace, **Casa de los Marqueses del Carpio**. A few paces further

house adjoining los Arquillos, and displayed the brothers' severed heads above the archway.

Continue to a junction and turn left down Caldereros. Keep ahead through Plaza de la Pescadería past its central palm tree, then continue to a T-junction with Calle de San Fernando.

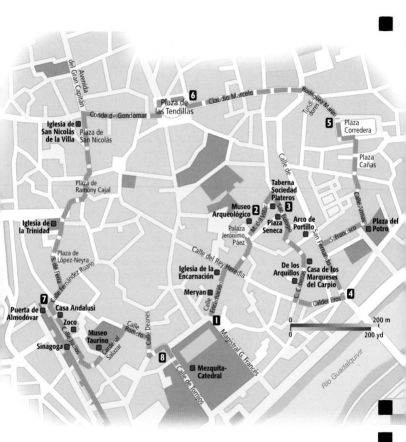

on is a narrow gated alleyway called **De los Arquillos**. On the wall to its left a plaque relates the harsh story of how a 10th-century knight took revenge for insults made to his bride by seven noble brothers. He had the seven killed, imprisoned their father in the

4–5

Turn left up Calle de San Fernando. Cross over and in a few paces go right and along Calle San Francisco past a junction (**Plaza del Potro**, ► 120, is down to the right) and bear round left along Calle Armas. At a junction keep along Calle

Sanchez Peña and through Plaza Canas to reach the Plaza Corredera. This 17th-century creation, rather over restored in recent years, has been the scene of *autos da fé* during the Inquisition, bullfights, festivals, and latterly rock concerts.

🔢–🔢

Leave the square by its far left-hand corner and go up Rodríguez Marín. At its top, cross the busy junction of Tundidores and Capitulares and keep ahead along Claudio Marcelo. On the right side of the road stands a cluster of reconstructed columns of a 1st-century Roman temple. Continue into **Plaza de las Tendillas** with its flamenco-chiming clock (► 121).

🔢–🔢

Cross Plaza de las Tendillas and go down the shopping street of Conde de Gondomar to the right of the flamenco clock tower. Reach the top of the broad Avenida del Gran Capitán and the **Iglesia de San Nicolás de la Villa**. This is one of Córdoba's finest churches, notable for its handsome bell tower. Turn left down San Felipe, to the left of the church. Pass through Plaza de San Nicolás to reach Plaza de Ramón y Cajal. Bear round right into Tesoro and reach Plaza Trinidad and the **Iglesia de la Trinidad**, which has magnificent gilded altarpieces set off by pristine white walls and roof. In front of the church is a statue of the 16th-century Cordoban poet Luis de Góngora. Cross in front of the church and continue down Sánchez de Feria, passing the little Plaza Profesor López-Neyra.

Turn right at a junction and go along Calle Fernández Ruano, with a great collection of *tapas* bars, to reach **Puerta de Almodóvar** (► 120).

🔢–🔢

Return through Puerta de Almodóvar, then go right down Calle Judíos. On the left, a short way down the street, is the splendid bar Bodega Guzmán, A short way down the street is the splendid **Casa El Malacara**, a local favourite. Just past here is **Casa Andalusí** an unusual museum in which the patios and rooms are furnished as they would have been in the 12th century; in the cellar are Visigothic reliefs and a fine Roman mosaic. Further down the street you pass the **Zoco** craft market, the **synagogue** and the **Maimonides statue** (all ► 119). Reach Plaza Maimónides and turn left past the **Museo Taurino** (► 119). Keep ahead along the narrow alleyway of Cardenal Salazar to reach Plaza del Cardenal Salazar, which is overlooked by the monumental doorway of the Facultado de Filosofía y Letras. Turn right out of the plaza and into crowded Calle Romero. Turn right at the next junction into Calle Deanes, then bear left, past a traffic barrier of little posts, to go along Judería to the Mezquita.

Insider Tip

TAKING A BREAK

There are numerous bars and cafés along the way. The **Taberna Sociedad Plateros** (Calle San Francisco 6) is popular and has a splendid covered patio. **Bodega Guzman** (Calle Judios 7) is definitely worth a stop, even if its superb wines persuade you to abandon the rest of the walk.

WHEN?

Mid-morning, or early evening if you want to tie in the walk with visits to the Museo Arqueológico and to the other attractions in the Calle Judíos area.

PLACES TO VISIT

Casa No 12 Andalusí
✉ Casa No 12 Calle Judíos
🕐 Daily 10–7

3

SIERRA DE GRAZALEMA
Tour

DISTANCE 80km (50mi)
TIME 4–5 hours
START/END POINT Grazalema ✚ 199 D2

The pueblos blancos, the "white towns" of Málaga and Cádiz provinces, are in reality small mountain villages of whitewashed houses set amid the spectacular mountains of the Parque Natural Sierra de Grazalema. This tour takes you to some of the finest.

1–2
Leave **Grazalema**, sheltering beneath the rocky peak of Peñón Grande, by the Ronda road and keep ahead at a junction, following signs for Ronda and Ubrique. The road winds uphill beneath huge overhanging cliffs. At a

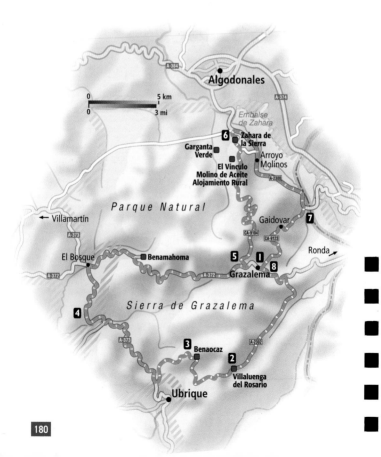

junction, keep ahead along the A374, signed Ubrique. Follow the road beneath the impressive rocky crags of the Sierra del Caillo and pass **Villaluenga del Rosario**, the highest village in Cádiz province.

2–3

Continue through a flat-bottomed valley where rocky slopes rise to either side and stone walls wriggle along the base of the cliffs. The valley is known as La Manga (The Sleeve). Soon, the road bends sharply to the right just after a picnic spot and viewpoint. In about 1km (0.5mi) turn off right at a junction, signed **Benaocaz**, and enter the village. There is parking for a few cars in Plaza de Vista Hermosa on the outskirts. The village, an 8th-century Moorish settlement, is a typical *pueblo blanco*, with whitewashed houses clustered on the hillside against a background of limestone crags and wooded slopes. Encircling the main square, Plaza de las Libertades, are pillars with small ceramic tiles picturing local landmarks.

3–4

From Plaza de Vista Hermosa, keep left down Calle Lavadero and on through Plaza de las Libertades. Turn left down Calle San Blas, then at the main road turn right, signed A373 Villamartín. In 3km (2mi) turn right at a junction. The large town of **Ubrique** lies down to the left below the dramatic cliffs of Cruz de Tajo. Continue along the wider and faster A373 for 8km (5mi).

4–5

Watch for signposts for El Bosque and for a junction on the right, signed Benamahoma and Grazalema. Bear right here, then keep right at the next junction on to the A372, signed Benamahoma, Ronda and Grazalema. The road now climbs towards the Sierra del Pinar, passing above **Benamahoma**,

another attractive *pueblo blanco*. It celebrates its Moorish heritage with a colourful festival that includes mock battles between "Moors and Christians" on the first Sunday of August. Continue along the A372 with views of limestone crags on your right. In 8km (5mi) turn left, signed Zahara de la Sierra.

5–6

You now enter a beautiful area of mountains swathed in cork oak and holm oak and large numbers of pinsapo pines, a conifer that has had a tenuous continuity since the last European Ice Age but which now flourishes in the Parque Natural Sierra de Grazalema. The road climbs steadily through a spectacular series of S-bends to reach the Puerto de Palomas (Pass of the Doves) at 1,357m (4,452ft), from where it descends through more S-bends. About 4km (2.5mi) below the pass, there is a car park

THE GARGANTA VERDE

If you have 2–3 hours to spare, a walk into this magnificent area of the Sierra is immensely rewarding. However, you need a permit from the information offices at El Bosque or Grazalema (► 66). The path to and from the roadside car park is well signposted and takes you high above the deep gorge of the Garganta Verde. Just before the path begins its descent into the bed of the gorge, divert up a steep, signposted path to the spectacular **Las Buitreras de Garganta Verde**, a viewpoint into the upper gorge and to the huge cliffs that are the roosting and nesting site of dozens of griffon vultures. Be patient and quiet and you should be rewarded by the sight of these magnificent birds with a 3m (10ft) wingspan cruising past. The main path takes you down into the stony bed of the gorge which leads to the great cavern of the **Garganta de la Ermita** with its multicoloured rock formations.

Walks & Tours

on the left from where a path leads for several kilometres to the spectacular Garganta Verde ravine (► 181). Continue towards Zahara de la Sierra and soon pass an olive oil production centre, **El Vínculo Molino de Aceite Alojamiento Rural**, which is open for visits during normal working hours (► 74). In a further 4km (2.5mi), reach the village of Zahara de la Sierra.

6–7

Enter **Zahara de la Sierra** by a winding uphill road. There are parking spaces just before you reach the narrow entrance to the village and it is advisable to park here, or further downhill. Zahara, one of the loveliest of the *pueblos blancos*, was declared a national monument in the 1980s. The village clings to a rocky hill crowned by a 12th-century castle. Its narrow main street leads to a central plaza overlooked by the baroque church of Santa María de Mesa and with a *mirador* giving fine views of the reservoir, the Embalse de Zahara, below. The castle is reached from the square by a rocky path; the views from its battlements are well worth the effort. Leave Zahara along the main street. At the central plaza keep right, and then left, round a tiny roundabout, before following exit signs down very steep and narrow streets. On reaching the one-way approach road that you came up earlier, go sharply right and down a short side road to a T-junction with the main road. Turn right, signed Grazalema, and at the next junction turn left onto a road signed Arroyo Molinos. At the next T-junction turn right, signed Arroyo Molinos, and follow the road above the reservoir.

7–8

Just past where the reservoir ends, turn right, signed Grazalema, and continue through wooded mountains to reach a T-junction. Turn right to return to Grazalema.

The restored 12th-century Moorish castle dominates the village of Zahara de la Sierra

4 POTTERY VILLAGES & COWBOY COUNTRY
Tour

DISTANCE 100km (62mi)
TIME 3 hours (longer if time is spent at Níjar and Mini Hollywood)
START/END POINT Almería ✚ 201 E2

First stop on this tour is the village of Níjar, one of Andalucía's most important pottery-making centres. From here the route continues through remote mountains and into Almería's astonishing desert canyons. This is where film-makers produced a string of "spaghetti westerns", including *A Fistful of Dollars*, and where the Wild West lives on in the theme parks.

❶–❷
Drive east out of Almería from the big roundabout at the bottom of the Rambla de Belén, following signs for Murcia and Mojácar. In 17km (10.5mi) join the A7. Once clear of Almería's outskirts and beyond its airport, you approach the world of *plasticultura*, the intensive production of fruit and vegetables inside

The arid landscapes around Tabernas exude the romantic flair of the Wild West

plastic greenhouses (➤ 184). Behind the plains of the Campo de Níjar rise the mountains of the Sierra de Alhamilla. In 30km (19mi) turn off left, signed Níjar, and, in a few kilometres, enter **Níjar** (➤ 101) by its main street, Avenida García Lorca, where there are numerous parking bays. Níjar's ceramics industry has flourished since

TAKING A BREAK
In the pretty main square of the old part of Níjar are the **Café Bar La Glorieta** and the **Bar Restaurant El Pipa**. There is also a café, bar and restaurant at Mini Hollywood.

Walks & Tours

Moorish times and there are numerous craft shops along Avenida García Lorca and the adjoining Barrio Alfarero. While in Níjar stop off in Plaza la Glorieta, the main square of the upper town, reached by continuing uphill from the top of Avenida García Lorca. The 16th-century church of Santa María de la Anunciación, which overlooks the square, has a fine *mudéjar* coffered ceiling in the central nave.

2–3

Leave Níjar by returning down Avenida García Lorca, and then turning left at the T-junction, signed Campohermosa and Murcia. At the next T-junction turn left, signed Lucainena, AL103, and drive uphill. Stop at the next junction before turning right, signed Lucainena. (The signpost indicating Lucainena on the corner opposite may be obscured by a tree.) Continue into the heart of the hills of the **Sierra de Alhamilla** where you

soon reach uninhabited country, a dry mountain landscape made appealing by its numerous oak trees and low scrub. From high above Níjar you can see the expanse of the plastic *invernaderos* that cover the plain of the Campo de Níjar below. Watch out for potholes in the road ahead. About 16km (10mi) from Níjar, the road descends from the hills to the village of **Lucainena de las Torres**, where whitewashed houses surround a pretty church beneath the soaring crags of the Peñón de Turrillas. Continue for 9km (5.5mi) finally descending a long, straight stretch of road lined with eucalyptus trees to a junction with the N-340a.

3–4

You have the option of turning right here to reach the village of Sorbas in 8km (5mi). **Sorbas** (➤ 103) is perched dramatically on the cliff edges of a rugged gorge. Its tradition of ceramics is similar to that of Níjar, but Sorbas pottery is more functional and less decorative. The limestone cave complex **Cuevas de Sorbas** (tours available, ➤ 103) is about 2km (1.25mi) southeast of the village. On the main route, turn left at the junction with the N-340a, signed Almería. Continue for 17km

Mini Hollywood, west of Tabernas, is the best known of the Wild West theme parks

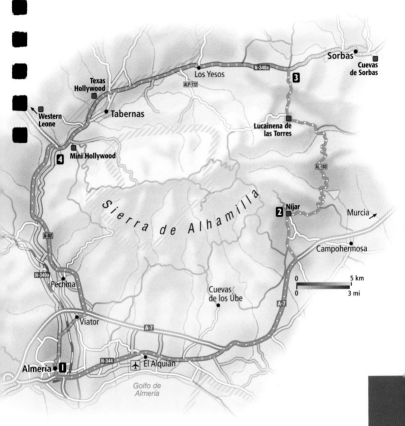

(10.5mi) through country that becomes increasingly arid and desert-like, its grey-brown sandstone hills barren of vegetation and sculpted into fantastic shapes by the wind. The road bypasses **Tabernas**, overlooked by a Moorish castle which may look impressive, but is disappointingly ruinous. You are now in the land of Wild West theme parks, the legacy of decades of film-making during the mid-20th century when the surrounding landscapes were used to replicate the cowboy country of North America. The first of three Wild West attractions is **Texas Hollywood**, reached down a dirt track. There's a dusty cowboy town, complete with a cavalry fort and

Native American wigwam village. Mock gunfights are staged at set times and you can hire horses and dress up in cowboy gear. The best organised (and most expensive) is **Mini Hollywood** (➤ 103), about 6km (4mi) west of Tabernas. About 1km (0.5mi) further on, the N-340a joins the recently constructed Granada–Almería Autovía. Turn right to reach the approach track to a third cowboy "town", named **Western Leone** after Sergio Leone, the maker of *A Fistful of Dollars* and *The Good, the Bad and the Ugly*. The cheapest of the Western attractions, this has the most authentic setting, above a dry gulch. To return to Almería, head south on the *autovía*.

185

SIERRA DE ARACENA

5 *Tour*

DISTANCE 60km (37mi)
TIME 2–3 hours (longer if stops are made at villages and points of interest along the way)
Start/End Point Aracena ✚ 198 B4

The Sierra de Aracena is a world of wooded hills traversed by roads that wind lazily between delightful villages where cobbled streets spill down to a central plaza, its fountain brimming with crystal-clear water even in high summer.

❶–❷

Leave Aracena by Plaza San Pedro, just beyond the car park, and take the road leading south-west, signed Alájar. Drive down an avenue lined with plane trees. Keep ahead at the next junction,

signed Alájar, and immediately enter the beautiful hill country of the **Sierra de la Virgen**.

You need old-fashioned driving skills here: there are lots of gear changes as the road, the A470, twists and turns through woods of chestnut, ash and oak. Soon you catch glimpses of the tiny village of **Linares de la Sierra**, in the valley below. The village is worth a short diversion. Park on the road above Linares and stroll downhill to the main square; every household has an individual

View of Almonaster la Real framed by the spring colours of Sierra de Aracena

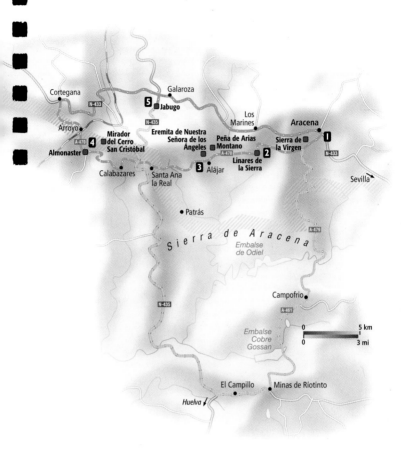

mosaic of pebbles, like a stone doormat, outside its door.

2–3

Continue along the A470 to reach a turn-off on the left that descends to the larger village of **Alájar**. Above is the rocky outcrop of **Peña de Arias Montano**, with caverns said to have served as human shelters from prehistoric times. A side road leads off right from the main route to the **Ermita de Nuestra Señora de los Ángeles**. This was the retreat of 16th-century cleric and scholar Benito Arias Montano. He was confessor to Philip II, who visited the hermitage and meditated in a nearby cave (below the modern car park). A large rock beside the cave has been known ever since as the King's Chair.

3–4

Back on the A470, carry on to a junction with the Huelva road, the N435. Opposite is the Hostal el Cruce, which has a good *tapas* bar. Go straight across, and take the road opposite, the continuation of the A470, signed Almonaster la Real and Cortegana. Continue through wooded country towards Almonaster. A detour just before

DIVERSION TO MINAS DE RÍOTINTO

The drive can be extended to take in a visit to dramatic landscapes of the Río Tinto mining area (▶ 165). Leave Jabugo by its southern exit, signed Huelva, and join the south-bound N345. In 25km (15.5mi), turn left onto the A461, signed Río Tinto and Nerva. Follow signs into **Minas de Ríotinto** (▶ 165). From the village take the exit road signed Sevilla and continue on the A461 through hills. Cross an embankment over a reservoir, the Embalse de Cobre-Gossan. Soon go left onto the A479, signed Campofrío and Aracena, and in 18km (11mi) reach Aracena. This extension adds 60km (37mi) to the main drive.

the village takes you up to the right along a side road with a gravel surface through a series of hairpin bends to reach the **Mirador del Cerro San Cristóbal**. There are two viewpoints on the summit: one overlooks Almonaster from below a thicket of radio trans-mitters; the other is reached along a track that leads off from near the road end and offers tremendous views to the west across the Sierra Pelada and to the northeast, the Picos de Aroche. From here, you have a good chance of spotting black vultures drifting past.

To continue direct to **Almonaster**, keep to the main road for a short distance, then turn left. There is parking at the entrance to the village, where you turn off. Almonaster has a 10th-century **mosque**, built partly into a rock face and left virtually intact after it was converted to Christian wor-ship in the 13th century. It has little horseshoe arches in brick,

supported by what are probably Roman and Visigothic columns, recalling, in miniature, the arches of Córdoba's Mezquita. From the adjoining minaret tower you can look down into the bullring (take care at the top: the window vents are unguarded). To view the inside of the mosque ask for the key at the town hall in the village square.

❹–❺

Continue from Almonaster on the A470 and in about 3km (2mi), at a junction, turn right down a side road, signed Estación FFCC. Keep left at the next junction, then ignore a turning, signed Canaleja. Reach a junction with the main N433, the Portugal–Seville road, and turn right, signed Aracena and Sevilla. In about 2km (1.25mi) turn off for Jabugo.

❺–❻

The otherwise quiet little village of **Jabugo** is the centre of the *jamón* (ham) curing industry. On reaching the first buildings of the town, turn right, signed Centro Urbano, into a quiet, cobbled street where you have a fair chance of parking. Walk up the street and keep left at a junction, then go immediately left and up Calle Silencio to meet a road lined with bars and shops selling an astonishing variety of *jamón* and other meats. From Jabugo return to the N433 and turn right to reach Aracena.

TAKING A BREAK

In the **Calle de Alfonso VI** you can enjoy a good lunch in the Mesón Jabugo. The bars and cafés in Jabugo offer snacks and meals featuring local *jamón*. But, be warned: the often high prices may spoil your appetite.

Practicalities

Practicalities

WHAT YOU NEED

		UK	USA	Canada	Australia	Ireland	Italy	Netherlands
● Required	Some countries require a passport to							
○ Suggested	remain valid for a minimum period							
▲ Not required	(usually at least six months) beyond the date of entry – check before you travel.							
Passport/National Identity Card		●	●	●	●	●	●	●
Visa (regulations can change – check before your journey)		▲	▲	▲	▲	▲	▲	▲
Onward or Return Ticket		▲	▲	▲	▲	▲	▲	▲
Health Inoculations (tetanus and polio)		▲	▲	▲	▲	▲	▲	▲
Health Documentation (► 194, Health)		●	●	●	●	●	●	●
Travel Insurance		○	○	○	○	○	○	○
Driver's Licence (national)		●	●	●	●	●	●	●
Car Insurance Certificate (if own car)		●	n/a	n/a	n/a	●	●	●
Car Registration Document (if own car)		●	n/a	n/a	n/a	●	●	●

WHEN TO GO

High season		Low season

JAN	FEB	MAR	APR	MAY	JUN	JUL	AUG	SEP	OCT	NOV	DEC
16°C	17°C	18°C	21°C	23°C	27°C	29°C	29°C	27°C	23°C	19°C	17°C
61°F	63°F	64°F	70°F	73°F	81°F	84°F	84°F	81°F	73°F	66°F	63°F

☀ Sonnig　　🌦 Wechselhaft　　🌧 Regnerisch　　☁ Bewölkt

Temperatures are the **average daily maximum** for each month. Easter is usually bright and sunny without being too hot; however, accommodation in cities is heavily booked. The best time to visit is in May and early June when there is plenty of sunshine, and the average daytime temperature is 23 to 25°C (73–77°F). Visitor levels are not too high and there is a choice of accommodation. Peak tourist times are in July and August, when the weather is hottest. Andalucíans holiday in August, and there is a huge exodus to the coast. September and October can be delightful, with the sunny weather lingering well into autumn. Winter temperatures on the coast and in low-lying regions are pleasant, but in the mountains expect chilly to very cold weather. Winter can also bring heavy rain and high winds.

GETTING ADVANCE INFORMATION

Websites
■ Tourism office of Spain:
www.tourspain.es

■ Links to other
Andalucían sites:
www.Andalucía.org

■ General information
about Andalucía:
www.Andalucía.com

GETTING THERE

By Air From the UK There are inexpensive flights to Málaga Airport with easyJet from Bristol, Luton, Stansted and Liverpool; Monarch Airlines from Luton and Manchester and with Jet2 from Leeds, Newcastle, Blackpool and Manchester. Monarch also flies to Gibraltar from Luton. Scheduled flights to Málaga, Seville and Gibraltar are available with BA from Heathrow and Gatwick, and to Málaga and Seville with Iberia from Heathrow. Iberia flies from Heathrow to Madrid for connections to Almería, Granada and Jerez de la Frontera. Charter flights from the UK to Málaga, Almería, Seville and Jerez de la Frontera often have spare seats.

From Dublin and Belfast Aer Lingus has direct flights from Dublin and Belfast to Málaga, while easyJet has cheap flights from Belfast to Málaga.

From Australia, New Zealand, America and Canada There are no direct flights, but national carriers from all four countries fly to Madrid and Barcelona where connections can be made.

Approximate flying times to Málaga: UK airports (2.5 hours–3 hours), Dublin and Belfast (3.5–4 hours), West Coast USA (12 hours), Vancouver (10 hours), Montreal (8 hours), Sydney (24 hours + connections), Auckland (22 hours + connections).

By Rail Travelling by train from the UK to Andalucía is time-consuming and can take anything up to 30 hours. You need to first travel to Paris, then change trains, changing once more at the Spanish border for connections to Madrid. There are further connections from Madrid to Córdoba, Seville and other main Andalucían cities.

Travel **by bus** from the UK to Andalucía is also time-consuming; at least 24 hours to Madrid, over 30 hours to Málaga. The cost can be more expensive than the cheaper flights.

TIME

Spain is one hour ahead of Greenwich Mean Time (GMT +1), but from late March until the last Sunday in September, summer time (GMT+2) operates.

CURRENCY AND FOREIGN EXCHANGE

Currency The **euro** (€) is the official currency of Spain. Coins are issued in denominations of 1, 2, 5, 10, 20 and 50 cents and €1 and €2. Notes are issued in denominations of €5, €10, €20, €50, €100, €200 and €500. Travellers' cheques are accepted by most hotels, shops and restaurants in lieu of cash.

Exchange The best places to exchange **travellers' cheques** are banks, bureaux de change at airports, main railway stations or in some department stores, and exchange booths. All transactions are subject to a commission charge. Travellers' cheques can also be changed at main city post offices.

Credit cards are widely accepted in shops, restaurants and hotels. VISA, MasterCard and Diners Club cards with four-digit PINs can be used in most ATM cash dispensers.

SPANISH TOURIST OFFICES

In the UK
22/23 Manchester Square
London W1M 5AP
☎ (020) 7486 8077
www.tourspain.co.uk

In the US
35th Floor, 666 Fifth Avenue
New York, NY 10103
☎ (212) 265 8822
www.okspain.org

In Canada
34th Floor, 2 Bloor St West
Toronto M4W 3E2
☎ (416) 961-3131
www.tourspain.toronto.on.ca

Practicalities

CLOTHING SIZES

UK	Spain	USA	
36	46	36	
38	48	38	
40	50	40	Suits
42	52	42	
44	54	44	
46	56	46	
7	41	8	
7.5	42	8.5	
8.5	43	9.5	Shoes
9.5	44	10.5	
10.5	45	11.5	
11	46	12	
11	46	12	
14.5	37	14.5	
15	38	15	Shirts
15.5	39/40	15.5	
16	41	16	
16.5	42	16.5	
17	43	17	
10	36	8	
12	38	10	
14	40	12	Dresses
16	42	14	
18	44	16	
4.5	38	6	
5	38	6.5	
5.5	39	7	Shoes
6	39	7.5	
6.5	40	8	
7	41	8.5	

NATIONAL HOLIDAYS

1 Jan New Year's Day
6 Jan Epiphany
28 Feb Andalucían Day (regional)
March/April Easter Monday
1 May Labour Day
24 June St John the Baptist (regional)
25 July St James (regional)
15 Aug Assumption of the Virgin
12 Oct National Day
1 Nov All Saints' Day
6 Dec Constitution Day
8 Dec Feast of the Inmaculate Conception
25 Dec Christmas Day

OPENING HOURS

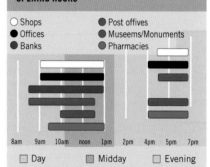

○ Shops   ● Post offives
● Offices   ● Museems/Monuments
● Banks   ● Pharmacies

8am 9am 10am noon 1pm 2pm 4pm 5pm 7pm

☐ Day   ■ Midday   ☐ Evening

Department stores, large supermarkets and shops in
tourist resorts open from 10am to 8, 9 or even 10pm.
The vast majority of shops close Sun and some close
in Aug. Some banks open Sat (Oct–May only) 8:30am
to 1pm. The opening times of museums is just a rough
guide; some open longer in summer, while hours may
be reduced in winter. Many museums close Sun afternoon, some also on Sat afternoon, as well as Mon or
another day in the week. Some museums offer free
entry to EU citizens (take your passport).
Remember – all opening times are subject to change.

TIME DIFFERENCES

Andalucía (CET)
12 noon

←
London (GMT)
11am

→
New York (EST)
6am

→
Los Angeles (PST)
3am

→
Sydney (AEST)
9pm

PERSONAL SAFETY

Snatching of handbags and cameras, pickpocketing, theft of unattended baggage and car break-ins are the principal crimes against visitors.

Any crime or loss should be reported to the national police (Policía Nacional), who wear blue uniforms. Some precautions to take are:

- Do not leave valuables on the beach or poolside.
- Place valuables in a hotel safety-deposit box.
- Wear handbags and cameras across your chest.
- Avoid lonely, seedy and dark areas at night.

Police assistance:
☎ 091 from any payphone

ELECTRICITY

 The power supply is: 220/230 volts. British visitors will need an adaptor and US visitors a voltage transformer.

TELEPHONES

All telephone numbers throughout Spain now consist of nine digits (incorporating the former area code, preceded by 9), and no matter where you call from, you must always dial all nine digits. Many public telephones (teléfono) take phone cards (credifone), which are available from post offices and some shops for €6 or €12.

International Dialling Codes Dial 00 followed by:

UK:	44
USA/Canada:	1
Ireland:	353
Australia:	61
New Zealand:	64
Spain:	34

POST

Post offices (correos) are generally open 9–2 (1pm Sat); closed Sun (tel: 952 35 90 08 Málaga). In main centres they may open extended hours. Málaga's main post office is at Avenida de Andalucía 1. Stamps (sellos) can also be bought at tobacconists (estancos).

TIPS/GRATUITIES

Tipping is not expected for all services and rates are lower than those elsewhere. As a general guide:

Restaurants (if service not included)	5–10%
Cafés/bars	Change
Tour guides	Change
Taxis	2–3%
Chambermaids	Change
Porters	Change
Cloakroom attendants	Change
Toilets	Change

POLICE (Policía Nacional) 091 (Policía Local) 092	
FIRE (Bomberos) 080	
AMBULANCE (Ambulancía) 061	

Practicalities

HEALTH

Insurance Citizens of EU countries receive reduced-cost emergency health care with relevant documentation (European Health Insurance Card), but private medical insurance is still advised and essential for all other visitors.

Dental treatment normally has to be paid for in full as dentists operate privately. A list of *dentistas* can be found in the yellow pages of the telephone directory. Dental treatment should be covered by private medical insurance.

The **sunniest** (and hottest) months are July and August, when daytime temperatures are often into the 30s. Try to avoid the midday sun, use a high-factor sun cream during most months, and become used to the sun gradually.

Drugs Prescription and non-prescription drugs and medicines are available from pharmacies (*farmacias*) distinguished by a large green cross. In emergencies, they will dispense prescription drugs without demanding a prescription.

Safe Water Tap water is generally safe to drink. Mineral water (*agua mineral*) is cheap and widely available. It is sold *sin gas* (still) and *con gas* (carbonated).

CONCESSIONS

Students/Youths Holders of an International Student Identity Card (ISIC) can get some concessions on travel, entrance fees etc, but the Costa del Sol is not really geared up for students.

Senior Citizens The Costa del Sol is an excellent destination for older travellers. Travel agents offer tailored package holidays, and in winter there are special low-cost, long-stay holidays. The best deals are through tour operators who specialise in holidays for senior citizens.

TRAVELLING WITH A DISABILITY

Facilities in Andalucía for travellers with disabilities are slowly improving as more hotels install ramps, special lifts and toilets, etc. For information and advice contact RADAR (tel: 020 7250 3222, www.radar. org.uk) or Cruz Roja (tel: 902 22 22 92).

CHILDREN

Children are revered in Andalucía, and welcome almost everywhere. Special attractions for children are indicated with the logo shown above.

TOILETS

There are few public toilets. Bars and cafés do not mind you using their toilets. Signs are *Aseos*, *Servicios*, and *Señoras* (Ladies) and *Caballeros* or *Señores* (Men).

CUSTOMS

The import of wildlife souvenirs from rare and endangered species may be either illegal or require a special permit. Before purchase you should check customs regulations.

CONSULATES AND EMBASSIES

UK	**USA**	**New Zealand**	**Australia**	**Canada**
☎ 952 35 23 00	☎ 952 47 48 91	☎ 915 23 02 26	☎ 954 22 09 71	☎ 952 22 33 46
(Málaga)	(Fuengirola)	(Madrid)	(Seville)	(Málaga)

Useful words

SURVIVAL PHRASES

Yes/no **Sí/no**
Please **Por favor**
Thank you **Gracias**
You're welcome **De nada**
Hello **Hola**
Goodbye **Adiós**
Good morning **Buenos días**
Good afternoon **Buenas tardes**
Good night **Buenas noches**
How are you? **¿Qué tal?**
How much is this? **¿Cuánto vale?**
I'm sorry **Lo siento**
Excuse me **Perdone**
I'd like **Me gustaría...**
Open **Abierto**
Closed **Cerrado**
Today **Hoy**
Tomorrow **Mañana**
Yesterday **Ayer**
Monday **Lunes**
Tuesday **Martes**
Wednesday **Miércoles**
Thursday **Jueves**
Friday **Viernes**
Saturday **Sábado**
Sunday **Domingo**

DIRECTIONS

I'm lost **Me he perdido**
Where is...? **¿Dónde está?**
How do I get to...? **¿Cómo se va...?**
  the bank **al banco**
  the post office **a la oficina de correos**
  the train station **a la estación de trenes**

Where are the toilets?
  ¿Dónde están los servicios?
Left **a la izquierda**
Right **a la derecha**
Straight on **todo recto**
At the corner **en la esquina**
At the traffic-light **en el semáforo**
At the crossroads **en la intersección**

IF YOU NEED HELP

Help! **¡Socorro!/¡Ayuda!**
Could you help me, please **¿Podría ayudarme, por favor?**
Do you speak English? **¿Habla inglés?**
I don't understand **No comprendo**
I don't speak Spanish **No hablo español**
Could you call a doctor? **¿Podría llamar a un médico, por favor?**

ACCOMMODATION

Do you have a single/double room?
  ¿Le queda alguna habitación individual/doble?
with/without bath/toilet/shower
  con/sin baño propio/lavabo propio/ducha propia
Does that include breakfast?
  ¿Incluye desayuno?
Could I see the room?
  ¿Puedo ver la habitación?
I'll take this room **Me quedo con esta habitación**
The key to room..., please **La llave de la habitación..., por favor**
Thanks for your hospitality **Muchas gracias por la hospitalidad**

NUMBERS

1 **uno**	11 **once**	21 **veintiuno**	200 **doscientos**
2 **dos**	12 **doce**	22 **veintidós**	300 **trescientos**
3 **tres**	13 **trece**	30 **treinta**	400 **cuatrocientos**
4 **cuatro**	14 **catorce**	40 **cuarenta**	500 **quinientos**
5 **cinco**	15 **quince**	50 **cincuenta**	600 **seiscientos**
6 **seis**	16 **dieciséis**	60 **sesenta**	700 **setecientos**
7 **siete**	17 **diecisiete**	70 **setenta**	800 **ochocientos**
8 **ocho**	18 **dieciocho**	80 **ochenta**	900 **novecientos**
9 **nueve**	19 **diecinueve**	90 **noventa**	1000 **mil**
10 **diez**	20 **veinte**	100 **cien**	

Useful words

RESTAURANT

I'd like to book a table ¿Me gustaría reservar una mesa?

Have you got a table for two, please ¿Tienen una mesa para dos personas, por favor?

Could we see the menu, please? ¿Nos podría traer la carta, por favor?

Could I have the bill, please? ¿La cuenta, por favor?

service charge included servicio incluido

breakfast el desayuno

lunch el almuerzo

dinner la cena

table una mesa

waiter/waitress camarero/camarera

starters los entremeses

main course el plato principal

dessert postres

dish of the day plato del día

bill la cuenta

MENU READER

aceituna olive

ajo garlic

alcachofa artichoke

almejas clams

almendras almonds

anguila eel

arroz rice

atún/bonito tuna

bacalao cod

berenjena aubergine

biftec steak

bocadillo sandwich

boquerones anchovies

calamares squid

caldo broth

callos tripe

cangrejo crab

cebolla onion

cerdo pork

cerezas cherries

cerveza beer

champiñones mushrooms

chorizo spicy sausage

chuleta chop

churros fritters

ciruela plum

cochinillo asado roast suckling pig

codorniz quail

conejo rabbit

cordero lamb

crema cream

criadillas sweetbreads

crudo raw

endibia chicory

ensalada (mixta) mixed salad

ensaladilla rusa Russian salad

espárragos asparagus

espinaca spinach

fideos noodles

filete fillet

flan crême caramel

frambuesa raspberry

fresa strawberry

fruta (de temporade) seasonal fruit

galleta biscuit

gambas prawns

garbanzos chick peas

gazpacho andaluz gazpacho (cold soup)

grosellas red/ black currants

guisantes peas

habas broad beans

helado ice cream

hígado de oca goose liver

huevos fritos/ revueltos fried/ scrambled eggs

jamón ham

judías verdes French beans

jugo fruit juice

langosta lobster

langostino crayfish

leche milk

lechuga lettuce

legumbres vegetables

lengua tongue

lenguado sole

liebre hare

lomo de cerdo pork tenerloin

manzana apple

mariscos seafood

mejillones mussels

melocotón peach

melón melon

merluza hake

mero sea bass

morcilla black pudding

pan bread

pato duck

pepino cucumber

pepinillos gherkins

pera pear

perdiz partridge

perejil parsely

pez espada swordfish

pescado fish

pimientos red/ green peppers

piña pineapple

plátano banana

pollo chicken

puerro leek

pulpo octopus

queso cheese

rape monkfish

riñones kidneys

rodaballo turbot

salchicha sausage

salchichón salami

salmón salmon

salmonete red mullet

solomillo de buey fillet of beef

sopa soup

tocino bacon

tortilla española Spanish omelette

tortilla francesa plain omelette

trucha trout

verduras green vegetables

zanahorias carrots

Road Atlas

For chapters: see inside front cover

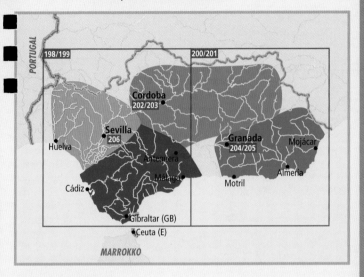

PORTUGAL

198/199

200/201

Cordoba
202/203

Sevilla
206

Huelva

Antequera

Granada
204/205

Mojácar

Almería

Málaga

Motril

Cádiz

Gibraltar (GB)

Ceuta (E)

MARROKKO

Key to Road Atlas

A-7	Motorway	Castle, Fortress / Ruin
A-381	Dual carriage-way	Monestary, church, chapel
A-369	Trunk road	Place of interest
A-2226	Main Road	Archaeological site
	Secondary road	Radio or TV tower / Windmill
	Road under construction	Cave / Lighthouse
	Dirt road	Peak / Pass
	Lane	Skiing area
	Footpath	Windsurfing / Marina
	Ferry	Beach
	National boundary	
	Regional boundary	TOP 10
	National park	26 Don't Miss
✈	International airport	
✈	Regional airport	22 At Your Leisure

1 : 3.700.000

0	50	100 km

0	25	50 mi

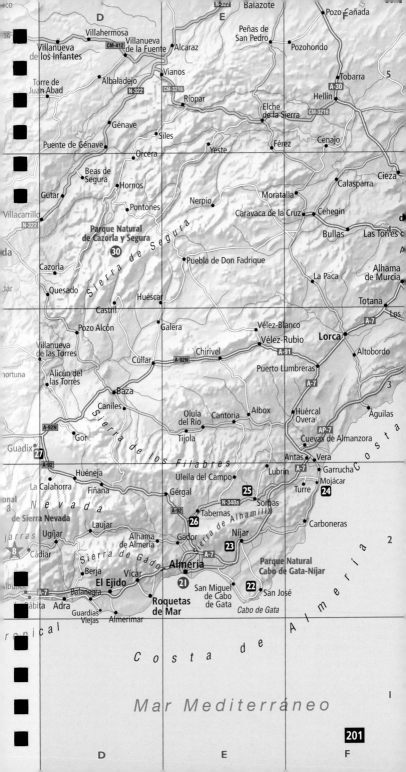

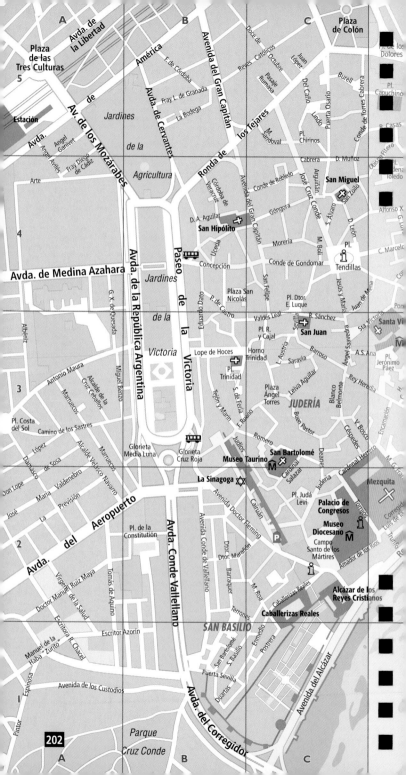

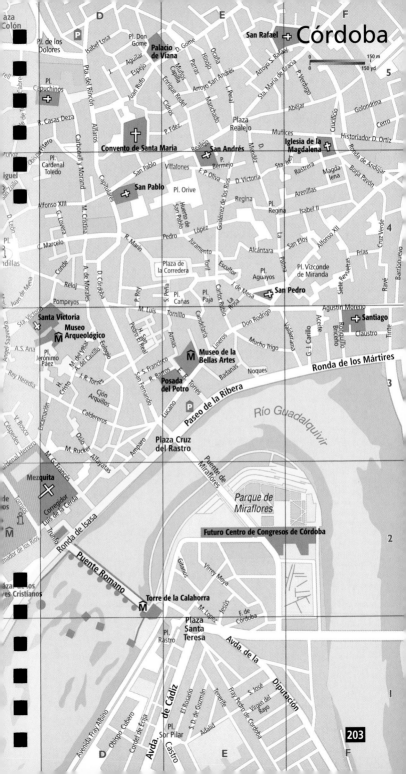

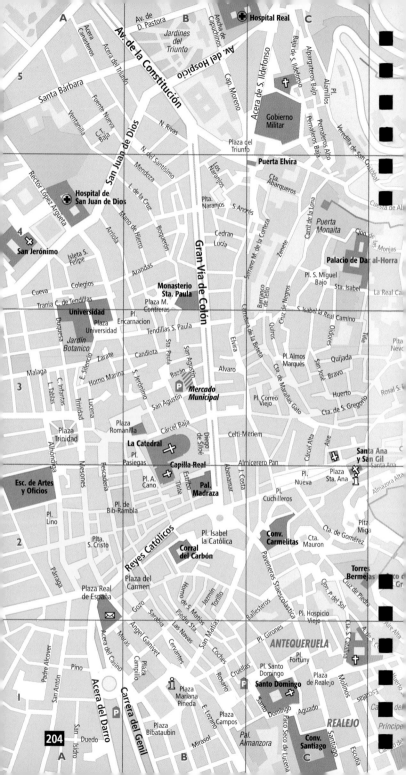

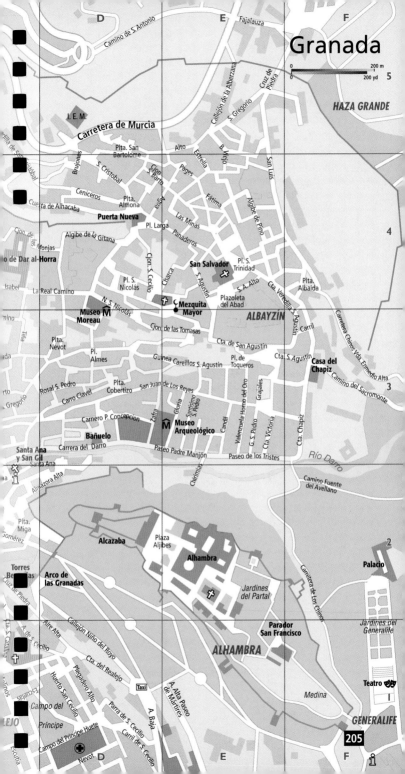

Granada

HAZA GRANDE

Camino de S. Antonio
Fajalauza
Carretera de Murcia
I. E. M.
Brujones
S. Cristóbal
Ceniceros
Cuesta de Alhacaba
Plta. San Bartolomé
Cjon S. Barto
Plta. Almona
Puerta Nueva
Pl. Larga
Algibe de la Gitana
Cjon. de las Monjas
o de Dar al-Horra
Isabel
La Real Camino
N.S Nicolás
Museo Moreau
Pl. S. Nicolás
Plta. Nevot
Pl. Almes
Rosal S. Pedro
Plta. Cobertizo
Carro Clavel
Carnero P. Concepción
Bañuelo
Carrera del Darro
Santa Ana y San Gil
Santa Ana
Almazora Alta
Plta. Miga
Gomérez
Torres Bermejas
Cruz de piedra
Arco de las Granadas
A. de S. Cecilio
Aire Alta
Cta. del Realejo
Callejón Niño del Royo
Plegadero Alto
Huerto San Cecilio
Taxi
Parra de S. Cecilio
A. Baja
Campo del Príncipe
Príncipe
Campo del Príncipe Huete
Nevot
Escuela
LEJO
Alto
Estrella
Pages
Fátima
Las Minas
Panaderos
Charca
S. Agustín
San Salvador
Mezquita Mayor
Cjon. de las Tomasas
Cta. de San Agustín
Guinea Careillos S. Agustín
San Juan de los Reyes
Gloria
Santísimo S. Pedro
Zafra
Museo Arqueológico
Paseo Padre Manjón
Chirimías
Callejón de la Alberzana
S. Gregorio
B. Viejo
San Luis
Algibe de Pino
Pl. S. Trinidad
S.A. Alto
Plazoleta del Abad
ALBAYZÍN
Pl. de Toqueros
Valenzuela Homo del Oro
Candil
G. S. Pedro
Cta. Victoria
Paseo de los Tristes
Cruz de Piedra
Plta. Albaida
Cta. Veredilla S. Agustín
Carril
Cta. S. Agustín
Casa del Chapiz
Camino del Sacromonte
Cta. Chapiz
Río Darro
Camino Fuente del Avellano
Carretera China Vda Ermedio Alta
Alcazaba
Plaza Aljibes
Alhambra
Jardines del Partal
Parador San Francisco
ALHAMBRA
A. Alta Paseo de Mártires
Medina
Carretera de los Chinos
Palacio
Jardines del Generalife
Teatro
GENERALIFE

200 m
200 yd

205

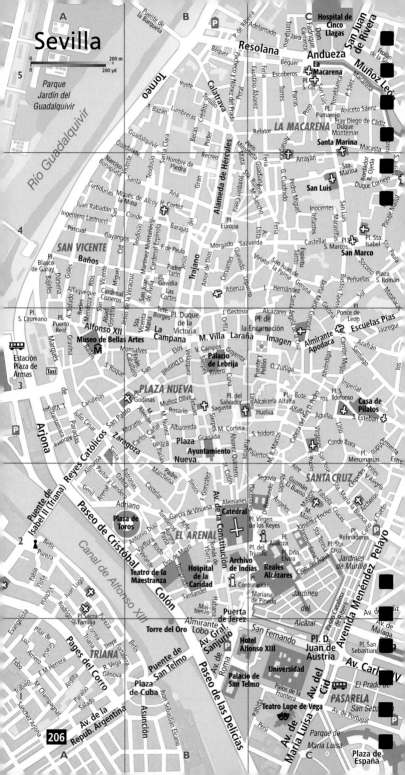

Index

Index

Index

Index / Picture Credits

Picture Credits

Credits

1st Edition 2015

Worldwide Distribution: Marco Polo Travel Publishing Ltd
Pinewood, Chineham Business Park
Crockford Lane, Chineham
Basingstoke, Hampshire RG24 8AL, United Kingdom.
© MAIRDUMONT GmbH & Co. KG, Ostfildern

Authors: Des Hannigan, Josephine Quintero, Achim Bourmer
Editor: Robert Fischer (www.vrb-muenchen.de)
Revised editing and translation: Sarah Trenker, Munich
Program supervisor: Birgit Borowski
Chief editor: Rainer Eisenschmid

Cartography: © MAIRDUMONT GmbH & Co. KG, Ostfildern
3D-illustrations: jangled nerves, Stuttgart

Printed in China

Despite all of our authors' thorough research, errors can creep in.
The publishers do not accept any liability for this. Whether you
want to praise, alert us to errors or give us a personal tip –
please don't hesitate to email or post:

MARCO POLO Travel Publishing Ltd
Pinewood, Chineham Business Park
Crockford Lane, Chineham
Basingstoke, Hampshire RG24 8AL
United Kingdom
Email: sales@marcopolouk.com

FSC
www.fsc.org
MIX
Paper from
responsible sources
FSC® C020056

10 REASONS
TO COME BACK AGAIN

1. Andalucía offers **history galore**: ancient cities, Moorish palaces and Renaissance towns.

2. There are **stunning beaches** – on two different oceans, the Mediterranean and the Atlantic.

3. **Delicious** tapas can be eaten instead of a big lunch or evening meal.

4. **Fino**, a sherry, tastes best after visiting a reputable *bodega!*

5. You can **experience** flamenco in a truly authentic and exhuberant setting.

6. Andalucía bares its true soul during the **fiestas**.

7. **Hiking**, **cycling**, **skiing and windsurfing**: the region is an eldorado for people who enjoy sport.

8. Watching the **Andalucían horses** dance in Jerez de la Frontera is a breathtaking experience.

9. Where else in Europe can you see as many **whales** as in the waters off the coast of Gibraltar?

10. In the Parque Nacional Coto de Doñana with **over 300 different species of bird** everyone becomes a hobby ornithologist.